"Ken Waters's new book brings light rather than heat to understanding the complexity of 'white evangelicals in America.' It provides careful analysis of the content of four well-known periodicals sponsored by self-defined evangelicals through the last three election cycles. The result is to find some unity amid considerable diversity, somewhat more caution about MAGA than in the white evangelical population at large, and many serious questions about a future characterized by declining evangelical numbers and continuing evangelical divisions based more on education and class than Christian doctrine. It is a most illuminating study."

—**Mark A. Noll**, Professor Emeritus, University of Notre Dame

"*Words That Shape Us* is a timely and groundbreaking study of white evangelical culture. While secular media depicts American evangelicalism as a white, right-wing bloc, Ken Waters looks at four evangelical news outlets to reveal nuanced perspectives among the movement's thought leaders. Examining coverage of key events, such as the 2016, 2020 and 2024 presidential elections, the murder of George Floyd, and the repeal of Roe v Wade, Waters shows how conservative evangelical journalists have wrestled with issues of racism, homophobia, and religious integrity through biblical lenses. Waters's study, similar to the work of David French and Tim Alberta, explores the politicization of evangelical churchgoers and the problematic impact of certain extremists who call themselves evangelicals but are unchurched. Waters has written an important book that ought to help readers understand that evangelicalism is a more complex and Christian—in the most positive sense of the word—movement than the secular media would have us believe."

—**Diane Winston**, Knight Chair in Media and Religion,
Annenberg School for Communication and Journalism, University of Southern California

"Ken's book is a tour of well-intentioned media no longer viable. The journals which did survive served nervous audiences divided along party, social, and cultural lines, readers often as upset at their favorite editors as the publishers were upset at the fickle loyalty of subscribers and funders. Unlike legacy media, these evangelical journals labored to tell their stories with biblical boundaries and eschatological endgames far more ultimate, yet confounding to their secular cousins and often to their churched constituents. Did they succeed? Waters, always the good teacher, invites us to ponder."

—**Mark Fackler**, Professor of Communications Emeritus, Calvin University

"Ken Waters brings five decades of experience studying the world of evangelical magazines to analyze how four publications—*Christianity Today, World, Sojourners* and *The Christian Post*—navigated the contemporary political terrain while striving to stay true to their biblical vision and journalistic values. Waters raises important questions of how faith-based publications can balance objectivity and prophetic critique, and his analysis illustrates the growing divide between the evangelical elite and the rank and file. This is a must-read text for everyday churchgoers and scholars interested in lived religion, media, culture, and politics."

—**Christina Littlefield**, Associate Professor of Journalism and Religion, Pepperdine University

"Professor Ken Waters provides a detailed look at popular periodicals that the evangelical subculture often read to make sense of a dizzying news vista. Like society at large, readers and viewers who identify as Christian and the publications designed to serve them run a colorful spectrum where observation and perspectives often are at loggerheads. The voices are anything but monothetic. Waters helps identify the wide variety of opinions with specifics and offers his opinion on which ones meet the test of offering the best reporting and interpretation in a digital world. While each periodical he studied offers a novel voice of advocacy for what it means to be active in piety in the public square, Waters isn't shy about when the publications rise to the laudatory role of nailing down the accuracy of a report, making sense of it and bearing witness to modest and grand doings of the church and the state and when they fail. He identifies those on the highway of hope and those who have steered into the ditch of despair. Readers may not agree with his analysis, but they will profit from a wide-ranging review of the leading faith-based publications and their approach to news."

—**Michael Ray Smith**, Professor of Contemporary Communication, LCC International University

"We are what we read. Christians know this and many make the study of Scripture a discipline they combine with prayer and reflection. But this discipline requires biblical literacy. There is also a literacy of Christian culture, magazines serving as part of it, that paved the way for the spread of churches across the newly forming United States. Ken Waters digs into this literacy. He shows Christian magazines' power to shape understanding of politics and faith in public spaces. Does Christian journalism still matter? Oh yes, Waters says. And he proves it chapter after chapter."

—**Michael A. Longinow**, Professor of Digital Journalism & Integrated Media, Biola University

"Ken Waters's new book offers a fascinating exploration of how four evangelical publications, with diverse approaches and perspectives, have covered the Trump era, both in news stories and editorials. Putting aside my own biases about these publications (I love the world-class reporting of *Christianity Today*, for example, while I've complained more than once about the aggregation-machine *The Christian Post* lifting my reporting without proper credit), I appreciated Waters's methodical and even-handed approach to his research. Ultimately, a complicated picture emerges that will help readers gain a better understanding of the vital role, challenges and competing interests faced by these publications' journalists."

—**Bobby Ross, Jr.**, Editor-in-Chief, *The Christian Chronicle*

"Ken Waters combines his skills as journalist and scholar in a thoughtful historical analysis of how *Christianity Today*, *World*, *Sojourners*, and *The Christian Post* approached coverage of a tumultuous era. In doing so, he will inform and enlighten those who thought they knew the publications well, and those who have little knowledge of them. Perhaps most importantly, the differences among the four, some nuanced and some striking, should allay any misguided assumptions about a congruent lockstep among evangelical journalists or evangelicals writ large. In chapter after chapter, Waters describes how events, personalities and politics shaped the publications' theology and coverage and how their journalists sought to shape readers' understanding of the tumultuous Trump era. A great read."

—**Cheryl Bacon**, Professor and Chair Emerita, Department of Journalism and Mass Communication, Abilene Christian University

WORDS THAT SHAPE US

How America's Most Influential Evangelical Magazines Craft the Narrative of Christian Culture

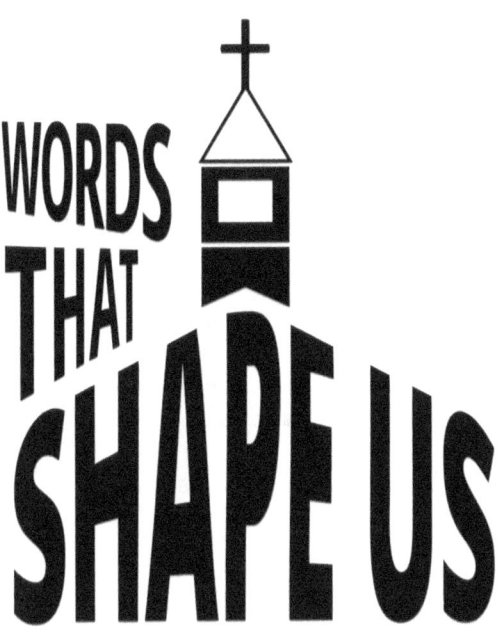

WORDS THAT SHAPE US

How America's Most
Influential Evangelical Magazines
Craft the Narrative of Christian Culture

Ken Waters

Foreword by John Ferré

Integratio Press
Pasco, Washington

WORDS THAT SHAPE US: How America's Most Influential Evangelical Magazines Craft the Narrative of Christian Culture

This is a publication of Academe, a Division of Integratio Press.

integratiopress.com

Integratio Press is an Imprint of the Christianity and Communication Studies Network.
11503 Easton Dr.
Pasco, WA 99301

www.theccsn.com

Cover design: Carol O'Callaghan
Interior design: Carol O'Callaghan

paperback isbn: 978-1-959685-29-6
ebook isbn: 978-1-959685-30-2

Library of Congress Control Number: 2025939787

Dedication

To Julie, Katie, and Alison
for your continued support and insight.
Your love sustains me.

TABLE OF CONTENTS

Acknowledgments

THIS BOOK WAS decades in the making. Many mentors, colleagues, and former students contributed advice and encouragement as it percolated in my mind and finally came to fruition.

Thanks to Cliff Christians, Mark Fackler, Bill Faith, Terry Lindvall, Michael Longinow, Martin Marty, Quentin Schultze, Michael Ray Smith, and Ron Wilson for your insight, encouragement, and feedback over the years. Without the nudging of Robert H. Woods Jr., friend and Editor-in-Chief of Integratio Press, this book would never have made it to press. Two other scholars directly affected the words and thoughts of the book—John Ferré and Stephen Perry. Colleagues over the years have likewise made suggestions advancing the narratives contained herein. Those colleagues and friends include the late Michael Casey, Lee Kats, Christina Littlefield, Denise Edwards-Neff, Rodney Reynolds, Gary Selby, Elizabeth Smith, and Courtenay Stallings. Student researchers Hayley Gotelli and Josh Fleer also contributed important information and insights. I'm grateful beyond words for your time and counsel.

Foreword

THE HISTORY OF AMERICAN JOURNALISM is filled with faithful reporters and editors who considered their work a prophetic calling. Elijah Lovejoy was one of them. A Presbyterian minister who came to understand the evils of slavery, Lovejoy published the abolitionist *Alton Observer* in Illinois, just across the Mississippi River from the slave state of Missouri. Outspoken and relentless, Lovejoy was threatened and attacked multiple times, until he was shot to death by a mob in 1837. Ten weeks later, defendants arrested for Lovejoy's murder were found not guilty. A monument to honor Lovejoy erected in Alton sixty years after his death bears this quotation: "If the laws of my country fail to protect me I appeal to God, and with him I cheerfully rest my cause. I can die at my post but I cannot desert it."[1]

No doubt early visitors to the Lovejoy monument were reading the best-selling novel of the era, *In His Steps* by Charles Sheldon, pastor of Central Congregational Church in Topeka, Kansas. *In His Steps* follows the lives of a congregation that vowed to follow the example of Jesus by asking the simple question, "What would Jesus do?" before making decisions in their personal and professional lives. Edward Norman, editor of the *Daily News*, was one of the church members who took the pledge. Under his leadership, the *Daily News* dropped tobacco and alcohol advertising; stopped lurid and sensational coverage, instead focusing on social problems; ceased publishing on Sunday; published articles with bylines; and supported candidates and policies based on their goodness, regardless of political party. Intrigued, the *Topeka Daily Capital* let Sheldon serve as editor for a week in 1900. Publicity for Sheldon's Christian issues increased circulation from 12,000 to 360,000, but the newspaper dialed up its editorial excitement when Sheldon returned to his church.[2]

A third prophetic news enterprise emerged in the depth of the Great Depression when Dorothy Day co-founded *The Catholic Worker*. Sold for a penny a copy then and still today, the newspaper promotes the cause of the Catholic Worker Movement, communities across the United States that seek to "live in accordance with the justice and charity of Jesus Christ."[3] In practice, *The Catholic Worker* focuses on poverty, houselessness, pacifism, racism and antisemitism, unemployment, and working conditions and labor movements, giving a voice to people too often overlooked by churches. Day's pacifism led *The Catholic Worker* to lose readers during World War II, especially her insistence that all Americans bore responsibility for the obliteration of Hiroshima and Nagasaki. For Day, the mystical body of Christ is everyone—poor, rich, enemy, friend—and all of us share responsibility for what everyone does. This commitment led to strategic civil disobedience, for which she was arrested multiple times.

In a thoughtful essay about prophetic journalism, Judith Valente reflects about her career reporting for the *Washington Post, Wall Street Journal*, public radio, and public television before leaving daily journalism to write books about spirituality such as *How to Live: What the Rule of St. Benedict Teaches Us about Happiness, Meaning, and Community.* "My work as a 'messenger' in both print and broadcast media . . . was never merely a job or even a career, but a calling," she explains.[4] "I considered it a privilege to tell the stories of people, especially those who live on the margins of society, and to invite to speak for themselves those whose voices are often muted or ignored."[5] Prophetic journalism, she says, drawing from the Trappist monk Thomas Merton, focuses on "the value, the rightness, the truth of the work."[6]

In *Words that Shape Us*, journalism scholar Ken Waters examines four important evangelical Christian publications to see the prophetic direction they took in reporting and evaluating Donald Trump's presidency and to determine their impact on the faithful. In 2016, Trump was an unlikely candidate to win favor among evangelical Christians. True, he chose the evangelical Mike Pence as his running mate and promised to appoint anti-abortion Supreme Court justices, but his history of sexual promiscuity, fraudulent business dealings, racism, and xenophobia were well known. Eight in ten white evangelical voters supported Trump in 2016, but where did *Christianity Today, Sojourners, World,* and *The Christian Post* stand?

From its founding by Billy Graham in 1956, *Christianity Today* has sought to be the voice of American evangelicalism. As church historian Douglas A. Sweeny observed, "*Christianity Today* would prove to be a medium unparalleled in promoting the message of the new evangelicalism and in reflecting the cultural and religious attitudes of its constituency."[7] Currently, *Christianity Today* has a print circulation of 110,000, with 1.5 million visits monthly to ChristianityToday.com. Does this popularity suggest that *Christianity Today* actually speaks for American evangelicalism? Does it promote a timid witness, one that acquiesces to evangelicalism's alliance with the GOP? The pages that follow answer these questions and suggest what we can expect from *Christianity Today* during Trump's second term as president. Current editor-in-chief Russell D. Moore has made prophetic stands for refugee resettlement and racial reconciliation, but as president of the Ethics & Religious Liberty Commission of the Southern Baptist Convention, he publicly apologized for his outspoken criticism of Trump.

From its scrappy beginning in 1971 as *The Post-American* magazine, *Sojourners* has self-consciously positioned itself as a prophetic Christian publication. It was founded by disaffected students at Trinity Evangelical Divinity School, who dropped out to do theology instead of just learning it. Resisting the cultural captivity of the church was their charge. Founding editor Jim Wallis put it this way: "Christians must be active in rejecting the values of our corrupt society, radical in our resistance and activism against the injustice of a racist society, warfare state, and materialistic system."[8] Today, *Sojourners* reaches 42,000 readers a month with its print edition and 2.5 million page views of its sojo.net. Its stated mission today is less jeremiad than in 1971, but prophetic still: "Our mission is to inspire hope and action by articulating the biblical call to racial and social justice, life and peace, and environmental stewardship."[9]

With its motto, "Sound journalism, grounded in facts and biblical truth,"[10] *World* magazine began publishing in 1986, and has since expanded from its print magazine to include a web presence and podcasts. In 1999, *World* magazine launched the World Journalism Institute, an effort to teach what it calls "Biblically objective journalism" to evangelical news reporters, who have subsequently reported for such evangelical outlets as Baptist Press News Service, *Christianity Today*, and Salem Broadcasting and for such commercial outlets as *The New York Times*, *USA Today*, and *The Washington Post*. *World* magazine's current co-chief content officer Lynn Vincent co-wrote *Going Rogue: An American Life*, the 2009 memoir of Republican vice-presidential candidate Sarah Palin, so it remains to be seen whether *World*'s prophetic journalism extends to the Republican administration.[11]

The newest of the four evangelical publications that Waters examines is *The Christian Post*, the online news source founded in 2004. From its headquarters in Washington, DC, christianpost.com delivers news and commentary to its audience of evangelical Christians, 2.2 million of whom visit the site monthly. Culture warrior Richard Land is *The Christian Post*'s Executive Editor, having previously led the Southern Baptist Convention's

Ethics and Religious Liberty Committee, the denomination's political lobby. Under Land's direction, *The Christian Post* describes its journalism as objective and its editorials as diverse, although the news analysis company Ad Fontes Media reports that *The Christian Post* skews right.[12]

Using the ways that evangelical publications have responded to Donald Trump as an extended case study, Ken Waters explores the degree to which they reflect the values and beliefs of evangelical Christian voters. Understanding the character of both the publications and the American evangelicals they serve provides an important perspective on the faith of a full quarter of American believers over the past decade. *Words that Shape Us* tells the story of faithful witness and compromise, of promise and disappointment, of prophecy and capitulation. It is a story of our times.

John P. Ferré, PhD
University of Louisville

Author's Preface

YEARS AGO, A MENTOR invited me to a luncheon sponsored by a thriving Christian book publisher. The publisher dreamt of starting a Christian version of the *New York Times* or the *Christian Science Monitor*. I lacked the funds to invest, but I put my name on a list of potential writers.

A few months later, I received a call from an editor of that fledgling newspaper, the *National Courier*, a newspaper that hoped to compete with tabloids at the supermarket checkout. She asked me to interview the president of World Vision for a Thanksgiving feature story encouraging readers to help hungry children. I wrote several other features for the newspaper during the next few years. Unfortunately, the *National Courier* was short-lived, lasting all of three years. However, I parlayed that experience into a year of serving as a writer and editor of the *National Catholic Register* while taking a sabbatical from my graduate program.

After the *National Catholic Register*, I served on staff at another start-up publication, *Inspiration*. It, too, attempted to reach Christians and spiritually interested people. It was a glossy, full-color magazine circulated on national newsstands. Petersen Publishing, an imprint responsible for *Hot Rod*, *Motor Trend*, *Teen*, and *Guns & Ammo*, felt the time was right for a feel-good magazine targeted to a mass audience.

Inspiration lasted four issues before being shut down because of poor readership and infighting among Christian staff members (including me). The publisher wanted a glossy version of *Guideposts*, while the staff wanted to compete with the popular evangelical publications of the day like *Eternity*, *Christian Herald*, and *Christian Life*.

The *National Courier* and *Inspiration* attempted to reach a broad audience of religious and non-religious people, combining *The Christian Science Monitor* and *Guideposts* for the Christian believer. The editorial plan for those failed publications looked great on paper. Unfortunately, the execution suffered from the need for better management decisions, a better-identified audience, more advertisers, and more robust financial backing to sustain them.

At the University of Southern California, I wrote my doctoral dissertation on how four publications—*Christianity Today*, *Christian Herald*, *Inspiration*, and *National Courier*—survived or failed during the heady era of the 1970s. The election of Jimmy Carter as president led *Time* magazine to call 1976 the "year of the evangelical." My research focused on how those four magazines attracted readers through their editorial content and, more importantly, how their circulation and financial decisions impacted their survival or demise. At that time, *Christianity Today* and *Christian Herald* were thriving, while the recent start-ups, *Inspiration* and *National Courier*, lasted a few short years. A few years after I completed my research, the *Christian Herald* also succumbed to a downturn in subscribers and insufficient advertising revenue.

During that era, inexpensive new publishing technology revolutionized the publishing industry. As a result, specialized publications flooded the market. If an entrepreneur thought he could reach a niche audience interested in the editorial content and advertising for products the audience desired, they started a magazine to reach that audience.[1] The advent of specialty publications, I thought, should benefit Christian entrepreneurs, denominations, nonprofit advocacy organizations, and even churches interested in reaching audiences with their carefully crafted messages delivered through glossy, well-designed magazines. Most failed, but that didn't stop would-be publishers from trying.

Since the publication of my dissertation, the Christian magazine trade has changed dramatically. At one time, a few religious publications commanded an audience of over one million print readers in any given month. Today, circulation and subscriptions to magazines such as *Decision* (sent to donors of Billy Graham's crusades), *World Vision* (sent free to donors and advocates for Christian humanitarian assistance), and even *Christianity Today* (founded by Billy Graham to define and shape the emerging evangelical movement) are down considerably. The former two publications downsized due to changing readership habits and increasing publishing and mailing costs. Publications such as *Christianity Today* and others that charge an annual subscription have likewise been affected by changing readership demographics and printing costs. Unable to attract advertising from mainstream companies like automakers or consumer product manufacturers, *Eternity*, *Moody Monthly*, the *Other Side*, and many more magazines folded as subscription revenue decreased.

During the early part of my teaching career, I used my knowledge of the religious press and journalism to serve as a judge for numerous annual competition awards bestowed by the Evangelical Press Association and the Associated Church Press. My admiration for the work of these editors and their publications is immense. They do not enter the world of religious publishing for fame or money. Instead, they are called by God to present readers with cogent analysis that enlightens those readers' daily walk with the Lord.

Meanwhile, the influence of Christian messaging switched from print to electronic. In the 1970s, televangelists reached millions of viewers with weekly sermons or daily news programs such as Pat Robertson's 700 Club. Jim Dobson's radio program and ensuing empire, "Focus on the Family," used the airwaves to reach millions of listeners interested in how to raise their children to love God and their country. Radio behemoth Salem Broadcasting morphed from featuring Christian music and talk shows to selling programming space to conservative pastors and political pundits. These programs and their influential leaders became spokespeople not only for a conservative brand of Christianity but for suggesting an approach to interacting with the culture and politics of the time in a much more confronting manner than the magazines of the late twentieth century.[2]

These changes pre-dated the Internet, which radically changed how we get our information and created even more challenges to print-based publications seeking adequate revenue to continue. Although I wrote an occasional chapter for edited books focused on religious communication, my interest in Christian publishing waned as we entered the new century. Then came Donald Trump.

Conservative Christians overwhelmingly supported his bid for the presidency in 2016 (and again in 2020 and 2024). His stretching of the truth, multiple marriages and affairs, and confronting rhetoric seemingly mocked the communication and lifestyle standards promoted by Jesus and other writers of the New Testament. In the era of Christianity I had studied for my doctorate, Trump's candidacy would have been unanimously rejected. Few faithful Christians would have voted for the controversial businessman, especially those who professed to advocate for a pro-life stance, family values, and Christian moral behavior. But most evangelicals voted to elect him president on three different occasions and seemed happy with their choice as he began 2025 by attempting to cut waste in portions of the federal government and impose tariffs on the importation of goods and commodities from most of the world's countries.

That raised a question I could not easily answer: Why? Dozens of books documented the politicization of evangelical believers and the attraction of Trump.[3] He courted a segment of evangelical voters by promising to appoint anti-abortion Supreme Court justices, build a border wall to curtail illegal entries into the U.S., and return manufacturing jobs to the U.S. In reading these books, one segment of the evangelical voice seemed to be missing—that of the publications I had studied years ago. What did they say about Trump's candidacy, election, and dominance of the political and cultural landscape over the decade from 2015 to 2025?

And what about the other "culture war" skirmishes of the era? Immigration? The COVID-19 pandemic? Increased racial tensions, especially after the murder of George Floyd? What did the publications say about the continued rise of Christian nationalism, a potential threat to the American experiment? And how should believers respond to the increasingly vocal LGBTQ+ advocates? Were these publications silent? Did they analyze and educate readers using the Bible as the basis for their reporting and commentary?

The following pages are my attempt to examine some of these questions. Dozens of public opinion polls during the first few decades of this century provide us with the opinions of people who say they are evangelicals. But what did the publications that reported on conservative Christian beliefs and their intersection with culture have to say? Did they support Trump and the values of the Religious Right? If so, did they do so mindlessly? Or did they provide readers with solid reasons backed by critical thinking? In short, what—if anything—did these influential publications contribute to the evangelical history of the early twenty-first century?

As I did with my dissertation, I focused on Christian print and online media that give readers news about Christianity's interaction with mainstream culture and politics. News covered in mainstream media often appears on Christian media sites, but that news is presented from the standpoint of a Christian worldview. The publications chosen had to adhere to journalistic practices and ethics. This included vetting sources for their expertise and truthfulness while strictly hewing to the quest for accuracy. I also wanted to study publications that occasionally sought truth, even when that truth reflected negatively on their own actions or the actions and potential corruption within other Christian organizations.

My search of Christian media for this analysis excluded publications focused on ending hunger and poverty or advancing loyalty to a denomination or other ministry. Many of the publications are excellent at what they do. For this analysis, however, I sought publications presenting a variety of perspectives and a variety of news.

Four publications appearing in print and online met these criteria. *The Christian Post, Christianity Today, Sojourners,* and *World* represent a snapshot of what concerned and agitated evangelicals while occasionally giving readers advice on responding to a rapidly changing world. Studying the educational and advocacy role of these Christian publications, their convergence and divergence with the opinions of believers captured during national polling, raises the essential question of this book: What is the future of the evangelical movement itself? That's what I hope to examine in the following pages.

There's a fine line between providing helpful analysis of a scholar's discoveries and imposing bias into the narration of the study's results and implications. That is particularly true of a book focused on the intersection of religion, culture, and politics in our age of polarization.

I read thousands of articles and essays published in four evangelical periodicals. As a journalist and historian, I tried to use the widely accepted ideas of thoroughness, accuracy, fairness, transparency, and vetting sources for their credibility. After reading these articles, I've chosen a selection to highlight as representative of the how these magazines portrayed essential issues of the day. Several colleagues read the final draft of this book and were kind enough to point out, with graciousness, that my word choices and selection of magazine articles as examples seemed at times to betray my ideological and theological biases. The use of biased wording and article selection does not support Christian unity, a goal the New Testament writers emphasized. The issue of this bias led me to consider influences on my scholarship and writing.

Most of my worldview results from my education and work experiences. I received B.A. and M.A. degrees from a Christian university, one aligned with a theological and educational philosophy of the American Restoration Movement of the early nineteenth century. That movement started as a reaction to the many splits within American churches. The antidote proposed by frontier preachers such as Barton Stone and Alexander Campbell included encouraging believers to return to the New Testament as an example of church organization, theology, and doctrine. Doing this allowed believers to unite in worship and service to God. One outgrowth of this worldview was the rejection of existing church rituals not expressly described in the New Testament.

The Restoration Movement ultimately split into three denominations: the Disciples of Christ, the independent Christian churches, and the churches of Christ. The latter group, which I am now a member, still adheres to distinctives they say arise directly from the New Testament examples. These include weekly communion; baptism for the remission of sins; *a capella* worship; the priesthood of all believers; and congregational autonomy. With no national organization to dictate doctrine, believers are encouraged to study the Bible for themselves, to determine what the scriptures are saying about how to worship together and live out the Christian life.

I'm indebted to scholars Richard Hughes and Christina Littlefield who recently noted how a Restorationist worldview might differ from the expectations of an evangelical scholar. Restorationists generally do not identify as evangelicals, but might be considered "evangelical adjacent."[4] They are "deeply influenced by the Scottish Enlightenment and a high view of scripture," rejecting credal statements common in Protestant churches.[5] They also reject Calvinist teachings on predestination. Restorationists, especially those in the churches of Christ, are amillennial, "so they avoid a lot of the apocalyptic elements within conservative evangelical circles."[6] Finally, a strong pacifist mindset from the nineteenth century lingered into the twentieth century. Several of my professors served in non-combatant roles in World War II and the Korean War because of their pacifism. Conversations with these professors affected me deeply.

The high view of scripture that characterizes the churches of Christ means prioritizing the biblical teachings of Jesus and the Apostles when the proclamation of a megachurch pastor or a social media influencer seems at odds with those New Testament teachings. Whether consciously or not, that means the Sermon on the Mount, advice to turn the other cheek, and to prioritize love over hate, are my expectations for all people who say they are Christians. Thus, I'm uneasy with the mindset of a minority of evangelicals I've worshipped with over the years who say Christians need to dominate politics and culture, and restore Christian values to the nation.

The other life experience informing my worldview is the ten years I spent as a communication executive at the international aid organization World Vision, a ministry founded by American evangelicals. Over the years, I wrote about sitting with the poor and oppressed in garbage dumps, refugee camps, and feeding centers. I heard their horror stories while marveling at their resilience and hope. I still maintain a mindset that sees the church falling far short of Christian compassion, and sometimes needlessly spending money in pursuit of political power and culture war victories in our increasingly polarized environment.

These educational influences and life experiences inform the analysis you'll find in the following pages. I have tried diligently to practice fairness and accuracy befitting the professional ethics of journalism and historical studies. My goal is to be a messenger of what the evangelical publications said on these topics of importance. I hope their words challenge and encourage you, and you overlook or forgive the interjection of bias into the narrative and analysis I present.

Introduction

IN JANUARY 2016, U.S. presidential candidate Donald Trump told supporters at an evangelical Christian college in Iowa, "I could stand in the middle of Fifth Avenue and shoot somebody, and I wouldn't lose any voters. Okay? It's like incredible."[1]

Many in the room identified themselves as Christians. According to journalists, the crowd laughed and clapped at Trump's statement. They cheered him even though his life hardly depicted that of a person pursuing the fruit of the Spirit or even aware of Jesus's Sermon on the Mount.[2] Trump rarely spoke of love, joy, peace, patience, kindness, goodness, faithfulness, gentleness, or self-control throughout his three presidential campaigns of the early twenty-first century. Still, that day's crowd in 2016—and countless other crowds over the next eight years—roared approval, as did millions of other Christians who heard Trump's message as he campaigned. To them, it was time to take back America from cultural, political, and spiritual infidels and, as Trump said, "Make America Great Again (MAGA)." Trump was the perfect mixture of bravado and anti-government sentiment to restore a nostalgic return to a Christian America that historians say never truly existed. In short, Donald Trump became their protector, a mythical hero willing to fight for a nation governed by biblical values.

Some evangelicals didn't cheer Trump's words that night or in the following months. Among these were the editors and executives of the nation's leading evangelical publications. Around the same time Trump declared (perhaps satirically) his followers' loyalty, *The Christian Post* made its position clear to evangelicals: "Back away from Donald Trump."[3] Noting that it had not taken a stance on a political candidate in its past, the editors said they were "making an exception because Trump is exceptionally bad and claims to speak for and represent the interests of evangelicals."[4]

Even before Trump's speech in Iowa, Jim Wallis, founder of *Sojourners*, wrote, "I believe Donald Trump is deliberately and directly appealing to that white racist core of the Republican Party . . . He is selling racism, and he is winning."[5]

World editor Marvin Olasky analyzed the presidential race at the end of June 2016, noting that if Trump made a "credible profession of faith, that's wonderful for him and, down the road, the entire nation."[6] Then he flung this zinger: "But the key question now is whether Donald Trump can make a credible showing of not being incredibly fatheaded."[7]

Fatheaded or not, many Christian news publications reluctantly decided supporting Trump was the lesser of two evils. The businessman and reality TV star beat Hillary Clinton in the 2016 Electoral College vote for President, thanks in large part to the support of White evangelical Christians.[8] In 2020, Trump lost to former Vice President Joe Biden and claimed that he actually won because of voter fraud. In 2024, his campaign doubled down on his MAGA message and his claim that evil forces like Democratic nominee Kamala Harris were trying to cheat him out of regaining the presidency. His margin of victory in that election surprised some pundits and he assumed the White House again in 2025.

Trump's words and actions also contributed to raising the stakes of important issues evangelicals had discussed for decades before he appeared on the scene. Conservative believers discussed, and sometimes strongly disagreed, on abortion, LGBTQ+ issues, immigration, Christian nationalism, the role of women in the church, and racism.

These discussions spilled out onto the pages of Christian media which provide an important, but often overlooked, insight into the evangelical mind. *The Christian Post, Christianity Today, Sojourners,* and *World*—arguably the most influential evangelical news publications—claim to reach more than 15 million people per month.[9]

Millions of devout Christians read these print and online publications, and the social media discussions their content create. Those four, and others, provide insight, encouragement, biblical knowledge, and help in navigating an ever-changing cultural and political landscape. While they failed at convincing Republicans to nominate someone other than Trump in 2016, their wise counsel and broad analysis of world events continue to provide an invaluable service to the faithful.

In this book, I'll explore three major questions:

1. Is the divide I saw with Trump 2016 evident in the voting advice of the evangelical press and the voting behaviors of self-identified evangelicals in subsequent elections?

2. What can be learned about the evangelical movement if we widen the lens to examine the rhetoric of their news and opinions on how to live as a Christian in the modern world? How does the content of the evangelical publications compare and contrast with the beliefs and attitudes of people who identify as evangelicals? In

other words, is there a disconnect between the content of
the publications and the voting patterns of people who claim
to be evangelicals?

3. Finally, in looking toward the future, how might these findings
foreshadow the future of the evangelical movement? Numerous
scholars point out that the evangelical tent is big, including within
it the fundamentalists, charismatics, Pentecostals, people with a
strong identity to their chosen denomination and its teachings,
and faithful Christians attending community churches with no
denominational affiliation. This diversity is evident in the description provided by the National Association of Evangelicals, which
states that evangelical Christians come from "a great multitude
that no one could count, from every nation, tribe, people and
language."[10] But the news and opinion essays appearing in the
evangelical press from 2015 to 2024 appeared to show an increasing political and cultural divide between people who identified
themselves as evangelicals and its popular press. Are there hints
within this diversity of content that the broad tent of evangelicals
is fraying at the edges or in danger of tearing apart completely?

The study is confined to issues at the intersection of the church and
society. It excludes topics largely confined within the evangelical tent, such
as the role of women in the family and church; doctrinal and theological
disputes between and among churches and denominations; and how to improve Christian education, among a plethora of other topics.

The first quarter of the twenty-first century is especially ripe for study.
A simmering anger and distrust, and a dangerous populism, exploded into
American political and cultural dialogue. Uncivil dialogue became a norm
in many pockets of political and cultural conversations.[11] Evangelicalism
was challenged as it navigated these conflicts with a message of hope, peace,
grace, and salvation.

A seldom-studied window on this evangelical dialogue is found in the
editorial content of publications in print and online format that claim to
educate and advocate for Christian living within the larger society. Their
content is ideologically and theologically diverse, representing varied responses to the divisive nature of the current age. The content is also important because it is written and edited by a group of journalistically minded
Christians possessing both an undergraduate degree and quite often an
advanced degree in theology.[12]

To zero in on the best examples of evangelical communication today, I considered three essential criteria:

1. The current-day publications circulate widely (with hundreds of thousands of readers) through their web presence and printed magazine;

2. They are free from editorial constraints imposed on them by a denominational hierarchy or the management of an organization pursuing a particular charitable purpose. Within the confines of a Christian worldview, they are journalistically free;

3. Their articles allow us to dive deeply into various issues, opinions, and passions during one of the most divisive eras of the past century. Personal attacks, harsh rhetoric, and unsubstantiated claims are rarely found in their content. They are generally click-bait free.

The four publications examined here—*The Christian Post, Christianity Today, Sojourners,* and *World*—represent these criteria. Each approaches its editorial practices differently, and their content reflects varied standpoints on politics and culture. All provide readers with news, feature stories, opinion articles, and reviews of books, movies, and other cultural expressions. Each has a distinctive history and editorial philosophy shaped by their founders. One weakness in choosing these four is that they are traditionally targeted toward White evangelicals and their concerns. Recent efforts at inclusion are providing readers with an understanding of how people of color react to, and are affected by, the controversies discussed on their pages. A thriving press representing people of color does exist, but most of its publications are the product of specific denominations or advocacy groups and thus fall outside the criteria I've outlined above.[13]

What is an Evangelical?

Before considering the content and influence of these publications, we need to understand their audience. If you ask a dozen people, "What is an evangelical?" you'll get a dozen different answers. Those answers range from "a serious Christian," to "a believer that the Bible is the literal word of God," to "a hypocrite," to "someone who's out of touch with modern society." Of course, there would be answers in between and around all of these responses.

Years ago, journalist Terry Mattingly asked the Rev. Billy Graham to define evangelical. At the time, Graham was the most influential figure in Protestant Christianity. "Actually, that's a question I'd like to ask somebody, too," Graham replied.[14] Mattingly added that this vagueness in defining evangelical leads most mainstream journalists to assume the term refers to conservative voters with some ill-defined religious belief. Graham later helped convene an international group of hundreds of evangelical leaders who crafted the 1974 Lausanne Covenant which provides a detailed statement of the movement's key distinctives.[15]

In 1989, historian David Bebbington offered a definition which The National Association of Evangelicals (NAE) appropriated as an official definition:

1. The belief that lives need to be transformed through a "born-again" experience and a lifelong process of following Jesus;

2. A demonstration of the gospel in missionary and social reform efforts;

3. Obedience to the Bible as the word of God, the ultimate authority on all of life;

4. Stress on the sacrifice of Jesus Christ on the cross as making possible the redemption of humanity.[16]

The NAE added, "These distinctives and theological convictions define us—not political, social or cultural trends."[17] Historian Mark Noll observed, "These evangelical traits have never by themselves yielded cohesive, institutionally compact, or clearly demarcated groups of Christians. But they do serve to identify a large family of churches and religious enterprises."[18] Various doctrines and denominations exist within the broad umbrella of the movement, spanning both Roman Catholicism and Protestantism. The continuum runs from fundamentalists to charismatics to Pentecostals. Some sub-groups of evangelicals believe the miraculous gifts described in the New Testament ceased when the official canon of the Bible was adopted a few hundred years after the death of Christ. Others believe all "gifts of the Spirit" used in the Bible are available to enhance and extend the church's life today.

The NAE does not say evangelicals should belong to the American Republican political party or vote consistently with the Republican Party platform. Yet an overwhelming number of people who say they are evangelicals vote Republican.[19] In response to this, the NAE suggested researchers define respondents as evangelicals only if that person agrees with these statements:

1. The Bible is the highest authority for what I believe;

2. It is very important for me personally to encourage non-Christians to trust Jesus Christ as their Savior;

3. Jesus Christ's death on the cross is the only sacrifice that could remove the penalty of my sin;

4. Only those who trust in Jesus Christ alone as their Savior receive God's free gift of eternal salvation.[20]

It's vital in considering evangelicalism and its interaction with politics, culture, and society that we constantly ask if the people acting on behalf of the movement believe in its chief tenets. Or are they people who call themselves evangelicals, despite not striving to live as if the Bible is the perfect rulebook for Christian living?[21]

The Importance of Evangelicals in American History

Evangelical Christians have significantly influenced American history. Nearly every denomination and social movement published a newspaper or magazine to advance the cause and, often, to solicit funding. In the nineteenth century, Christian publications railed against slavery, evolution, and alcohol consumption while advocating for women's rights and conversion of the "lost" worldwide. Dennis Voskuil notes: "The Protestant perspective, at this time pervasively evangelical, reached to the very center of national life; and Protestant journalists took all of society to be their 'beat.'"[22]

Christian History, published from 1743 to 1745, was the first such publication. Its editors printed sermons from leaders of the Great Awakening sweeping Europe and the colonies. Preachers like Increase Mather, George Whitefield, and Jonathan Edwards wrote for the magazine, and it, in turn, chronicled their speaking engagements and crusades.[23] The German American *Ein Geistliches Magazien* ("A Religious Magazine"), published from 1764 to 1773 in Germantown, Pennsylvania, helped non-English speaking newcomers adapt to their new home while assisting them in preserving parts of their ethnic identity.[24]

Christian Scholars and Farmers Magazine claimed a three-part editorial focus: "to promote religion, to diffuse useful knowledge, and to help farmers in their work."[25] *The Advocate of Moral Reform*, published by the New York Female Moral Reform Society, supported the group's goal of assisting prostitutes and destitute women in the early nineteenth century. Without the journal, "there is every reason to believe the usefulness of the Society would have been greatly circumscribed, perhaps . . . wholly suspended . . . ."[26]

Publications against slavery and alcohol consumption appealed to Christian values and readers. "Abolitionism was a religious movement, emerging from the ferment of evangelical Protestantism . . . ," claimed historian Richard Hofstadter, then added: "The profusion of anti-slavery and abolitionist books, newspapers, pamphlets, reports, printed speeches and other publications which appeared in those three decades were an essential feature of this evangelical movement."[27]

The National Woman's Christian Temperance Union, the most visible anti-alcohol lobby of the time, started the well-read periodical *The Union Signal* in 1875. It shared how to advocate against alcohol consumption and in favor of what became the 18th Amendment to the Constitution (later repealed by the 21st Amendment passed in 1933).

In the twentieth century, some publications used their editorial space to rail against creeping secularism, the scientific method for finding truth (as opposed to literal acceptance of the Bible's explanation), and belief in evolution. Historians point to the seminal trial of a high school teacher, John Scopes, as a watershed moment in the history of religion in America. The trial arose after the state of Tennessee banned the teaching of evolution in the 1920s. The American Civil Liberties Union asked Scopes to test the law by teaching evolution. Scopes did. He was promptly arrested.

His 1925 trial captured national attention with prominent daily newspapers depicting the so-called Scopes Monkey Trial as an indictment of backward, uneducated Christians.[28] The trial caught national attention as the large-city newspapers ran articles from the courthouse detailing the battle for the spiritual soul of the nation. High-profile lawyers Clarence Darrow and William Jennings Bryant argued for and against the traditional religious view of creation.[29] At the end of the trial, Scopes was found guilty.

Conservative Protestants, who identified at the time as fundamentalists, lost more than Scopes, however. Stung by the mainstream press criticism, they withdrew from trying to interact with and influence the culture of that time. Instead, they started Bible colleges and publications to create a reality that ran parallel to mainstream culture. This alternative culture was certainly not a monolith. Elizabeth Nordbeck noted, "They are linked by no single organization, council, or bureaucracy. Indeed, historically, conservatives have often been separatistic, disputatious, and mutually hostile. Yet undeniably, they share a strong family resemblance that cuts across denominational and even deep theological boundaries."[30]

Magazines of the early twentieth century adopted "militant-sounding names like *The Conflict*, *The Crusader's Champion*, *Dynamite*, and *The Defender*."[31] Among these was *the Sword of the Lord*, which facilitated evangelism and encouraged believers to "earnestly avoid compromise in doctrine or yoking up with unbelievers."[32]

After World War II, evangelist Billy Graham captured worldwide attention for his crusades in massive stadiums, resulting in millions of Christian conversions. In his messaging, the term evangelical replaced fundamentalist, as Graham's preaching initially attracted young people returning from the horrors of fighting in World War II. In 1956, he founded *Christianity Today* to help scattered believers in various denominations better understand biblically based Christianity.

Editorially independent magazines *Sojourners* and *World* began in the 1970s. An internet-only news publication, *The Christian Post* debuted in the early 2000s. Over the decades, these and other religious publications have engaged "clergy and lay members of churches in vigorous conversations about important events, ideas and artistic expressions that are shaping culture far beyond the boundaries of the ecclesiastical channels."[33]

The four evangelical publications analyzed in this book follow many predecessors seeking to educate, motivate, and occasionally entertain readers. In doing so, they help evangelicals polish their identity amidst the permissiveness of today's culture. Lester Kurtz notes: "The beliefs of a religious tradition never stand in isolation, either from one another or from the life of the community."[34] For Quentin Schultze, these publications provide collective ways of knowing and interpreting the world through the eyes of faith: "In the United States, the religious press has been one of the most important vehicles for bringing people of faith into a shared public space to converse about the broader society."[35]

With the advent of the Internet, readers of evangelical publications live in nearly every nation worldwide, and some of the articles in these publications are posted online in multiple languages. Thus, "Tribal journals extend the specialized conversations across geographic space, organize collective sentiment, focus the discussion, and somewhat centralize how the participants imagine their faith in the world."[36] Sometimes the information comes from writers or editors assuming a prophetic role, providing "an on-going critique of the life of the church and the wider society," as we'll see in the following pages.[37]

Today's evangelical publications are read primarily by people who are interested enough in news about the movement to buy an annual subscription. These readers are not only invested in the future of the church and its relationship to the American experience, but they also tend to be opinion leaders whose viewpoints influence people in their social circles and their churches and businesses. If the evangelical press disappears, what will replace it as a trusted news source on all things Christian?

With changes in the future audience of these publications on the horizon, and the technological revolution showing no sign of abating, this question should interest students seeking a religious communication career and church leaders and influencers within the movement.

Media Influence and Their Audiences

How does this influence occur? Prominent communication scholars, summarizing thousands of studies about media influence, provide us with insight. A handful of media influence theories help explain why publications with a small print readership and a larger web readership might wield so much influence in a tribal culture.

The Two-step Flow says that media influence is more potent than we'd find by simply looking at subscription, circulation, or readership data. The idea is that opinion leaders read the publications' content and then pass it on to people in their circle of friendship and influence.[38] Pastors, lay leaders, elder board members, professors, teachers, and journalists are influential opinion leaders who are more likely to read religious publications and then pass on information they've learned to those they influence. This process can also be seen in the actions of social media influencers who might have thousands, even millions, of followers.

The Uses and Gratifications Theory says we read media content that reinforces what we already believe. During the early twenty-first century, as political and religious divisions increased, Fox News attracted evangelical audience members, while MSNBC and CNN attracted more liberal and progressive viewers. Very few news consumers switched between the two information sources. Instead, we ignore the media outlets whose content we disagree with or distrust.[39] Our human tendency, then, is to seek reinforcement to our beliefs, not challenges brought about by new information or cogent arguments.

Another media theory is Agenda Setting. By publishing certain news and opinions and downplaying or ignoring other events, editors indirectly tell readers, "This issue is important for you to be aware of."[40] We may not be told what to think about the issue, only that we should be thinking about it. It thus becomes an essential agenda item in public discourse. This phenomenon is why a topic of interest to only a few people gets magnified into a suddenly crucial cultural issue.

The idea of Framing is that the wording of the title or headline unconsciously sways our opinion. The placement of essential facts and quotes within the article provide a point of view, or a window, that can lead the reader to similar conclusions reached by the writer or the editor.[41] Framing is different from expressing an outright opinion, but it does influence the feelings and potential actions of the reader in subtle and, at times, unknown ways. Framing can result from a reporter's unconscious bias or the publication's editorial policy. This is particularly true with evangelical news media because their role is to illuminate current events through the lens of a Christian worldview.

We thus return to the questions posed at the beginning of this Introduction. How did the evangelical press, represented by four of its influential editorially independent media outlets, report on the critical and controversial issues dividing American society in the early decades of the twenty-first century? This required carefully reading hundreds of news articles, editorials, and columns printed in these magazines and on their websites and deciding which of these articles best represent the mindset of the editors, the gatekeepers of what readers know and believe about the evangelical movement.[42]

Examining the questions posed here will point us toward a better understanding of the evangelical movement and its future.[43] We'll begin that quest by introducing the four key publications that influence millions of people each month.

Chapter 1

Journalism through a Biblical Lens

THE PUBLICATIONS EXAMINED in this book have solid reputations for providing a variety of news and commentary aimed at readers who consider themselves to be evangelicals. In this and the following pages the magazines and their content are presented in alphabetical order.

The Christian Post

Korean pastor David Jang launched *The Christian Post* in Washington, DC in 2006. He claimed the world suffered from an information glut that his online-only publication could solve for Christians.[1] *The Christian Post* claimed to be "the nation's most comprehensive Christian news website," saying it delivers "up-to-date news, information, and commentaries relevant to Christians across denominational lines."[2]

The *Post* offers readers dozens of new stories daily, some in the form of regurgitated news releases from pastors and Christian organizations. Still, the amount of news and commentary it provides fuels healthy discussions among its primarily evangelical readers.

Richard Land, then-president of Southern Evangelical Seminary and a tireless crusader against abortion, signed on as executive editor. Nowhere on the website does the *Post* list information about its ownership. Rather than a legally constituted governing board, the publication lists only a board of advisers.

The publication's early days were marked by controversy over Jang's ministry and intentions. In 2012, *Christianity Today* published a 4,000-plus word exposé on Jang's ministry. The article claimed that Jang's followers said he was a "new messianic figure that would complete Jesus's earthly mission," a so-called "Second Coming Christ."[3] The heretical belief, if true, countered the carefully crafted view of himself and his ministries that Jang projected. Interviews with former members of Jang's church and details of investigations into his claims by Asian Christian groups seemed to validate the claims of his heresy.

The Christian Post immediately published a lengthy article disputing the assertions, noting that investigations by the Christian Council of Korea had twice cleared Jang of those charges.[4] The *Post* article called the charges by one of *CT*'s primary sources an "outright lie."[5]

That furor barely subsided before another controversy arose. A 2014 piece in *The New York Times* highlighted an announcement that two young entrepreneurs planned to begin publishing *Newsweek* in print again. Etienne Uzac and Jonathan Davis reportedly had ties to Jang, even though both denied the pastor had a business interest in their company. Nonetheless, *Christianity Today* claimed International Business Times, *Newsweek*'s parent company, was part of Jang's media empire. In *The New York Times* piece, the *Newsweek* owners called *CT*'s allegation "preposterous."[6]

In 2018, *The New York Times*, *Mother Jones*, *Buzz Feed*, and *The Wall Street Journal* reported that the Manhattan, New York, District Attorney's office indicted four followers and four organizations affiliated with Jang. The indictment listed five felonies: money laundering, fraud, conspiracy, falsifying business records, and criminal contempt. The charges stemmed from false loan applications submitted to several banks totaling $35 million. The indictment said a portion of the money fraudulently obtained by IBT's co-editor Uzac and Christian Media CEO William Anderson (the parent company of *The Christian Post*) did not solely purchase computer hardware, as the applications claimed. Instead, Jang-affiliated Olivet University and *The Christian Post* used some of the money to fund ongoing expenses. Adding to the intrigue, *Newsweek*'s editors published news about the indictment of their co-owner, which led to their termination for posting that story.[7] Uzac and Anderson pled guilty to the charges in February 2020 and the loan was eventually repaid.[8]

Buzz Feed then reported that *Newsweek* and *The Christian Post* used a malicious code that allowed the publications to claim exaggerated readership numbers.[9] This, then, led the publications to charge higher advertising rates.

The most comprehensive exploration of *The Christian Post*'s leadership and its editorial credibility appeared in a three-part series written by veteran Christian journalist Steve Rabey, editor of the *Ministry Watch* newsletter. The first article summarized the allegations of fraud, money laundering, and lying about actual readership by the *Post* and eight other Jang-affiliated publications.[10]

The second article charged, as previously reported by *Mother Jones*, that unpaid or poorly paid students attending Jang's Olivet University in northern California wrote much of the content. Rabey claimed articles on other websites were rewritten without crediting the original author and publication. Finally, he noted that much of the content was "more promotional than journalistic, and it tended to favor celebrities with large media platforms, both because their events were easier to cover and because these celebrities provided the kind of click-bait business model the *Christian Post* demanded."[11]

In his final piece, Rabey contacted prominent Christians listed as advisers to the *Post*, asking if they were aware of the guilty pleas of its former executives. According to his report, "It turns out that most of the advisors haven't been doing much advising—or having any personal contact—with anyone at the publication for years. But their names remained on the *Christian Post*, lending credibility to an organization trying to legitimize itself with evangelical Christians and padding their resumes."[12]

By 2024, Olivet University had relocated its main campus to southern California and opened branch campuses in several other states and Washington, DC. A New York branch closed earlier as it ran into trouble with state regulators. The *Los Angeles Times* reported in September 2024 that Olivet remained under state and federal investigation for its treatment of students.[13] Whether any of the allegations related to the university's use of students to prepare content for *The Christian Post* are true remains clouded.

So why did I choose *The Christian Post* for this analysis? First, the *Post* claims it reaches millions of readers with its free online-only content. The other three publications require a subscription to its print and online editions. Second, a typical day finds dozens of articles and op-ed articles posted, representing various perspectives. Thus, while it may be better thought of as an aggregator of content, it's an unparalleled evangelical bulletin board. Third, while it lacks the journalistic rigor of the other publications, the continuing presence of executive editor Land, a respected Southern Baptist leader and ardent crusader against abortion, gives it a modicum of credibility.

Christianity Today

Christianity Today is the oldest and arguably most influential of the publications. The first issue appeared in 1956. After World War II, young evangelist Billy Graham preached a simple but profound message about Jesus in large arenas worldwide.[14] As a rising star in the church and culture, Graham longed to redefine what it meant to be a Bible-believing Christian and to present Jesus to a new generation, particularly those physically and mentally ravaged by the war.

Graham said he woke up one morning in 1954 and quickly outlined an idea for a magazine explaining the beliefs of evangelicals.[15] He felt the national conversation over religion was mediated through the mainstream press and relied too heavily for its understanding of Protestantism by reading the nearly 100-year-old magazine *Christian Century*. He remarked, "I feel that there is needed in Protestantism today a magazine that is the counterpart to the *Christian Century*. Something that will be evangelical, theologically oriented, and will commend itself to the Protestant ministers of America. I feel it is desperately needed."[16] *Christianity Today*'s first managing editor, Larry Ward, revealed some of Graham's thinking when he wrote to a donor: "We all know how evangelicalism has been charged with second-rate scholarship and second-hand science, etc. Here, at last is something with both the weight of scholarship and the authority of the Scriptures behind it."[17]

Theologically dense writing and distrust of mainline Protestants and Roman Catholics characterized founding editor Carl F. H. Henry's editorial content.[18] At the same time, the leadership issued writers' guidelines that cautioned against such harsh rhetoric. The advice included striving for factual descriptions of religions outside of evangelicalism in a non-offensive manner: "We are out to win a hearing, not to condemn."[19]

Henry occasionally used the magazine's pages to dialogue with Protestant leaders with whom he differed. Early editions of the magazine featured articles by Charles Morrison, the long-time editor of *Christian Century*, and Eugene Blake, the head of the liberal National Council of Churches.

That editorial policy changed in 1968 under Harold Lindsell. Lindsell introduced more practical and readable articles sprinkled with personality features and testimonies. To reduce costs, the board voted in 1976 to move the magazine from Washington, DC to the Chicago suburbs.

Graham's desire to see evangelicalism move beyond its parochial cultural and political roots sometimes backfired. The most widely cited example is his relationship with President Richard Nixon. Graham delivered the prayer at the newly elected president's inauguration in 1969. Later, Graham discovered that Nixon had used their friendship to boast to others that the evangelist supported Nixon's conduct during the Vietnam War.[20] Years later when asked if he would change anything in his decades-long ministry, Graham replied, "I would have steered clear of politics."[21]

The publication has not been shy about speaking out on important moral issues. It voiced concern about abortion soon after the 1973 U.S. Supreme Court decision in Roe v. Wade allowed the practice nationwide.[22] On issues of sexual morality, the magazine insisted that any sex outside marriage—heterosexual or homosexual—was a sin. The magazine also opposed gay marriage.

Christianity Today generally avoided "investigative" news stories involving other Christian ministries.[23] But in 2020, it published a series of articles exposing the sexual misdeeds of the late evangelist Ravi Zacharias.[24] The magazine's editors explained: "*Christianity Today* doesn't undertake the long and expensive work of investigating accusations to create a list of notorious sinners. Our aim is correction—not just of the leaders we're reporting on, but of all of us."[25]

A few years later, the magazine turned its lens on itself, admitting that over 12 years, it allowed a pattern of sexual harassment by two men: its just-retired editor, Mark Galli, and former advertising director Olatokunbo Olawoye.[26] *Christianity Today* published the full text of an external investigation commissioned by its Board of Directors, along with an explanation and apology from the company president.[27]

Despite its slowness in recognizing harassment in its midst, the publication's readership did not appear to suffer. The journal claims over five million pageviews monthly through its digital and print resources. Its print edition appears bi-monthly while online content is updated daily.

Sojourners

In 1971, a group of disgruntled seminary students in suburban Chicago launched a movement for peace and justice that included the ideal of communal living. The students were troubled by the inconsistency between their understanding of biblical values and the support given by many evangelicals (including *Christianity Today*) to American involvement in the Vietnam War. They also felt Christians lacked action on racial and social injustice, human rights, and care for God's creation. They created a magazine, *The Post-American*, so named because they felt the church needed to move beyond the existing value system in America.

"We find ourselves in the midst of a radical awakening, among people who are raising basic and critical questions about the nature of our society and about the quality of life in the world we inherit," founding editor Jim Wallis wrote in the first issue.[28] In his inaugural column, he expressed disillusionment, alienation, and anger at an American system he regarded as oppressive. Yet his jeremiad firmly rested on a foundation of evangelical values: "We contend that the new vision that is necessary is to be found in the radical Christian faith that is grounded in a commitment to Jesus Christ."[29]

Some early articles were penned by people of color and explained their struggles with racism and poverty.[30] Other writers, such as John Howard Yoder, advised Christians to avoid paying taxes to protest heavy government expenditures on weapons.[31] In 1979, the magazine's name changed to *Sojourners*. The original 16-page quarterly publication was replaced with a 32-page, well-illustrated magazine published ten times yearly. *Sojourners* moved its center of operations to Washington, DC in 1975.

Reagan-era political alliances between evangelicals and the Republican Party intensified during the latter two decades of the twentieth century. In the 1980s, Wallis argued against the growing alliance of evangelicals and the Republican Party. He said this alliance compromised evangelicals' ability to address poverty and social inequity, adding that "aligning with a political party created division and bred animosity between Christians rather than promoting unity and cooperation."[32]

While the magazine challenged many conservative Christian beliefs, it remained staunchly anti-abortion. Wallis was once called "the most visible antiabortion cleric in the progressive movement . . . ."[33]

Wallis's emphasis on progressive evangelicalism caught the attention of national leaders after the publication of his 2005 best-selling book *God's Politics: Why the Right Gets It Wrong and the Left Doesn't Get It*. Both political parties sought his wisdom as they considered policies and legislation aimed at eradicating poverty.[34]

Cracks in the magazine's editorial independence created controversy in 2020, resulting in a shake-up of the publication's editorial leadership. A freelancer's article alleged that the U.S. Council of Bishops rejected wording in a document on race that would have condemned swastikas, Confederate flags, and nooses. The headline read, "The Catholic Church Has a Visible White-Power Faction."[35] Once published, the allegations incensed Catholic leaders participating with *Sojourners* and its larger movement in an advocacy campaign for the poor. Given what he called an unprecedented outpouring of protest from Catholic leadership, Wallis removed the article from the website, the first time the publication had taken such an action.[36] His decision led to the resignation of two editorial staff, both people of color, who felt his actions downplayed the racism reported on in the article.

Wallis explained that the article's allegations "seriously jeopardized our advocacy work, particularly through the Circle of Protection—our broadly ecumenical coalition over ten years that has been remarkably effective in preventing deeper budget cuts to the most vulnerable."[37]

Wallis also announced changes in editorial procedures and leadership because of the claims in the article (some of them questionable) and his removal of the article (temporarily) from the website. In the future, he said a more robust line would divide the publication's editorial team from *Sojourners* movement campaigns and his activism. The publication, he said, would put a hold on accepting freelance articles, presumably because verifying facts was difficult for the publication's small editorial team.

On the first day of 2021, Adam Russell Taylor, a former student of Wallis and long-time board chair of the *Sojourners* movement, succeeded his mentor as President of the overall organization. Several women assumed editorial leadership of the printed and online publication. Wallis remained an influential adviser while transitioning into a full-time teaching position at Georgetown University.

Scholar Hana Kim asserted that *Sojourners*, "has been an incredibly important source that has helped to shape and influence progressive evangelicalism in the U.S."[38]

WORLD

World traces its founding to 1986 when Joel Belz, owner of the *Presbyterian Journal* and *God's World* publication for kids, created a weekly news magazine for Christians.

Until 2021, *World* called its editorial philosophy "biblical journalism." Coined by its long-time editor, Marvin Olasky, biblical journalism teaches writers to report news events through a lens of what the Bible says about human existence. His justification for this approach is that all news media reflect the bias of their writers, editors, and publishers. Olasky encouraged his writers to recognize their bias as Christians and to present the information, quotes, and other facts with accuracy and integrity, but to do so through the lens of a Christian worldview. "[This] reporting is designed to show readers the salient facts in Bible-based contextualization and allow them to agree or disagree with the conclusions reached," he said.[39] In his ground-break-ing analysis of Christian journalism, he claimed, "A solidly Christian news publication should not be balanced. Its goal should be provocative and evocative, colorful and gripping, Bible-based news analysis."[40]

One distinctive of such an approach is that it "provides necessary insight for believers in a culture that has taken pluralism to new heights and has often pushed what's been called traditional Christian values into minority status."[41]

The North Carolina-based publication did not shy away from criticiz-ing the actions of church leaders or politicians, even Republicans. *The New York Times* noted, ". . . evangelical Protestant journalism is generally more public relations than reporting; *World* stands out as an exception."[42]

For instance, in 1997, the publication challenged Zondervan, the world's largest Bible publisher. "Femme Fatale" by Susan Olasky (Marvin's wife) charged that Zondervan and a well-respected translation committee quietly planned to introduce a gender-neutral version of the New Interna-tional Version of the Bible.[43] Susan Olasky charged that this signaled that the "feminist seduction of the evangelical church" was close to undermin-ing traditional understandings of the gender roles God had created.[44]

Zondervan immediately protested what it felt were unfair reporting techniques. That led to more *World* stories and a challenge for Zonder-van to refute the general truth of the articles.[45] Zondervan eventually filed an ethics complaint with the Evangelical Press Association (EPA). At face value, the reports were factual, an ad hoc committee of the EPA concluded, even if sensationalized inferences existed.[46]

World's article and the concern expressed by its more influential evangelical readers forced Zondervan to delay plans for the translation's release.[47] In retrospect, author Susan Olasky said the courageous decision to take on Zondervan and its owner, NewsCorp, threatened the ongoing existence of *World*.[48]

Rarely is a religious publication mentioned, much less lambasted, in *The New York Times*. In early 2000, *Times* columnist William Safire criticized the publication's depiction of Arizona Sen. John McCain who launched a short-lived campaign for the Republican Party presidential bid.[49] "The McCain Craze: Can Anything Stop Him Now?" by staff member Bob Jones claimed in its subhead that McCain's political views "should give Republicans pause."[50] Jones claimed that the senator was soft on supporting restrictions on alcohol companies because his wife, Cindy, was then heir to millions of dollars of Anheuser-Busch stock. The writer also reported that McCain was unaware of his wife's addiction to barbiturates until there was a federal investigation into her illegal drug use.

World's editors sent copies of that story to political and media leaders in Washington, DC. After reading these claims, the Times's Safire questioned Jones's word choice, particularly the statement that McCain ". . . claimed not to know about Cindy's addiction—even though she had at one point checked herself in for treatment at a nearby clinic."[51] Safire said this gave the impression that World thinks, "the senator did know, did not care, and is now lying about it."[52] The columnist called Jones's story a "repugnant anti-McCain political document," while saving his harshest words for editor Olasky:

> . . . when its editor is [Texas Gov. George W.] Bush's trusted Austin adviser; when its reporter bears the name of the school being abused as a Bush tool in the campaign; when its not-for-profit funds are used to print, illustrate and distribute a hatchet job on a political opponent to a list of officials and media biggies on a primary election eve—then such backdoor backing of candidate Bush strikes me as religio-political sleaze in action.[53]

In response to Safire, Olasky wrote: "his paranoia gained a broad audience and World suddenly had new enemies (and also new fans)."[54]

It's important to note that not all of World's content contained investigative pieces using an iconoclastic, no-holds-barred approach. Over the years, the publication published inspirational feature stories, dispassionate book and movie reviews of mainstream releases, sports stories, and articles lending helpful advice to individuals, families, churches, and organizations.

World's embrace of Olasky's biblical journalism philosophy altered in 2021 when its board voted to add an opinion section to the magazine and website. It said the new department would only accept opinions from conservative commentators. Olasky was not involved in the decision and moved his retirement date forward because he disagreed with the board's decision.

Albert Mohler, a leading figure in the Southern Baptist Convention, was named editor of World's Opinion section. He said the new section was a "bold venture into the battle of ideas" and that the standpoint would be "unquestionably conservative, and marked by a commitment to preserve and defend the unique contribution of Western civilization as established under the influence of Christianity."[55]

Olasky and several long-time staff saw the board's decision as a rebuke of *World*'s editorial approach and their hard work.[56] Olasky even charged that the publication abandoned its commitment to independent journalism and had adopted a "pay-to-play and editorial favoritism."[57]

Among those resigning was Mindy Belz, the sister-in-law of *World*'s founder and publisher Joel Belz. In her farewell column, she wrote: "For those who have read my work, it's no surprise that my framework is at times at odds with conservatism and liberalism, the strife and stridency that's befallen American evangelicalism, and with some directions *World* News Group is charting."[58]

In her resignation, staff writer Sophia Lee said, " . . . I feel uncomfortable about *World*'s Opinions, which has declared itself 'unquestionably conservative.'"[59] She said she was not comfortable with the "evangelical world and its tendency to mark certain political and cultural instincts as 'Biblical.'"[60] Angela Lu Fulton, the managing editor, said she resigned because ". . . . the leadership at WNG [World News Group] seems to be shifting its focus and resources away from biblically objective journalism toward politically conservative positions."[61]

The New York Times's Ben Smith reported that Olasky's departure "marks the end of a remarkable era at the publication, which has delivered a mix of hard news and watchdog articles about the evangelical realm."[62] Smith noted: ". . . these articles offered something old-fashioned and hard for any community to take: accountability reporting."[63] Olasky's departure, he added, meant another ". . . conservative news outlet, which had almost miraculously retained its independence, is conquered by Mr. Trump."

After quitting *World*, Olasky and several former staff members quickly pivoted to writing for *Christianity Today*. Olasky accepted a position as Executive Editor of News and Global at *Christianity Today* in December of 2024.

World is now published in print form on a bi-weekly basis. News and commentary are posted online daily. Its commitment to biblical journalism is difficult to find when reading news articles published after the departure of the core of *World*'s reporting staff. Its news articles continue to remain faithful to the practice of journalistic values such as accuracy and fairness.

Chapter 2

The 2016 Presidential Election: The Lesser Evil

THE PRESIDENTIAL ELECTION of 2016 presented Christians with two extremely unpopular candidates. Each publication found Donald Trump and Hillary Clinton lacking in adherence to Christian values. The challenges they faced in communicating with their readers took on a variety of different forms. Reading articles and opinion pieces prior to the election shows each publication's twisted and agonizing journey to make sense out of the options available to believers.

The Christian Post

Early in 2016, only one Republican candidate failed to meet the criteria for being a valid moral candidate according to *The Christian Post*. "Back away from Donald Trump," an editorial advised its readers.[1] Trump said he had never asked for forgiveness in his life, nor did his words and deeds display "the fruit of the spirit."

Further, the editorial alleged, "Trump is a misogynist and philanderer. He demeaned women and minorities on several documented occasions. His preferred forms of communication were insult, obscenities, and untruths."[2] Additionally, the article cited Trump's racism and embrace of dictators and White supremacists.

The editors acknowledged that Trump supporters had legitimate complaints about the political landscape in the nation and the fear of more years of politically liberal policies. But they said that Trump changed his positions on the issues to suit the moment and that "questionable business practices, reported association with organized crime, and abrupt changes in fundamental positions" dogged his professional life.[3] "We already have a Protector, and He is not Trump."[4]

The publication asserted that if elected, Trump might use the levers of government to silence leading evangelical voices who have already spoken out against him. The article ends with this statement: "This is a critical time in American history, and we call on all Christians to pray for personal repentance, divine forgiveness, and spiritual awakening in our nation. It is not the time for Donald Trump."[5]

Frequent contributor Michael Brown criticized candidate Trump, although he finally backed the reality TV star as the lesser of two evils. Brown raised the issue of Trump's statement that he had never asked for forgiveness, suggesting the presumptive candidate attend an evangelical church to hear "some fresh new sermons from some fine contemporary pastors . . . ."[6]

In March 2016, commenting on a Trump rally protestors shut down in Chicago, Brown asserted that Trump bore some responsibility for the situation because of "his inflammatory and irresponsible rhetoric."[7] Brown later urged Trump to humble himself before the Creator so he might use more acceptable language, suggesting Trump had crossed the line into uncivil discourse.[8] He encouraged Trump to utter three words that would transform his candidacy, "I WAS WRONG."[9]

A month before the election, Brown said of Clinton that she would appoint "disastrous" judges and curtail religious liberties.[10] He said that when she began telling Christians that their pro-life, pro-marriage beliefs must change, that Christians would "finally awaken from our complacency and lethargy."[11] Of Trump, he said, "It would be very hard to look to him as the savior of the nation."[12] He concluded: "So, what will it be, a great or rude awakening? The choice is ours to make."[13]

Editor Richard Land was a reluctant convert to Trump's candidacy. In June 2016, he agreed to serve on Trump's evangelical executive board, which allowed evangelical leaders to advise the candidate. Land was careful to tell readers that while he agreed to serve on the committee, it did not constitute an endorsement of Trump for President. "We as Christians often ask ourselves 'what would Jesus do?' Frankly, I cannot imagine our Savior would draw His robes around Himself and walk on the other side of the street and spurn Mr. Trump's request for spiritual counsel and advice."[14] He added that he would have said yes to Clinton if she had asked him to join an advisory board.

On July 7, he made his position on Clinton clear as he reacted to the news that FBI Director James Comey decided not to prosecute her for using personal computers to send and receive classified government emails. Land alleged that this just showed how both Bill and Hillary Clinton had dodged prosecution for several incidents over the years, writing "They corrupt, corrode, and seduce everything they touch."[15]

A week later, Land wrote an Open Letter to Trump on behalf of evangelical voters. Land urged Trump to show his loyalty to evangelical causes by naming a vice-presidential candidate who was strongly pro-life, someone like eventual nominee Mike Pence.[16] Then Land suggested that Trump release the names of his potential Cabinet choices, people amenable to evangelical values, and to empower these men and women to campaign on Trump's behalf. (Of the names mentioned, only Ben Carson and Rick Perry served in the Trump administration). Finally, Land suggested that Trump signal his intention to nominate Sen. Ted Cruz to the Supreme Court after receiving a solid endorsement from Cruz.

By the end of August 2016, Land acknowledged that the election posed "an excruciating choice."[17] He told evangelicals voting was a moral obligation. He cited the Romans 13 mandate to support civil society and Matthew 5:13–16, calling believers to become "salt and light" to the world. Acknowledging that Trump may not be a good president, he feared Clinton would destroy America. "Consequently, with sadness of heart, I will cast my vote for Donald Trump and pray that God will have mercy on him and on my beloved country."[18]

Despite its reluctant support for Trump, the *Post* published a few opinion pieces by writers endorsing Clinton's candidacy. Frequent contributor Eric Sapp argued that Clinton was the best choice for voters who opposed abortion. He reasoned that Christians "should not be single-issue voters since Christ's ministry wasn't a single issue."[19] He also hinted that hypocrisy might be present in the way pro-life adherents approached their endorsements, saying "When Hillary Clinton allows for these exceptions, evangelicals are told she 'supports late-term abortion,' but when Republicans make some same exceptions, they are awarded 100% Pro-Life voting records."[20]

Deborah Fikes, a former National Association of Evangelicals board member, gave readers a personal and passionate plea for respecting Clinton's work on behalf of people experiencing poverty and lauded her solid religious character.[21] She argues, "There is nothing in a Christian's political engagement or love for our country that justifies the hateful words and deeds that Hillary Clinton has been subjected to for the past 25 years. Even if you could never see yourself voting for Hillary Clinton, if you are follower of Jesus, you cannot be a member of anyone's Hate Club, including Hillary Clinton's."[22]

The Christian Post's editorial page editor suggested that neither candidate should receive a vote. The editor's note introducing Natt Nazworth's article said only two options existed for evangelicals—vote for Trump or cast a protest vote. Nazworth said Trump's imperialistic impulses would ruin the country, stating "*CP* has taken many controversial stances over the years on issues like homosexuality and abortion, but it was only after our anti-Trump editorial that threats became a security issue. The main office of *The Christian Post* recently had to increase security due to death threats. This is the type of behavior Trump encourages."[23] The publication's reluctant support for Trump's candidacy didn't budge after revelations that Access Hollywood leaked his crude comments about women.[24]

As columnists and editors provided their perspectives, the *Post* ran dozens of news articles giving readers a blow-by-blow account of the latest information. These included a report that respected evangelical minister and author John Piper had called on both Trump and Clinton to quit the race.[25] The *Post* also featured a news article detailing influential evangelical leader Franklin Graham's defense of Trump.[26]

If the editors of *The Christian Post* had their way, neither Donald Trump nor Hillary Clinton would have been nominated to run for president in 2016. Still, with great reluctance, they supported Donald Trump as the lesser of two evils.

Christianity Today

Christianity Today faced the same dilemma. What should their readers do when both candidates failed the test of character and lacked genuine evangelical commitment?

Early in 2016, writer Christina Cleveland foreshadowed how the vote might finish. She differentiated between people who need and crave structure and those who are more comfortable with ambiguity. Those who need structure tend to be politically conservative. She also noted that a powerful personal experience, such as a college semester or academic year of international study, an impactful Bible study, or a meaningful life transition, influenced how readers might vote.[27] While she did not come right out and say it, her observations predicted that most religious conservatives, i.e., evangelicals, would likely vote for Trump as they fell into the psychological camp of those needing black and white answers.

As the presidential election heated up, a report on a Pew Research study found only 1% of people who attended church (both evangelicals and mainline Protestants) heard their pastor speak favorably about Donald

Trump. In comparison, 6% said they heard positive comments about Hillary Clinton.[28]

Perhaps the most prescient data reported was that 78% of White evangelicals responding indicated they would vote for Trump, even though their pastors said little or nothing in support or opposition to his candidacy.[29] Even before the election, the divide between Christian leaders (lukewarm on both candidates) and evangelical laity (fervently pro-Trump) became evident.

Recognizing that its editors could not formally endorse a presidential candidate, the publication asked three noted evangelicals to share their election choices with readers. The September 2016 issue of *Christianity Today* featured articles in support of Clinton, Trump, and "neither." Ron Sider, founder of Evangelicals for Social Action and a long-time professor at Eastern University, kicked off the special section with his endorsement of Hillary Clinton. Noting that he had not endorsed a presidential candidate in 44 years, he did so in 2016 because this election was the "most important" in his lifetime.[30]

While opposing Clinton's pro-abortion stance and support for gay marriage, Sider said that he found her "decades-long history of working hard for racial and economic justice" worthy of endorsement.[31] He also cited her support for more funding for college affordability, her desire to raise the minimum wage, and her pledge to change tax policies favoring the rich. Sider criticized Trump's statements on taxes, his racist comments, and his position on immigration. America needed a wise statesman as president, not someone even senior Republican national security leaders said lacks "character, values, and experience."[32]

Supporting Trump was the founder of the powerful radio ministry Focus on the Family, James Dobson.[33] To Dobson, the most crucial key to the 2016 election was that the new president would pick at least one Supreme Court judge, perhaps more. He remarked, "Unelected, unaccountable, and imperialistic justices have a history of imposing horrendous decisions on the nation."[34] He cited the Roe v. Wade decision of 1973 by the U.S. Supreme Court that "divided the nation and led to the murders of 54 million innocent babies. This killing goes on every day."[35] Dobson also praised the selection of vice-presidential candidate Mike Pence.

Dobson admitted that Trump "speaks in hyperbole, clearly. His rhetoric has been inexcusable, and I don't defend it."[36] He added that he felt public and private criticism of Trump's comments already led him to moderate what he said in public, saying "If Trump turns out to be an incorrigible demagogue, we can hope he will be reeled in by the political process."[37]

Sho Baraka, an African American rapper and a founding member of the AND Campaign, explained his endorsement of "neither" candidate: "As an African American, I'm marginalized by the lack of compassion on the Right. As a Christian, I'm ostracized by the secularism of the Left. As a man, I'm greatly concerned by subversive attempts to deconstruct all 'classical' definitions of manhood."[38] Baraka called on Christians to stand against the anti-Christian policies of both parties, saying "I believe that soon there will be a movement of folks who protest both police brutality and abortions without feeling disloyal to one party or the other," noting that he hopes that more people would adopt an "unabridged concept of life, that it is to be protected from the cradle to the grave."[39]

Evangelicals reacted with surprise and disappointment when *The Washington Post* revealed an audiotape of Trump bragging to TV host Billy Bush about his prowess with women. *Christianity Today's* editor, Andy Crouch, felt compelled to speak out, noting that Christians should not be silent when a potential national leader voices "blatant immorality."[40] Crouch added that Trump remained unrepentant despite his claims of being a Christian believer who should have put aside idolatry and repented, concluding that "He is, in short, the very embodiment of what the Bible calls a fool."[41] Crouch also rued the impact Trump's statement and evangelical silence might have on non-believers, voicing that "Enthusiasm for a candidate like Trump gives our neighbors ample reason to doubt that we believe Jesus is Lord."[42]

While Donald Trump's lack of morality was the central point in Crouch's op-ed, he did not spare Clinton. He pointed out that using personal email to conduct government business demonstrated her desire for secrecy and "the path to power preferred by the global technocratic elite . . . ."[43] He condemned policy positions incompatible with evangelicals' positions on the sanctity of human life. Finally, he expressed evangelical fear that Clinton was "hostile" to Christianity.

After thousands of words and dozens of articles about the 2016 election, readers of *Christianity Today* did not find an endorsement of any candidate. Both fell short of biblical Christianity's expectations for the leader during such a critical time in world history.

Sojourners

Donald Trump and Hillary Clinton are mentioned once in the print content of *Sojourners* during the contentious 2016 election.[44] Hundreds of online articles, however, discuss the relative qualities of each candidate.

Sojourners began its barrage of anti-Trump analysis more than a year before he was even nominated. Editor Jim Wallis sounded the alarm about Trump in May 2015. In a blog post on the *Sojourners* website, he described Trump with words that would be used consistently by mainstream media and progressive Christians: narcissist and egomaniac.[45]

Wallis took Trump to task for his race-baiting and lying about the impact of undocumented immigrants on the economy and crime in America. Wallis speculated that part of the acceptance of Trump's racial bigotry resulted from the Republican Party's acceptance of racism and its desire to keep the party and America White.[46] Wallis ended this first of 149 overwhelmingly negative blog posts on Sojo.net, calling Republicans to wake up and push back against Trump. Wallis added that party leaders "not only have my challenge—they have my prayers."[47]

Meanwhile, Hillary Clinton, who became the Democratic nominee for president, received passing mention in a 2015 Wallis post about her support for the Iraq war. Wallis noted, "While she had the same intelligence as the others, she wrongly voted yes on the Iraq war. She has since admitted her mistake."[48]

By February 2016, Trump appeared headed for the eventual nomination, buoyed by polling numbers showing massive support for his candidacy among White evangelicals. Wallis speculated that Americans were confused by Trump calling himself an evangelical, writing "I find it's best to use the words of Jesus himself, words white evangelicals need to listen to if they are, as they claim, believers in Christ."[49] He quoted Luke 4:18, where Jesus talks about his anointing to encourage the poor, release captives, provide sight to the blind, and free the oppressed. He contrasted those words of Jesus with the stances of Trump and his closest competitor, Sen. Ted Cruz of Texas. He concluded, "In other words, the mission statement of Jesus in Luke 4 has almost nothing to do with the voting practices of white evangelicals in this election year. Or we might say that white nativism has trumped the faith of the evangelicals—or at least what Jesus meant by 'evangelical.'"[50] Wallis also cites then-current polling numbers showing that most Trump supporters were overwhelmingly White and male.

In spring 2016, Wallis wrote in support of Russell Moore, then-president of the Ethics and Religious Liberty Commission of the Southern Baptist Convention. Moore wrote a negative op-ed about Trump in *The New York Times*. In response, Trump tweeted that Moore was a "terrible" representative of evangelicals and "a nasty guy with no heart!"[51] In his defense of Moore (who later became editor of *Christianity Today*), Wallis responded, "Well, Donald, many of us are right with Russell on this, and you will face strong opposition to your political use of bigotry from Christians across the political spectrum."[52] Wallis asked if the presumptive Republican candidate dared to meet with faith leaders to talk about bigotry and racial issues, adding "But I don't think you have such courage or honesty."[53] In conclusion, Wallis referenced another quote from Moore: "The man on the throne in heaven is a dark-skinned, Aramaic-speaking 'foreigner' who is probably not all that impressed by chants of 'Make America Great Again.'"[54]

Later, Wallis quoted from a manifesto signed by 23,000 evangelicals. It read, in part: "Whether we support Mr. Trump's political opponent is not the question here. Hillary Clinton is both supported and distrusted by a variety of Christian voters. We, undersigned evangelicals, simply will not tolerate the racial, religious, and gender bigotry that Donald Trump has consistently and deliberately fueled, no matter how else we choose to vote or not to vote."[55]

In this post, it appeared that Wallis was once again attempting to salvage the term evangelical from cultural misunderstandings about the difference between White conservative Christians who self-identify as evangelical and Christians of all ethnicities who believe historical definitions of evangelical. He added that he found the opinions of younger, multicultural evangelicals to be "good news indeed."[56]

Sojourners also responded to Trump's bragging about his sexual power over women. Correspondent Nish Weiseth chronicled the reaction of evangelical female leaders like Beth Moore and Lisa Sharon Harper who condemned Trump's comments. Weiseth noted, however: "Yet, even with the unearthing of Trump's comments about sexual assault, many evangelical Christian leaders, particularly white women, have remained silent."[57]

Thus, the editorial strategy of *Sojourners* during 2016 mainly focused on Trump's shortcomings. Clinton received a rare mention, although the publication highlighted her lifelong devotion as a social justice Methodist and how her faith animated her values and actions.[58] Later, the publication covered her Catholic support and the ongoing FBI investigation into sending government emails from her personal email accounts.[59] While *Sojourners* and its editor, Wallis, did not publish articles endorsing Clinton for the Presidency, they made it crystal clear that Donald Trump was anathema to Bible-believing Christians.

WORLD

World used an ingenious monthly poll of just over 100 evangelical leaders to chronicle the evolving loyalties of the 2016 Presidential election, what they called a snapshot of how "well-connected evangelical insiders are leaning."[60]

The first poll from July 2015 found Florida Senator Marco Rubio as the top choice, with nearly 20% of those responding voicing support. Former Florida Gov. Jeb Bush came in second with almost 15%, and Wisconsin Gov. Scott Walker and Texas Sen. Ted Cruz tied for third with just under 14%. *World* also asked its evangelical panel who they would not vote for: Democrat Clinton led that tally with 86.8%. Trump finished fourth. Nearly 75% said they would not vote for the New York City businessman.[61] The preferences of this group underwent dramatic changes in the 16 months to follow.

By February 2016, Rubio (48.8 %) and Bush (26.7%) were the *World's* panel Republican front-runners. Trump garnered 8% of favorable votes from evangelical leaders, but nearly 76% said they still would not vote for him. The article does note that by February, national polls showed Trump was the favored Republican nominee of potential voters of all beliefs and values.[62]

A few weeks after this poll was released, Rubio exited the presidential race, and Cruz emerged as the leader with a 76% favorability rating. Consistent with past polls, Donald Trump received a 5% positive rating. The March article noted in its lead, "a large majority of participants ready to vote for a third-party candidate if Donald Trump wins the Republican nomination."[63] Mirroring the opinions of *World's* poll respondents, reporter D. C. Innes asked what Christian values and policies remained in the Republican Party. Acknowledging that Christians had a different worldview than typical voters, he said: "The Christian's freedom to live consistently as a Christian—to worship but also to speak, to do business, to educate—is more important than the economy, illegal immigration and even national security."[64] He concluded that perhaps the Republican Party benefited greatly from evangelical Christian support but had abandoned Bible-believing Christians.[65]

World editor Marvin Olasky addressed his disappointment with both presidential candidates in a March 2016 column. The occasion was a claim by Focus on the Family founder James Dobson that evangelist Paula White mentored Trump, and thus the candidate understood and practiced Christian values. Olasky expressed skepticism of the claim, noting that Trump's statements and behavior did not comport to a person attempting to live a Spirit-filled life. He asked, "Shouldn't Trump show some signs of understanding that he, like all of us, is a sinner who needs God?"[66] Olasky hoped that Trump would temper his rhetoric and showmanship, "but his performance during the past month suggests he can't help himself."[67]

While admitting he was scared of a Hillary Clinton administration and the addition of more liberal judges to the Supreme Court, Olasky expressed hope that Trump would eventually temper his rhetoric and pick a strong vice-presidential candidate. If he did so, the nominee "could still impress rather than depress me and many *World* readers."[68]

During summer 2016, *World*'s long-time editorial leadership expressed frustration with both candidates. Publisher Joel Belz lamented that all the professed evangelicals had lost out in Republican state primary ballots. Why? Belz suggested that voters preferred the simplistic message and promises made by Donald Trump, saying "In state after state, pragmatism trumped principle—even among principled evangelicals."[69] He added that evangelical malaise was not confined simply to politics. With vibrant colleges and universities, more than 250 varied evangelical publications, and more than 1,000 radio stations, evangelicals had not only failed to nominate strong candidates for public office, but they had also barely influenced the professions of law, business, healthcare, education, and science.[70]

While *World*'s editors and columnists remained skeptical of Trump, their reporting and commentary on Clinton's failings went into high gear after the nominating conventions. International reporter Mindy Belz headed *World*'s investigations into the past actions of the former secretary of state. The subhead for the piece said it all: "You can't spin Hillary Clinton into the more respectable candidate."[71]

Mindy Belz concluded that her reporting had "uncovered multiple ties between the Clinton Foundation, Hillary herself, and Nigerian business interests who benefitted from the United States not cracking down on terror."[72]

Meanwhile, the survey of evangelical insiders consulted by *World* in late August said they were leaning toward voting for the recently nominated Republican Trump or would write in a candidate. Some 44% said they would support Trump after he released names of pro-life justices he might nominate to the U.S. Supreme Court. Still, J.C. Derrick noted that 48% of evangelical leaders said they would write in a name or not vote.[73]

On the eve of the elections, *World* called on Trump to step aside after the leak of his comments to Access Hollywood. On behalf of *World*'s editors, Olasky noted: "Although *World* over its 30 years has been more critical of Democrats than Republicans, particularly because of the abortion issue, we are not partisan."[74] The publication applied the same standards in 2016 when asking Trump to step aside as in 1998 when it suggested President Bill Clinton resign or face impeachment, stating "A Clinton resignation would have been good for America's moral standards in 1998. A Trump step aside would be good for America's moral standards in 2016."[75] Olasky said he understood that the magazine's stance might offend Trump's supporters, adding "Our regular surveys of evangelical leaders during the primary season showed almost no support for Donald Trump. Only when Clinton became the alternative did Trump gain majority evangelical support in public opinion polls."[76]

Olasky concluded by acknowledging that *World* might lose readers and donors because of its criticism of Trump (while remaining consistently critical of Clinton): "We don't know if He [God] will rescue *World* from the ire some Trump supporters will feel. We hope and pray that He will—but if He doesn't, He is still God, holding the future of individuals and nations in His hands. May His name be praised forever and ever."[77]

A few days later, Olasky wrote that both Trump and Clinton supporters faced the dilemma of choosing between two unfit candidates. He noted that *World* could impact the votes of its conservative Republican readers as the publication and its competitor, *Christianity Today*, had called for Trump to step down so Republicans could nominate someone else.[78] He also criticized progressive Protestant publications that had not pointed out the corruption of Clinton and called on her to step down, remarking "If they've had enough of the Clinton campaign's lies and are suggesting that Hillary Clinton step aside—a development we at *World* would welcome, although we have no influence regarding that—we'll be glad to reprint their comments."[79] Ultimately, *World* found both candidates unacceptable, acknowledging that most readers would vote for Trump.

The Aftermath

Trump won the Electoral College vote with Clinton winning the popular vote. While mainstream media expressed shock, evangelical media sighed.

The Christian Post reported on the Wednesday morning after the election that in his acceptance speech, Trump had vowed to represent all Americans, and he praised Clinton's hard-fought campaign and service to the nation.[80] Columnist Carmen Fowler LaBerge, president of the Presbyterian Lay Committee, recognized that Trump's victory left half of the U.S. feeling like they didn't belong, remarking "Four out of five white evangelicals voted for Trump, while evangelicals of color largely preferred Clinton. Does this difference define us? Or does the Gospel?"[81] She later added, "We have allowed the term 'evangelical Christian' to become a political classification. That's not OK."[82] She proposed that Christians get on their knees and repent for putting politics ahead of unity in Christ and then put God first in their lives and politics.

Likewise, *Christianity Today* announced Trump's victory without laudatory comments, writing in an objective news style that the candidate had gained sufficient Electoral College votes to become president-elect. Kate Shellnutt reported, "Exit polls suggest that 'Never Trump' was never a likely outcome for white evangelical voters, who showed up to support President-elect Donald Trump by their highest margin since 2004."[83]

A few days after Trump's victory, editor Mark Galli noted in a long (nearly 1,700-word) opinion piece that some prominent evangelical leaders, including the editors of *World* and *Christianity Today*, had "serious reservations" about Trump's candidacy, but evangelical voters chose Trump anyway.[84] Galli said this showed a vast gulf among evangelicals, with many asking in the hallway at work or on social media, "How could you, as an evangelical, possibly support your candidate?"[85] Galli asked, "We wonder if we can go on sharing the same name—evangelical."[86] In answer to the query, he reminded readers that the primary calling of an evangelical was not to culture or politics but to Jesus and the word of God found in the Bible. Galli also called on all believers to try to "make space for those with whom we disagree, while continuing to champion the causes we believe further justice."[87]

The disappointment in Trump's victory appeared on *Sojourners*'s webpage the day after the election. The editors wrote: "Last night, the United States elected Donald J. Trump as the 45th president of the United States. The vote comes at the end of a grueling 18-month election season, one that put misogyny, racism, homophobia, and bigotry in the spotlight . . . Trump's win is an endorsement of his divisive language and his slogan to 'Make America Great Again.'"[88]

A few hours later, Jim Wallis spared no words in criticizing Trump and, by extension, the people who voted for him. Wallis saw nothing positive about America or the church in Trump's wide margin of victory among White voters, writing "Most white evangelicals didn't seem to mind that they sold their souls to a man who embodies the most sinful and shameful worship of money, sex, and power, and—perhaps more than any other public figure in America—represents the very worst values of what American culture has become. We have never witnessed such religious hypocrisy as we saw in this election . . . ."[89]

Wallis suggested two practical steps for Christians after Trump's victory. First, he encouraged people to help protect those most vulnerable, including people of color, undocumented immigrants, and Muslims. Second, Christians must be public in their condemnation of racism, "especially from white Christians, who must call for the replacement of white identity politics with faith identity politics."[90]

Sojourners's mourning of the Trump victory continued throughout his first term in office. A March 2018 cover story by William Barber II advised readers on "How to Handle a Power-Hungry Narcissist."[91]

World's response contained four initial posts. The first noted, "Trump routs Clinton, wins the presidency."[92] The publication could not resist the opportunity to criticize mainstream media, as it began with: "In a stunning rebuke of polls and pundits . . . ."[93]

The article also called into question the contention that more than 80% of evangelical voters favored Trump. *World* reminded readers that mainstream media and pollsters allowed people to self-identify as evangelicals, even though not all those people attended church regularly or understood the central claims of the gospel, noting "Still, it's likely that plenty of true evangelicals joined the Trump constituency, whether reluctantly or enthusiastically."[94]

Another article appearing the day after the election said "'Never Trump' Republicans" commended Trump on his victory but continued to advocate for ethical campaign reform and the protection of the rights of all Americans, regardless of race, religion, or gender identity.[95]

Based on their commitment to enlightening readers about important biblical values, Christian publications warned against Trump because his actions and rhetoric did not conform to biblical values of love, forgiveness, honesty, fidelity, and justice for all races, genders, and ethnicities. Slightly more than 80% of self-identified White evangelicals voted for Trump anyway.

The 2016 presidential vote illuminated a schism within the evangelical movement. That is, the influence of its most respected publications held little sway compared to the communication power of right-wing media, conservative bloggers and radio hosts, and the influence of friends and colleagues. With the election over, would the intense disagreements fade?

Chapter 3

The Challenge of Immigration

For I was hungry, and you gave me something to eat; I was thirsty, and you gave me something to drink; I was a stranger, and you invited me in; I needed clothes, and you clothed me; I was sick, and you looked after me, I was in prison, and you came to visit me . . . Truly, I tell you, whatever you did for one of the least of these brothers and sisters of mine, you did for me.

Matt. 25:35–40

Give me your tired, your poor,
Your huddled masses yearning to breathe free,
The wretched refuse of your teeming shore.
Send these, the homeless, tempest-tost to me,
I lift my lamp beside the golden door!

—Statue of Liberty, New York City harbor

Few topics evoke such strong passion as those related to immigration. In 2015, Lifeway Research polled 1,000 evangelicals. Nearly half believed immigrants drained American economic resources. Seventy percent felt it essential for Congress to pass "significant" new immigrant legislation that should protect the unity of the immediate family. Border security should be tightened, according to an overwhelming majority of respondents. At the same time, nearly two-thirds supported a pathway for legal residency and citizenship for those who met "certain qualifications for residency."[1] Over 40% said the arrival of refugees provided an opportunity for evangelism.

Surprisingly, only 12% of evangelicals polled said their views on immigration came from the Bible.[2] The most decisive influence on evangelicals' attitudes was interaction with immigrants, media reports, and discussions with friends. The lack of Bible knowledge meant a daily diet of mainstream media stories, conservative media influencers, and interactions with friends and family could erase the compassion for immigrants expressed in the Bible.

Seven days after his inauguration, President Donald Trump issued an executive order banning immigrants, even those possessing valid visas, from seven majority-Muslim countries. People from Iraq, Iran, Libya, Somalia, Sudan, Syria, and Yemen could not enter the country for 90 days. The order also indefinitely suspended all Syrian refugees from entry, even those with previously approved visas. The Department of Homeland Security noted, "The Executive Order protects the United States from countries compromised by terrorism and ensures a more rigorous vetting process. This Executive Order ensures that we have a functional immigration system that safeguards our national security."[3]

A Pew Research Center study found 76% of White evangelicals supported Trump's ban. Fifty percent (50%) of White mainline Protestants approved of the President's actions, while only 10% of Black Protestants agreed.[4]

A day after Trump announced his ban, federal courts began issuing orders to pause implementation. The issue took months to resolve. Finally, in a 5-4 ruling in June 2018, the U.S. Supreme Court upheld Trump's third attempt at banning immigration from predominantly Muslim countries. The government did agree to process people still caught in limbo and to unite families separated by the ban.[5]

The controversy over immigration didn't end with Trump's first executive order and the dozens of lawsuits and court decisions that followed. Later, in 2017, he moved to eliminate the five-year-old Dreamers order issued by President Obama. The Deferred Action for Childhood Arrivals (DACA) order allowed young, undocumented immigrants brought to the country when they were very young children to remain without fear of deportation and receive official work visas, but not citizenship.[6]

Trump also sent to Congress that fall a request for billions of dollars to construct a border wall separating Mexico and the United States (more on that in Chapter 4) and increase the number of Immigration and Customs Enforcement officers, immigration judges, and federal prosecutors.[7] He also asked Congress to ban current legal immigrants from bringing extended family members into the country while penalizing so-called sanctuary cities and establishing an E-Verify program to prevent undocumented immigrants from getting jobs.

Early in 2018, CNN reported that in a White House meeting to discuss potential immigration reform, Trump recoiled at a proposal allowing more immigration from some African countries and Haiti.[8] He reportedly asked: "Why do we want all these people from 's---hole countries' coming here?"[9]

The Christian press had reported on immigration issues and Jesus's teaching in Matthew 25 long before the arrival of Donald Trump in the White House. His comments, however, kept news writers and pundits busy during the early part of his presidency.

The Christian Post

In 2014, *The Christian Post* reported that the U.S. Conference of Catholic Bishops had expressed concern about national leadership's inaction on immigration reform, noting that "By not acting, we alienate a generation of young persons who are future leaders of our country. We are saying 'we do not want you or your families.'"[10] The Bishops also noted that immigration is about human beings, "not economic or social issues."[11] The article is among a handful the *Post* printed expressing compassion for refugees.

President Obama issued his executive order on the Dreamers at the end of 2014. Two headlines give clear evidence of the *Post*'s reaction: "Obama's Executive Order Will Authorize Work Permits for 5 Million Illegals; Immigration Plan is 'Unconstitutional' Top Republicans Say," and "Obama Bypasses Congress on Immigration Reform: 5M Illegal Immigrants Given Temp Legal Status But No Pathway to Citizenship."[12] Only Republican politicians served as sources for the articles.

In early 2015, conservative columnist Phyllis Schlafly urged Republicans to read then-Alabama Senator Jeff Sessions's "Immigration Handbook for the New Republican Majority."[13] Schlafly praised Sessions's recommendations and slammed President Obama's issuance of work permits for five million "illegal aliens" taking jobs Americans could perform.

Frequent contributor Dan Delzell warned readers that immigration must follow existing laws lest terrorists be allowed to enter the country and kill innocent people.[14] He remarked, "Those who push for immigration without appropriate requirements demonstrate their lack of concern for everyone who lives here. It is extremely unpatriotic and typically motivated by nothing more than a selfish desire to 'buy' the votes of unvetted immigrants. This approach flows from a genuine lack of wisdom and compassion and an insatiable hunger for power and control."[15] He also stated that America could become great again, but only if it maintained law and order while extending the compassion of Christ to others.[16]

Before the election of Donald Trump, then, *Post* writers presented a steady dose of claims that immigrants stole American jobs, did not contribute to the welfare of the country, would only vote for Democratic candidates, and could potentially be terrorists.

When Trump issued his ban on immigration from Muslim-majority countries, the *Post* seemingly changed course. A month later, it pointed out that President Trump said at a rally that he planned to cut off government welfare support for people seeking entry to the United States and that newly arrived immigrants must be able to support themselves for the first five years they are in the country. Writer Kristinova V. Justimbaste noted with irony, "The President, who claims to be interested in such a legislation, must not be aware that laws on benefits of immigrants currently exist."[17]

Soon after President Trump's DACA announcement, Samuel Smith presented five facts about the program and comments from its supporters and opponents.[18] Among the various news articles published during 2017 and 2018, one stands out for its passion. Frequent contributor Selwyn Duke questioned why Dreamers needed more protection. He ridiculed the use of the name Dreamers, calling it a "sickening, manipulative propaganda term if ever there were one (how about Schemers)?"[19] Duke asserted that Dreamers had not enriched the American experience as "almost a quarter are functionally illiterate, 71% live in low-income housing, and only 4% complete college."[20] Part of the statistics for his claims came from Breitbart News, a conservative publication known as anti-immigrant and a questionable source of truth in its reporting.[21]

Jonathan Wilson-Hargrove, author of *Reconstructing the Gospel: Finding Freedom from Slaveholder Religion*, criticized the lack of moral leadership in Washington, DC when he wrote in the *Post*:

> We have not seen this level of institutional racism in our federal government since Woodrow Wilson re-segregated federal offices and played "Birth of A Nation" in the White House, celebrating the Ku Klux Klan. It is no accident that such blatant white supremacy a century ago was followed by the Literacy Act of 1917 and the Johnson-Reed Act of 1924, both of which aimed to reduce immigration from non-white countries.[22]

Wilson-Hargrove said the most ardent supporters of the current administration's immigration policy were Christian nationalists who celebrated "policies that demonize God's people."[23] He called this a "capitulation to the racial logic of the plantation economy. Slaveholder religion is not new, but it is spiritually lethal."[24]

The Christian Post gave editorial space to an executive of the American Immigration Lawyers Association. He refuted President Trump's assertion that gang violence and criminal activity resulted from immigrants.[25] He also asserted that a healthy immigrant workforce was "critical to the future growth of our economy."[26]

Christianity Today

Over the decades, hundreds of articles and opinion pieces about refugees have appeared in *Christianity Today*. Most are indexed in a searchable database.[27]

In the months leading up to President Trump's attempts to limit immigration, the publication relied on World Relief, the humanitarian arm of the National Association of Evangelicals, for updates on refugee resettlement activities in the United States. *CT* said that the agency had resettled almost 10,000 refugees through its network of 1,180 churches nationwide. A large portion of these refugees came from civil-war-torn Syria. "The milestone comes at the same time as major setbacks to the effort to ban Syrian refugee resettlement in Indiana and Texas," author Timothy C. Morgan noted.[28] Morgan reported that a federal court had just struck down a state of Indiana order from then-governor Mike Pence to ban Syrian refugees because they may be terrorists. "No evidence of this belief has been presented," the federal appeals court said.[29]

The article also quoted contributor Ed Stetzer, organizer of a refugee summit at Wheaton College, who said "It's a counter-cultural moment for the church. How do we sit out the greatest refugee crisis in history and still say that we love our neighbor?"[30] Stetzer attacked a central anti-immigration talking point, noting that a person had a 1 in 3.64 billion chance of being killed by a terrorist attack on American soil. He also stated a Pew study that found that since 2000, the U.S. had admitted 400,000 Christian refugees and less than 300,000 Muslim refugees. Why include this fact? Presumably, to correct the fearmongering from the pundits warning that immigrants were murderers and terrorists and that the U.S. under President Obama had admitted more Muslim than Christian refugees.[31] *Christianity Today* reported on a petition signed by more than 500 conservative evangelical pastors urging Trump to reverse his order.[32]

A few weeks later, the publication noted that a record number of Muslim refugees came to the United States in 2016. Some evangelicals, especially those representing missionary groups, saw that immigration as an opportunity for evangelism. "This is the best chance we've had in human history to share the love of Christ with Muslims," said David Cashin, intercultural studies professor at Columbia International University.[33]

Trump revised the initial executive order a few weeks after its release. *Christianity Today* detailed the new order while reminding readers that most self-identified evangelicals approved of the temporary ban while most evangelical leaders opposed it.[34] It also reported that World Relief was forced to lay off 140 staff and close five refugee resettlement locations due to the cuts in the number of refugees allowed to resettle in the country.[35]

Christianity Today reported on a widely circulated letter and a full-page ad in *The Washington Post*.[36] Russell Moore, a signee, said: "As Christians, dreamers are not some abstract category for us. Dreamers are teaching Sunday school . . . Dreamers are leading churches. When we see Dreamers in jeopardy, we see all of us in jeopardy."[37] Shirley Hoogstra, president of the Council of Christian Colleges and Universities, added: "We love our DACA students. These students are courageous, they are brave, and they are resilient. These students deserve an opportunity to pursue an education without fear of deportation."[38]

Kate Shellnutt's extensive article on the DACA crisis included supportive quotes from evangelical leaders. She cited the previously mentioned Pew poll that found more than half of naturalized U.S. citizens of Hispanic background feared deportation for themselves or others close to them.[39]

Christianity Today chose to educate rather than criticize. Kent Annan, an author of several books on refugees, presented six points about the president's comments. Annan agreed with Trump that life is hard in countries such as Haiti, where history, poverty, and corrupt governments contribute to difficult living conditions.[40] He disputed assertions that immigrants to America take from the nation rather than contribute to the richness of the culture and economy. He also reminded readers that when people struggle, the Christian logic of love asks, "How can I help?" Without naming Trump specifically, Annan concluded, "Our neighbors, who are especially vulnerable right now, deserve our continued welcome without disparagement and without hesitation."[41]

Amid the battle of words and legal wrangling, *Christianity Today* editor Mark Galli gave readers a recipe for countering evangelical beliefs about immigration.[42] He reminded readers that surveys showed that evangelicals who were reporting resentful attitudes toward Mexicans, Muslims, and non-Whites were not regular church goers. They may self-identify as evangelicals, but the answer is often "no" when asked if they attend church regularly and consistently. Galli suggested that his readers start with that question when engaging with people who claim to speak as evangelicals. Then, he said, try inviting them to a church that teaches love and compassion for others.

Christianity Today presented a full-throated defense of compassionate immigration, sidestepping the problematic discussions about the economic impacts (both real and imagined) noted by a few writers of *The Christian Post. CT* also pointed readers toward biblical values of compassion and the opportunity to share Jesus with newly arrived immigrants.

Sojourners

In 2015, Jim Wallis of *Sojourners* wrote that new refugee laws were a "moral imperative" for U.S. immigration policy.[43] Wallis also hailed the creation of the Evangelical Immigration Table, a group of evangelical leaders and organizations concerned with keeping immigration issues front and center in American political policy.

Days after Trump's victory, Wallis asked: What now? Should Trump follow through on his campaign pledges to stop most immigration?[44] Wallis instead touted The Matthew 25 pledge, "I pledge to protect and defend vulnerable people in the name of Jesus."[45] Those who took the oath agreed to stand up to government officials attempting to arrest undocumented immigrants at "places of sanctuary such as churches," protect the religious rights of Muslims, and help stop racial profiling of people of color.[46] Wallis claimed, "Over the past 30 years, our immigration system has become increasingly ineffective, illogical and inhumane."[47]

Wallis also criticized the executive order and its evangelical supporters. These refugees fled terrorism in their own countries; they weren't moving to the U.S. to foment terrorism, he claimed. "Religious leaders who supported Donald Trump must now speak up against anti-religious policies, or they will be guilty of religious hypocrisy and tying their religion to the power of the state," he concluded.[48]

Sojourners also reprinted a Religious News Service article reporting statements from Chaldean Christian Patriarch Louis Raphael I Sako of Bagdad, who argued "Every reception policy that discriminates [among] the persecuted and suffering on religious grounds ultimately harms the

Christians of the [Middle] East, because among other things [it] provides arguments to all propaganda and prejudice that attack native Christian communities of the Middle East as 'foreign bodies,' groups supported and defended by Western powers."[49]

Sojourners published dozens of articles opposing Trump's order. Additionally, the publication offered free educational materials suitable for small-group study. Several *Sojourners* articles advised the undocumented on how to renew DACA applications and what might happen should the program end completely. The publication also profiled the lives of Dreamers, showing them making essential contributions to the church and society.[50]

An opinion piece in *Sojourners* challenged the president to "meet the people directly impacted by the stroke of your pen."[51] The article added, "Once you've looked into the eyes of those caught in the wake of our broken systems, heard their stories, and confronted the facts on the ground, I trust your compassion will grow, and your decisions will be shaped by factual reality."[52]

Several articles reported that Christian groups and colleges condemned the President's comments. Jim Wallis summed up the overall response: "He was a political candidate who ran on, and is a president who continues to run on, the racial bigotry of white nationalism."[53]

A personal reflection on Trump's insult came from former *Sojourners* staffer David Beltran. He recalled moving from Colombia to the U.S. as a young boy. His family, he noted, had lived in America for 17 years. His parents were law-abiding taxpayers who refused any government handouts. They also sent their two boys to college. He also noted that the president of Colombia, Juan Manuel Santos, won a Nobel Peace Prize for ending the nation's long internal war with narcotics cartels and guerilla groups. Perhaps President Trump could learn something from leaders of nations like Colombia, one of those sh—hole countries, Beltran concluded.[54]

WORLD

World's Marvin Olasky noted the inconsistency of American immigration policy. He also reminded readers that potential U.S. citizens must disavow "forever all allegiance and fidelity to any foreign prince, potentate, state or sovereignty."[55] Muslim theology, he noted, does not believe in separating religion and the state. They are the same. Thus, a Muslim who wants to become a U.S. citizen must forsake loyalty to portions of the

Koran and Muslim theology, including Sharia law, if they were to apply for U.S. citizenship.

Joel Belz, the long-time publisher of *World*, acknowledged Protestant Christians' ambivalent attitude toward refugee arrivals even as the Bible contained "many passages about [how] we were all refugees once and needed a helping hand."[56] Belz recalled a conversation with former U.S. Secretary of Education William Bennett. Bennett told Belz that *World* seemed to have an open spirit about immigration, something rare among conservatives. Belz said he told Bennett he gave conservative Protestants too much credit, adding "Neither at that point in our history, nor even now, could we claim a well-conceived biblical exegesis to govern and define our position on the delicate, explosive issues of immigration, refugees, globalism, and related matters."[57]

Belz admonished readers to return to the Bible, even though it did not offer exact formulas for how many refugees to accept or what countries to accept refugees from; "But if you do no more than pursue a quick word study of the term 'sojourner,' you'll learn the lay of the land."[58]

Mindy Belz emphasized that previously vetted and approved refugees from the Middle East posed no danger to America. The article's subhead said: "Trump's executive order on immigration leaves a wake of unintended consequences."[59] The ban was expected, but the way it happened was surprising.[60] She added that Trump should have consulted with Congress and members of his Cabinet. Her story ended with a quote from a World Relief executive: "For a lot of reasons, we don't think this order will help protect persecuted Christians, and our Christian faith compels us to help others as well."[61]

World reporter Evan Wilt reported on a petition signed by 3,000 evangelical leaders asking Trump to reconsider the ban.[62] One source, World Relief CEO Scott Arbeiter, claimed, "We are closing our doors during the height of the greatest refugee crisis in recorded history."[63]

Trump supporter Franklin Graham, however, noted that compassion must be balanced with obeying the law: "Because of the dangers we see today in this world, we need to be very careful."[64] Tony Perkins, president of the Family Research Council, told Wilt the Bible "never suggests that you are to indiscriminately let people into your country who want to do you harm . . . This is about those countries who have been producing people who want to undermine America, attack America, and we're simply saying, 'pause this.'"[65]

Finally, Wilt quoted a Baptist pastor from Oklahoma: "We may not say it out loud, but I think many conservative Christians almost believe Muslims deserve their suffering. If our security is a priority and they happen to suffer as a result, that's just collateral damage we can't avoid."[66]

Olasky wrote in an October 2017 issue of *World* that resolutions changing Dreamers' status suffered because President Obama's original executive order by-passed Congress.[67] Olasky noted that *World* spoke to four evangelical senators who all favored some type of DACA legislation. He did not hold out hope that such legislation would appear, however. "If Congress does let the 800,000 stay, maybe they'll have more appreciation for our Bill of Rights than some who are native-born" he added.[68]

Trump's question about "sh--hole" countries did not amuse *World*'s staff. The publication reported that one evangelical leader said of Trump, "He speaks for our country on the international stage. We want and deserve to have him act with dignity. Just once, I would like to hear him say that he was wrong and ask for forgiveness."[69] The story also quoted Ed Stetzer: "Trump has courted evangelicals, some of whom have had access to him and his administration. I hope those evangelical leaders will speak clearly, reminding Trump that all people are worthy of dignity and respect because they are made in the image of God."[70]

Reporter Wilt interviewed Johnnie Moore, head of Trump's evangelical advisory council. Moore said comments attributed to the president were "absolutely suspect and politicized."[71] Another strong Trump supporter, Robert Jeffress, pastor of First Baptist Church Dallas, said he supported the president's views but not his choice of words.

World's Mindy Belz slammed Trump's statements: "Our president, with his tweeted and spoken words, has embarrassed and diminished the nation's highest office. He has done so particularly on foreign policy matters, drawing high and low international scorn. Those who defend him amid these escapades seem to be counting on his contrariness, or God's, to triumph in the end."[72] She continued, "It's part of an emerging pattern: a president who can't be anything but center stage, the one it all hinges on. Call his policies right or wrong, he seems simply not to accept the United States as a nation ruled by laws, not by man."[73]

Conclusion

Each of the publications, then, expressed dismay, if not outright condemnation, of Trump's call for limiting the number and nationality of people entering the United States. The actions and words of the president challenged the deep biblical call for believers to extend hospitality and compassion to those less fortunate, which includes people fleeing for their lives from hostile environments. This ethos, of course, must be balanced with government responsibility to ensure the safety of its citizens by only allowing law-abiding people, vetted in advance, to enter legally. As several writers admitted, this balancing act is difficult. The majority of the comments in the articles drew heavily from the teaching of the Bible, which stands in contrast to the 2015 opinion poll of self-identified evangelicals, only 12% of whom looked to God's Word as their source of beliefs about immigration. That number rose to 26% by 2024, a sign that perhaps the flood of articles advocating biblical actions by the U.S. government had their intended effect.[74] Still, despite 77% of evangelicals favoring immigration reform in 2024, the prospect of realizing that reform—even after four years of Democratic control of the White House and Senate from 2021 to 2024—failed to materialize.[75]

While President Trump's initial efforts to limit immigration met with occasional criticism from evangelical publications, his signature campaign pledge to virtually stop the entry of people from Mexico attracted even more negative commentary from believers concerned with balancing compassion with the rule of law. We turn to that topic in the next chapter.

Chapter 4

Build That Wall?
Evangelicals, Trump, and the
Southern Border Controversy

As THE NATION'S DEBATE over immigration raged, one of President Trump's central campaign promises—to build an impenetrable wall between the U.S. and Mexico—created dozens of conspiracy theories and misinformation campaigns. One such approach said waves of immigrant caravans walking up from Central America to the U.S. were organized and funded by leftists like George Soros, a frequent bogeyman of the far right.

Seeking truth, *World* reporter Sophia Lee went to Tijuana, Mexico, on the border with California.[1] She interviewed immigrant organizers and Central American immigrants. Who was funding the immigrant caravans, she asked? What she found on the ground differed from the misinformation in the States. In their home countries, immigrants said they faced oppression, poverty, and perhaps even death for themselves and their families. They left behind family and friends, seeking safety and the hope of a better life. They survived hostile villagers along the way and often walked for days with minimal water and food. They said no one had organized them; they walked in groups for protection from bandits and gangs.

One asylum seeker told Lee that Donald Trump probably organized the caravans to get more American support for his anti-immigration policies and border wall funding. Musing on what she found (and didn't find) at the border, Lee wrote: "Maybe the truth is messier and more nuanced than a simple theory that some group or individual is financing these caravans for an unknown agenda."[2] She concluded, ". . . maybe what's happening is less historic and critical than how we and our leaders will choose to respond to it."[3]

Lee's investigation at the border gave Christian readers an eyewitness account of just a slice of the immigration puzzle. Other publications also ran articles and opinion pieces highlighting President Trump's quest to build a concrete wall between 30 and 50 feet tall.[4] Most self-identified evangelicals supported the wall, but evangelical publications told a different story.[5]

The immigration debate went into overdrive in 2018. Attorney General Jeff Sessions enraged many Christians when he decreed that all illegal immigrants caught by the U.S. Border Patrol would be treated as criminals with their children separated and treated as unaccompanied minors. This zero-tolerance policy sparked mainstream news media reports of children being forcefully torn from their parents in emotionally trying circumstances.[6]

Sessions used Scripture to defend his new policy. He told a group in Indianapolis, "I would cite to you the Apostle Paul and his clear and wise command in Romans 13 to obey the laws of the government because God has ordained the government for his purposes."[7] He reminded Americans that the law, if fairly applied, "protects the weak and protects the lawful."[8]

Each publication had a slightly different approach to reporting on efforts to build the wall and the controversy that erupted after mainstream press reports of the child separation policy.

The Christian Post

IN EARLY MARCH 2017, *The Christian Post* published the first of a dozen articles on the wall. This piece said that Trump proposed cutting the Transportation Security Administration (TSA) and Coast Guard budgets to help pay for its construction. During the presidential campaign, Trump said Mexico would pay for the wall.[9]

At the same time news media highlighted Trump's budget shuffling, the *Post* also published a news report from Reuters that the Catholic Archdiocese of Mexico had decreed that any company or individual in Mexico "intending to invest in the wall of the fanatic Trump would be immoral, but above all, its shareholders and owners should be considered traitors to the homeland."[10]

The publication also reported on a bill proposed by Congressman Mike Rogers of Alabama to tax outgoing remittances sent by legal and illegal immigrants back to their families remaining in Mexico, Central America, the Caribbean, and South America. The 2% tax on all funds sent abroad would help fund the border wall.[11]

More reports on the wall's progress appeared in September and October 2017, as the *Post* reported that numerous environmental impact studies and regulations were waived for the project.[12] The frequency of articles detailing the announcements via news releases, news conferences, and tweets indicates that *The Christian Post* knew the importance of this issue for its readers and provided them with continual updates on the wall's funding and potential construction.

The Christian Post also published several opinion pieces pushing back against the wall's naysayers. Foreshadowing a consistent theme from evangelicals opposed to most legal and certainly most illegal immigration, Texas pastor Selwyn Duke presented an *ad hominem* argument. He accused Sen. Ted Kennedy of pushing through an immigration bill in 1965 that resulted, 50 years later, in bringing in too many immigrants from Third World countries.[13] He decried that Pew Research projections for the year 2065 showed that less than half the people living in the U.S. would be White. This projection appeared to fill Duke with dread that White people would be in the minority in America in the not-too-distant future.

Another op-ed by David Ruzicka, pastor of a Baptist church in Katy, Texas, listed ten ways the Bible opposed illegal immigration.[14] He cited Romans 13:2: "Anyone who rebels against authority is rebelling against what God has instituted, and they will be punished" (NLT).[15] He also said allowing illegal immigration breeds corruption in encouraging the creation of fake IDs, driver's licenses, identity theft, slavery, and property destruction. He then criticized those who might use Scripture to justify allowing undocumented immigrants shelter in the U.S.: "You cannot use it [to] argue for any activity that is unfair to others, unjust to others, and disobedient to God."[16]

The Christian Post dove deeply into the family separation controversy in June 2018. Columnist and blogger Marvin G. Thompson blasted Sessions's comments, arguing "Once again, the Church finds itself, at the nexus of religion and politics, having to answer in defense because a high-ranking political official invoked his religious belief to justify a morally objectionable government policy."[17] He noted that some children separated at the border might never see their parents again.

Another article reported that 600 Methodist pastors and lay leaders accused Sessions of child abuse, immorality, and racial discrimination.[18] Of the criticism, Sessions, a Methodist, told the Christian Broadcasting Network (CBN), "I feel it. I think there's a legitimate concern there, and I'm pleased to work with the president to address those concerns."[19]

In another opinion piece, Tony Perkins wrote that Trump's critics tried to turn attention away from the President's North Korean diplomacy successes by dredging up the family separation issue. He accused Congress of failing to resolve the immigration crisis, thus leading to housing separated kids away from their parents.[20] He said the situation was tragic, and the children were innocent victims of their parents' breaking of the law: "But the origin of that pain and confusion isn't U.S. law or the Trump administration. That burden lies with their parents who knowingly put them in this position."[21] Perkins added: "I'm not suggesting our laws don't need work—or that this crisis isn't urgent . . . Maybe these new small faces of the immigration crisis will prompt Congress to work across lines and unite to reform an immigration system that's dividing families and our country."[22]

Columnist Michael Brown asked Christians a series of questions about the immigration debate.[23] He said he sought answers and was not pushing an ideological position, yet some of his opinions seem evident from his rhetoric. First, he asked what was so controversial about keeping illegal refugees out of the country. Second, he claimed the new phenomenon of refugee caravans was "ostensibly stirred up by leftwing activists" and that the U.S. should not be forced to take in those people.[24]

Third, Brown asked, what was wrong with wanting to preserve the national identity of the United States? He noted that European countries had opened their doors to Muslim immigrants, "many of whom have little or no desire to become incorporated into the host countries' national culture."[25] Finally, he asked why it would be so challenging to provide a path to citizenship, with penalties, for people who came to the U.S. in past years but had been working jobs, obeying laws, and contributing to the good of American society. Why must these people be deported, as hardliners were demanding?[26]

As the immigration debacle neared the end of its second year, *The Christian Post* published promising research results from a recent book on immigration.[27] Political scientists Ruth Melkonian-Hoover and Lyman Kellstedt reinforced previous research showing a greater acceptance of legal immigration and resettlement of legal immigrants among more frequent church attendees. In analyzing Christian responses to immigration, they identified a frequent theme of this book: evangelical leaders (regular church attendees) and self-identified evangelicals (infrequent church attendees) differed significantly on the issue of immigration. The book also called for more extensive, rigorous research that included better evangelical definitions.

At the same time, staff writer Samuel Smith noted that the Evangelical Immigration Table (EIT) called for immigration reform consistent with the principles of the Bible.[28] While educating its readers about the need to obey the laws of the nation, the authors of an EIT booklet noted that the current immigration system was difficult to navigate as a Christian. "We're called to love our neighbors (Luke 10:27) and to make disciples of all nations (Matthew 28:19), regardless of where we land on public policy," it said.[29] The authors of the 35-page booklet make clear that in tough issues like immigration—legal and illegal—the role of government differs from the responsibility of individual Christians.[30]

Christianity Today

Christianity Today carefully avoided criticizing the idea of the wall. Instead, it reminded readers that prejudice toward non-White Americans persisted. One opinion piece by Biola University Professor Octavio Javier Esqueda, a U.S. citizen, told of anti-Hispanic verbal abuse his children and other faculty children faced at school. "They are just victims of the political and social polarization of our times," he wrote.[31] God sees all people as equal, Esqueda reminded readers.

The zero-tolerance policy instituted by the government coincided with World Refugee Day 2018, noted *CT*'s Kate Shellnutt. She shared a World Evangelical Alliance prayer for refugees: "Abba Father, we lift to you the precious refugee children who have become separated from their parents and family."[32] The prayer asked that God keep those separated children protected from abuse and that they be quickly reunited with their families.

Shellnutt also noted that evangelicals had long advocated for immigration reform to protect people legitimately fleeing gang violence and oppression in several Latin American nations. The Southern Baptist Convention urged American families to welcome and adopt refugees through their churches. She also said the zero-tolerance decision united Christians across partisan lines. Franklin Graham said, "I think it's disgraceful, it's terrible to see families ripped apart, and I don't support that one bit."[33] He blamed politicians, present and past, for the horrors unfolding.

Shellnutt concluded her article by noting that only 25% of White evangelicals said the U.S. was responsible for accepting refugees. That compared to 43% of White mainline Protestants and 63% of Black Protestants.[34]

Griffin Paul Jackson wrote that data from the United Nations showed an 82% decline in the admission of immigrants to the U.S. from 2016 to 2019. World Relief's president, Scott Arbeiter, responded, "We are gravely concerned that the U.S. has abdicated its role in exemplifying the moral leadership needed to meet the needs of the most vulnerable displaced around the world."[35] The publication also reprinted World Vision president Richard Stearns's Twitter post: "We turned away Jewish refugees fleeing the Nazis in WWII. I thought our national conscience had learned a lesson. Guess not."[36]

Sojourners

As the crescendo of national commentary on the border wall continued, Jim Wallis attempted to educate *Sojourners*'s readers why the wall "is obviously a terrible idea" and "a 2,200-mile-long monument to racism."[37] He urged his readers to tell Congress that Christians did not support the wall and to do so "until our shouts cause Trump's wall to come tumbling down before it's ever built."[38] He concluded: "It's time for Christians to show the strength of our convictions and put an early end to this poisonous racial project once and for all: Trump's wall would indeed be a monument to our worst instincts in this nation. Therefore, Christians must say that Trump's wall will not be built on our watch, not this week, not this year, not ever."[39]

In another essay, Wallis said the administration's actions would make orphans out of the children who could not be reunited with their families. He called the policy a "combination of cruelty and ineptitude."[40] The crisis, he added, was not the result of the broken immigration system, which needed reform, but a direct result of Trump's policies. Wallis said that the moral outrage expressed by people of all political persuasions should end the separation policy, stating, "We can do no other than to fight for a country that treats immigrants with empathy and compassion, tempering justice with mercy for those beloved children of God."[41]

WORLD

While other publications gave voice to the president's immigration policy critics, *World* editor Olasky decided to visit the border and talk to people who might be affected by the border wall. This "boots on the ground" reporting, like that of Sophia Lee's, demonstrated the publication's commitment to reporting from the scene of important events and providing a human angle to the story. Olasky spoke with several government agents at various towns and villages along the border. One agent told him it would be impossible to build a wall along multiple parts of the Rio Grande River because of seasonal flooding.[42] Another said people would continue to seek entry into the U.S. until the economic and political conditions improved south of the border.

Olasky ended his journey by positing that the U.S. might consider a return to the Bracero Program. This program allowed agricultural workers from Mexico to work temporarily during harvest season and then return home to Mexico. That comment is consistent with the biblical journalism ideal of providing context to human events, seeing the issue through God's eyes. It also mirrored the philosophy of solutions journalism, presenting problematic social issues and highlighting people and programs trying to minimize harm to those affected.[43]

World ran another immigrant-focused piece in August 2017.[44] Hispanics moving to Sioux City, Iowa, to work in a meat packing plant changed the nature of the city. Christians there helped as the newcomers encountered culture shock and poverty, "trying to make 'Love your neighbor' more than words."[45] The changes are evident as the *World* article describes the new shops featuring colorful piñatas in the storefront windows and new restaurants where the English language menus were infrequently consulted. The owner of the Hispanic market told *World* she and her family moved to Iowa from California 17 years previously to escape gangs and found helpful, polite, and friendly people. Nice, religious people, she added.

A news roundup in June 2018 reminded *World* readers that President George W. Bush instituted the zero-tolerance policy setting forth criminal prosecution for illegally entering the country.[46] A spokesperson for Homeland Security told *World* that the Obama administration also separated children from their families. The Trump administration, she said, was just enforcing that law.

The article added more facts to its coverage, noting that 55% of Republican voters supported the zero-tolerance policy. The story ends with a quote from Sessions: "If we build the wall, if we pass legislation to end the lawlessness, we won't face these terrible choices."[47]

What might a compassionate immigration policy look like? Olasky posed that question in *World* as 2018 came to a close.[48] While acknowledging that some Americans feared refugees could be radical Islamic extremists or MS-13 gangsters, he said America's history and values favor a biblical approach to caring for refugees. To prove his point, he reprinted three past articles he'd written on immigration and the educational milieu in the U.S. (1994, 2002, and 2008).

Olasky added that his ancestors left their country of origin to seek a better life for themselves and their children. He also dismantled four arguments against immigration popular during his lifetime, including one that claimed that immigrants are not accustomed to living in a democracy and expect the government to tell them how to act and what they should believe. Therefore, the argument goes, they will vote Democrat. Olasky challenged that argument by noting the reason that more Hispanics are Democrats is that the Democratic party has been more proactive in soliciting their support. He also stated that three-fourths of Latinos were Christians, and Korean Americans flocking to the U.S. were ten times more likely to be Christian than Buddhist. Olasky left no doubt that anti-immigration sentiment was not consistent with biblical Christianity.[49]

In another article, writer Harvest Prude said the President "now risks alienating and disillusioning Christians who want their persecuted brethren helped."[50] She recounted the dilemma facing legal Chaldean Christians living in the Detroit area. Because Trump promised to protect Christians in the volatile Middle East, many voted for him in 2016. Now, they were having second thoughts. Even Trump apologist Franklin Graham had spoken out against the deportation of Chaldean Christians.[51]

In response to the national outcry over the separation policy, President Trump signed an executive order in June 2018 ending the practice. The evangelical response was largely positive.[52] Tony Perkins praised the president and said that a group of evangelical leaders had recently met with AG Sessions to intercede with the president. The ruling "should not lessen the pressure for Congress to come together to overhaul our immigration system and secure our borders," he added.[53] The United Methodist Church leadership called the announcement of the decision "good news and a reversal of an inhumane and immoral practice."[54] Robert Jeffress, the pastor of First Baptist Dallas Church, tweeted: "Will hypocritical Democrats now put an end to the ULTIMATE separation of children from parents—abortion?"[55]

The Aftermath

As the White House worked on new immigration proposals, evangelicals kept up the pressure for a comprehensive and fair policy. An op-ed in *The Christian Post* called Trump out for "empty noise on religious freedom and refugees."[56] The authors John Stonestreet and Roberto Rivera said overall immigration of Christians from the Middle East had fallen by a "staggering 98%" during the Trump presidency.[57] The duo said one former Trump administration executive pinned the blame for the lower admissions rate on Trump adviser Stephen Miller, who "would be happy to never let another refugee into the country again."[58]

Bekah McNeel's *Christianity Today* feature gave practical suggestions for readers.[59] The government limited access to detention centers, presenting news media with a challenge. McNeel suggested readers interested in providing legal assistance to asylum seekers donate to groups such as the American Civil Liberties Union, which pro-life Christians would usually avoid because of its advocacy of abortion rights. She also mentioned smaller groups providing legal assistance that did not pay for abortions.

Once children and families were out of detention, she noted, evangelical groups like World Relief could assist with resettlement. Throughout this article, the subtext appears to be a plea from *CT* and its reporter to care more about people and less about political ideology cloaked in biblical values. The editor's note at the end of the article said, in italics: "*This article was updated to clarify the position on abortion of several non-profits*."[60] That caveat was added, no doubt, to prevent readers from thinking that the publication's mention of agencies helping immigrants implied an acceptance of that agency's funding of abortion.

Most immigration-related articles in the evangelical press framed the controversy in a manner that implied criticism of the Trump administration's actions because those policies lacked compassion for refugees. While their writers offered hundreds of suggestions, a middle ground between compassionate protection and the safety and economic well-being of the nation proved impossible. Sophia Lee wrote in 2019, when she reported for *World* from Tijuana, that maybe the crisis at the border "is less historic and critical than how we and our leaders will choose to respond to it."[61] In other words, less rhetoric and indifference, and more compassion. Four years later, reporting from El Paso for *Christianity Today*, she found Christians attempting to bridge the information and compassion gap, but still, the situation remained vexing.[62]

So, too, is another topic that erupted into violence during the Trump years—race. The following two chapters explore that volatile topic.

Chapter 5

Charlottesville and the Problem of Christian Nationalism

ON AUGUST 12, 2017, a coalition of neo-Nazis, Ku Klux Klan members, and White supremacists calling themselves Unite the Right descended on Charlottesville, Virginia. They came to protest the city government's removal of a statue commemorating Confederate General Robert E. Lee. City leaders had recently voted to remove the statue from public view after years of pleas from anti-racism groups.

Television footage from Charlottesville showed white-hooded protestors carrying lit torches and chanting slogans denouncing immigrants, African Americans, and Jews. The scene was reminiscent of Klansmen marching to torch a Black family's home—or, worse—to lynch a Black man they deemed "troublesome." Unite the Right factions chanted slogans such as "blood and soil," a Nazi chant praising White Europeans, and "You Will Not Replace Us," a reference to the Great Replacement Theory, the fear of White nationalists that the U.S. would continue on its path toward becoming a majority non-White country and that people of color and new immigrants would consistently vote in support of Democratic Party candidates and platforms.[1] In the melee between warring factions that day in Charlottesville, a woman died when a White supremacist drove his car into a crowd of counter-protesters.

Before Christian editors could digest the incident and begin to educate their readers with commentary and context, President Trump said at a news conference a few days later that there were "good people" on both sides of the violent confrontation.[2] The idea that he would indirectly endorse any of the beliefs or tactics of Unite the Right inflamed the contentious dialogue in the U.S. over race and Christian nationalism.[3]

Within a few hours of the president's statement, Trump's evangelical advisory board condemned the violence. It noted that "white nationalism and white supremacism are anathema to the teachings of Christ."[4] Trump clarified his comment a day later and denounced racism in all its forms.[5] Some leaders reacted negatively, nonetheless. Pastor A.R. Bernard, head of the 40,000-member Christian Cultural Center in Brooklyn, quit President Trump's evangelical advisory board, saying: "When you vacillate like that, it means that there's not a set of core values that you have determined to guide your thinking, your decision making. Instead, it demonstrates that you are being tossed between opinions of those around you. And I've got a problem with that kind of lack of leadership."[6]

The Charlottesville violence led New York City pastor Tim Keller to warn Christians that the values displayed by the White nationalists in Charlottesville were likely present in their churches, asserting that often these values are held by those pushing "traditional values."[7]

Russell Moore, then president of the Ethics & Religious Liberty Commission of the Southern Baptist Convention, condemned the violence in an opinion piece for *The Washington Post*. Of the Unite the Right participants, he said: "Some of them speak of 'Christendom'—by which they mean white European cultural domination—and not Christianity. But many others are members of churches bearing the name of Jesus Christ. Nothing could be further from the Gospel."[8] Despite Trump's comments and an apology later in the week, most evangelicals on his advisory board promised to stick with the president.[9]

Unite the Right represented a coalition of groups with similar beliefs, some of which existed from the early days of the American experience. While the beliefs and motivations of those at the Charlottesville rally are many, some aspects of Christian nationalism were reflected in their rally cries. Controversial historian David Barton fueled claims that gave an aura of Christian approval to White supremacists. Barton argued that the Founding Fathers never intended the idea of the separation of church and state to be a part of the American political and religious experience.[10] Instead, they intended that the U.S. become a theocracy where the church and the government thrived together. Barton's appeal to White Christians is among the narratives of American history influencing the more radical ideas condemned by Keller, Moore, and thousands of other pastors. Nonetheless, the idea of America as a Christian nation founded by Western Europeans is a central doctrine of the alt-right.

Time magazine named Barton one of the "25 Most Influential Evangelicals" in 2005.[11] While Barton's work has detractors, his influence on individual Christians and churches has added to Christian nationalism narratives that lack verifiable factual truth.[12]

Among his promises to evangelicals in 2016, Donald Trump vowed to protect Christianity's pre-eminent position as the arbiter of values and laws governing the country. Evangelical publications noted his promises, occasionally setting straight the historical record. But in the days and weeks following the Charlottesville incident, dozens of articles in the Christian press dissected the meaning of the confrontation and violence, primarily condemning the alt-right and the racist intent of Unite the Right. Many linked the violence to the insidious ideology of Christian nationalism. Here's a deeper dive into their messages.

The Christian Post

The Christian Post published over 50 news and commentary articles after the Charlottesville violence. Most condemned the insurrection and linked it to Christian nationalism.[13] For Richard Cizik, president of the New Evangelical Partnership for the Common Good, part of the racial and social divide in the church resulted from Christians being drawn into this trap. Many people believed in unreliable media reports. Cizik claimed that some alt-right press and their supporters were atheists who spawned hatred against non-Whites and Muslims, adding, "A follower of Christ will neither sanction nor endorse racism and white supremacy . . . It's that simple. We must choose one or the other. Stand up. Speak out against hate."[14]

An editorial in *The Christian Post* urged Trump to distance himself from the movements that spawned the violence in Charlottesville. These actions jeopardized his Christian witness. The editorial ended with a plea for the president to become an ambassador of reconciliation during a time of violent tribalism in America.[15]

Post editors did give ample editorial space to Trump supporters. To separate the president from the violence, pro-Trump writers invoked the blame game. For instance, the editors praised Trump's "repudiation of white supremacists 48 hours after his initial bland tweet," noting that by this action, he "distinguishes himself from former president Barack Obama, who has yet to admit that radical Islamists are at the core of the Western world's terrorism problem."[16]

The Christian Post also featured Franklin Graham's defense of the president. The publication noted that Graham wrote a tweet blaming Satan for the unrest and Charlottesville's city leaders for allowing the protest. Of the media, he claimed,

Instead, they want to blame President Donald J. Trump for everything. Really, this boils down to evil in people's hearts. Satan is behind it all. He wants division, he wants unrest, and he wants violence and hatred. He's the enemy of peace and unity. I denounce bigotry and racism of every form, be it black, white, or any other. My prayer is that our nation will come together. We are stronger together, and our answers lie in turning to God.[17]

Post columnist Ryan Bomberger continued the attack on mainstream media, accusing them of asking inane questions. He inferred that they were trying to trap Trump into saying things that made him sound stupid or evil:

#FakeNews media will completely ignore hundreds of thousands of pro-lifers gathered in the nation's capital but will fixate on a handful of racist clowns craving relevance in a small college town in Virginia. The racist "Unite the Right" tiki-torch tantrum could have gone down like a tree in an empty forest, but instead, the Left made it into a spectator sport. Timber!!! That's the sound of civility crashing to earth as anarchists, racial activists, and social justice whiners clashed, enabled by police acting as bystanders.[18]

He also condemned mainstream media for ignoring the killing of one million "innocent human lives each year" through abortion.[19]

The *Post*'s habit of giving voice to those caught up in the blame game continued over the next few months. Columnist Rachel Alexander asserted (without evidence) that leftists infiltrated White supremacist organizations to encourage violence, stating "Don't let the left get away with the misinformation that these [the Charlottesville protestors] were conservatives; they were not."[20] She also claimed that conservatives did not support the violence that day in Charlottesville. The article is noteworthy because nowhere does she mention the church or the role of evangelicals in supporting or opposing conservative political ideology. Her take is entirely political.

The Christian Post, then, published dozens of news articles containing comments from pastors and politicians as the investigation into the violence continued. It also gave space to a wave of pushback by its conservative voices determined to condemn Unite the Right while quickly moving on to deflect blame from the claims of Christian nationalists and the rhetoric of President Trump. President Obama, the leftist mainline press, and abortion providers all fueled the continued racism in America.

Christianity Today

Christianity Today also published dozens of online articles analyzing the Charlottesville incident's implications for evangelicals.[21] Unlike *The Christian Post*, *CT*'s writers and columnists analyzed the deeper issues, often featuring voices from African American scholars. Theon E. Hill, a scholar of political rhetoric, said he understood Trump's reluctance to bite the hand that fed him (White nationalists). Still, the morality of Christianity dictated condemnation of the president's comments. He said of efforts to remove Gen. Lee's statue: "The goal of these removal efforts is not, as some argue, to whitewash the past, but to recontextualize it. Defense of an institution that legitimated forms of physical, psychological, and sexual trauma is not a cause to honor but lament."[22]

Clifton Clarke and Jarvis J. Williams addressed a historic issue within the Black church—the rhetoric of reconciliation between races. Their op-ed said using the term reconciliation was an inappropriate word to describe what needed to happen next: "The term *reconciliation* itself is a misnomer for race relations in America. Reconciliation implies a time when blacks and whites were 'conciliated' or 'in agreement.' A Latin derivative, the word conveys the idea of restoration or a return to a past ideal situation. Black people in America—brought here in slave ships—have never had such an ideal with the white majority."[23]

Additionally, the authors questioned White Christians' thinking that racism is a social issue, not a theological challenge. People who think racism is not a theological issue misunderstand God's Word.[24] This powerful piece should have provided great educational value for *CT*'s readers, both for its negation of the idea that Black and White Christians should (or could) reconcile at that point and for criticizing Whites who believed that racism was someone else's problem, not a problem of the heart or one's relationship with Christ.

Ed Stetzer, then executive director of the Billy Graham Center for Evangelism at Wheaton College, said some Christians would never criticize Donald Trump. But he reminded believers their Kingdom mandate was to have no political party and no higher allegiance than to Christ. He also asserted that if Trump could do no wrong in the eyes of his supporters, then he was their savior, not Christ, adding that "Our citizenship is in heaven, and we don't need a Rorschach test to tell us that the only perfect King is already on the throne. If your response is always one-sided, I'd ask why."[25]

Thus, while *Christianity Today* published some news about the ugly

Charlottesville rally, its primary focus, in keeping with its mission, was to add reasoned context and history to inform and educate Christian leaders seeking wisdom in a critical moment of crisis in the country.

The publication also had the opportunity to widen the lens of history and examine its coverage of racial issues over the years. *Christianity Today* editor Mark Galli wrote that he had read his magazine's reporting and opinion essays on racial issues since its founding in 1956. He concluded that the magazine's history was "checkered at best."[26] Instead, the content reflected the "moral ambiguity and confusion of that era's white churches."[27]

> In that era, we consistently argued that racism would never end without the spiritual transformation of each individual's heart. That was and remains true enough. But we were completely ignorant about the nature and stubbornness of structural injustice. We worried how "forced integration" would impinge upon the freedom of individuals (mostly, the freedom of whites) without recognizing that segregation already denied freedom to millions of African Americans.[28]

We "repent of this part of our history," he added.[29]

A few months later, New York Divinity School President Paul H. DeVries countered Galli's criticism of *Christianity Today*'s early reporting on racism. DeVries cited significant articles during the Civil Rights movement of the 1960s calling Christians to stand against racism. He also noted that the magazine's coverage of Billy Graham's crusades during the critical year of 1965 emphasized that Graham insisted on integrated choirs, integrated stadium seating, and the presence of people of color as spiritual counselors. As the evangelical magazine of note during the Civil Rights era, DeVries says that it was not devoid of focusing on its educational and advocacy role and that Galli's full-throated apology may not have been necessary.[30]

Sojourners

Jim Wallis of *Sojourners* wrote two articles in the wake of Charlottesville. One asserted that Donald Trump and Christian nationalists' positions were "theologically and morally indefensible" and that Trump spoke on "behalf of a myth, lie, ideology . . . deliberately fueling racial division."[31] For church leaders seeking some advice on how to respond, Willis suggested a five-fold path to churches:

1. Preach against racism from the pulpit;

2. Repent and call on the church to repent. Turn from going in the wrong direction. Consider reparations of some kind to atone for past actions;

3. Provide pastoral care. Even White people infected with the disease of White supremacy need pastoral care, and the church needs to develop strategies for helping White supremacists repent and recover;

4. Prophesize. People need to be prophetic about the insidious and comprehensive nature of White supremacy. It is underneath everything in America. Systems need to be transformed;

5. Support policy changes in the governance of churches and denominations and in the American body politic. This includes expanding voting rights and reforming the criminal justice system.[32]

Wallis's second column compared the actions of strangers rescuing their neighbors (regardless of their race) during deadly floods in Houston that summer to the hatred exhibited in Charlottesville. He noted, "White people, and white Christians in particular, must find the understanding and the courage to *speak out* and *intervene* in systems and structures of evil white supremacy"[33] (italics in original).

These comments from Wallis are consistent with the publication's teaching since its founding. While *The Post-American* and later *Sojourners* began with young students opposed to the Vietnam War, their focus on racial and social justice distinguished their editorial content from that of competing magazines at the time.

The fight against Christian nationalism remained an important topic for *Sojourners*'s writers. In 2023, Professor Jacob L. Wright wrote of the angst felt by his students at the growth of Christian nationalism, especially in the statements from then Speaker of the House Mike Johnson. Additionally, he said his students objected to the "simplistic use and cynical abuse of biblical texts."[34] Wright praised the Hebrew Bible for its community orientation and noted that its idea of nationhood—in contrast to that of the Christian nationalists like David Barton—is focused on openness toward others and hope for the future. Christian nationalism, he asserted, "feeds on insecurity, fear, and hate."[35] Diversity is an ideal emphasized in the Bible, not conformity, he added.

Sojourners continued its educational mission by noting even pro-gressive Christians employed symbols of Christian nationalism in their rallies. In an interview with Brian Kaylor and Beau Underwood, authors of *Baptizing America*, Mitchell Atencio asked them to provide a definition of Christian nationalism. Kaylor defined it as "an ideology that fuses and confuses American and Christian identities. That to be a good American, one must be a 'good Christian.'"[36] Kaylor further explained that in the U.S. the term Christian nationalism really refers to White Christian national-ism, which is tied to racist ideologies, presumably those on display in the Charlottesville incident.

WORLD

World editor Marvin Olasky lamented that situations like Charlottesville distracted believers from emphasizing "we the people."[37] His review of American history reminded readers that the United States is an experiment in government, and one of its chief virtues is that it has—albeit not without struggle—welcomed people of many religions and races.[38] He asked readers to remember the big picture of the nation's virtues and not be sidetracked by White supremacists.

In a backhanded manner, he criticized President Trump. He said the nation's chief executive should protect the American experiment and that, "He should advocate constitutional understandings and vigorously call out racists, particularly those who use violence to frighten opponents."[39] Olasky said of the White supremacists, "Some, even some who call themselves Christians, want to shrink the Bible and the Constitution by mandating racial and ethnic preferences—but their god and their constitution are too small."[40] Reinforcing a theme from *The Christian Post*, he said that getting sidetracked by the demonstrations took believers' eyes off the powerless-ness of aborted children.[41]

World's Jamie Dean reminded readers that it was not just the White supremacists whose actions in Charlottesville must be condemned. She quoted a *New York Times* reporter who tweeted during the violence that alt-left antifa protesters were also beating people. Dean veered off course by adding that leftist-leaning demonstrators had forced universities to take extreme measures to protect conservative pundits speaking on campus.[42] In other words, violence and intimidation was a two-way street.

Coverage of the events in Charlottesville focused primarily on what occurred on the day of the Unite the Right protest, which ended with violence. Believers in Christ populated both the warring groups of protesters and counter-protesters. The publications recognized this reality. Some reported what happened and let their columnists do the needed biblical reflections. Additionally, they all offered advice for diffusing future situations.

Conclusion

Charlottesville provided the publications an opportunity to explore racism and White supremacy in America. No exploration of the issue, however, was the final word. Even after the departure of President Trump, Christian nationalism remained a topic of interest for the editors of evangelical publications.

After the January 6, 2021 storming of the nation's Capitol, *Sojourners* reviewed *The Flag and the Cross*. The book by Samuel L. Perry and Philip Gorski tried to explain Christian nationalism by equating it with the idea that God divinely inspired the creation of the United States, the "city set on a hill."[43] That notion, while misguided, is not necessarily dangerous. Instead, the danger is that "white racial identity creates the political vision that seeks hegemonic power for white people."[44]

Despite the national media attention as late as 2024, a majority of Americans had still not heard of Christian nationalism, according to a 2024 Pew survey.[45] This included 58% of evangelicals. Most Christians do believe that the Bible should have influence over the nation's laws, although what that means in practice is up for debate. The lead researcher for the study noted that, "Even those who think the United States should be a Christian nation and the Bible should have a great deal of influence on the law, most of them are reluctant to say that they have a favorable view of Christian nationalism. So there seems to be some negative stigma with the term."[46]

Charlottesville brought the always simmering topic of race relations in America to the front of dialogue within the Christian church. The death of a young Black man at the hands of police in Minneapolis catapulted the discussion into overdrive.

Chapter 6

George Floyd and the Continuing Debate Over Racism in the United States

THE MURDER OF GEORGE FLOYD on May 25, 2020, by Minneapolis police officer Derek Chauvin shocked the world. Video of the incident went viral, and millions of viewers worldwide wondered what was going through Chauvin's mind as he ignored Floyd's pleas to let him breathe.

Public reaction to Floyd's death was fierce, as peaceful and not-so-peaceful protestors took to the streets of major American cities, demanding justice. Some protestors used the occasion to loot local businesses and attack police officers.

In the wake of the death of Floyd, *Christianity Today* and *Sojourners* turned over their digital and print pages to the personal and theological cries of racial minorities, told primarily by Black pastors, theologians, and authors. *The Christian Post* and *World* condemned Chauvin's actions while also condemning the violent protests that followed Floyd's death.

The Christian Post

Executive Editor Richard Land called Floyd's murder an "atrocity of unspeakable barbarity."[1] Police officers who kill a citizen in this way violate the biblical mandate that "divinely authorized civil magistrates" (quoting Rom. 13:1–7). He demanded punishment for Chauvin while noting: "As for me and my house, we will never abandon Dr. King's mesmerizing dream that our nation will fully live up to the promises of our founding documents, and we will produce a country where people will be 'judged not by the color of their skin, but the content of their character.' While I draw breath, this dream will never die."[2]

In a *Post* column, Ron Sider, founder of Evangelicals for Social Action, said the George Floyd murder presented evangelicals with an opportunity. Widening his lens from that of Floyd's death to racism in America, he referenced a recent poll asking people if police treated Blacks as fairly as

Whites. Forty-seven percent of White respondents said yes, while only 6% of Blacks agreed.[3] "But what especially grieves me as a white evangelical," Sider confessed, "is the failure of white evangelicals to deal with white racism. Indeed, it's much worse than that! White evangelicals have too often participated in, and even led, that racism."[4]

In another article, Leonardo Blair's comments mark one of the few times a writer linked pro-life ideology to include a concern for people faced with health disparities, racial injustice, and inferior educational opportunities: "Evangelicals are pro-life people, and I strongly believe, if nothing else, standing against anything which threatens the life of our brothers and sisters in Christ must also be treated as a pro-life issue."[5]

The *Post* also reported that evangelical leaders like Tony Evans and Joel Osteen had joined marchers in Houston, Floyd's burial place. Called Blackout Tuesday, the protest called for people to turn their anger into constructive action. Floyd's death "ignited something in me," Osteen said.[6] He asserted that the issue of racism was not a political issue but one of humanity and theology. He said he hoped God would bring good out of the tragedy.[7]

The *Post*'s columnist Michael Brown reminded readers of the pitfalls of the outbreak of violent protests after Floyd's murder. With city after city under assault, he charged, the portrait of Black Americans rioting reinforced racial stereotypes among Whites that "this is what they do."[8] He wrote that once the riots ended, he hoped America could refocus on the issues raised by Floyd's death.

Christianity Today

Christianity Today took seriously its editorial mandate to explore the "what" of Floyd's death, the "why," and how Christians might change American society's underlying problems. Four articles stand out. On May 29, 2020, guest columnist Dennis R. Edwards called on White Christians to respond with more than platitudes. "White America has long had its knee on our necks," he said.[9] He added that White America needed "to repent, rebuke and reorient itself against racial injustice."[10] He admonished Christians to stop watching their television screens or creating hashtags about racial justice and join a revolution with those who "seek and hunger for justice" (Matt. 5:6, NLT).[11]

Reporter Kate Shellnutt interviewed friends and former pastors of

George Floyd. "Big Floyd's" dedication to Christ and his unselfishness highlighted the comments of those in Houston who knew him best.[12] Shellnut attended the four-hour memorial service for Floyd. She noted how the songs and scriptures, delivered in Gospel, hip-hop, and other genres, dominated the service. The "you-are-there" description of the memorial gave an insider's perspective on the event and the sadness, anger, and hope emanating that day from the music and speakers. What distinguished Shellnutt's article from most others was her interviews with experts on African American music and how the history of Black struggles intertwined with the selection and pacing of the music at the service.

In another article, Daniel Silliman described how Minneapolis pastors responded to the violent protests on their city streets.[13] Christians in Minneapolis cleaned streets, handed out food, and comforted people traumatized by Floyd's death and the protests that followed. A Zoom meeting of Black and White pastors in Minneapolis heard a warning from Charvez Russell, a Baptist pastor: "We don't need saviors. What we need are partners."[14] He then added, "Yes, we need your help right now. Yes, we need your help cleaning up. Yes, we need your resources. But we also need long-term partners who are going to help us stand up for God and tear down the systems that hold people down."[15]

In the aftermath of Floyd's death, *Christianity Today*'s publisher, Timothy Dalrymple, acknowledged slavery and racial prejudice as America's original sin.[16] He quoted a recent poll showing only 42% of White Christians believed that the history of slavery impacted African Americans today. He acknowledged that *Christianity Today*'s record on race was mixed. The magazine founders asserted that Christians primarily needed to preach the Gospel and focus on individual salvation while letting others tackle racism and social inequalities that arose in politics and society. Dalrymple concluded, "What we thought righteous was unrighteous. We repent of our sin."[17]

Dalrymple then offered a partial solution that would have been considered radical just a few years before: that of reparations. Citing the story of Zacchaeus (Luke 19:1–10), the tax collector who repented and then made restitution, Dalrymple noted the current actions of churches trying to atone for their past support for slavery.

In addition to those four articles, *CT* began a 20-week series of online opinion pieces, "Race Set Before Us," edited by Vincent Bacote, associate professor of theology at Wheaton College. Sensing pushback from Whites tired of discussing racism, Bacote argued that Christians must continue to discuss racial inequity. While it's the path less traveled for many and leads to emotional discomfort, the "steady, marathon work [is] required for change."[18] He added that the series was not about guilting White people but providing a "politics of reckoning."[19] He encouraged readers to approach the series with ears to hear and eyes to see (Mark 4:23) so the Holy Spirit might transform them into disciples of justice and mercy.

Authors in the series focused on varied sides of the racial justice debate. Some authors wrote passionate essays calling out White pastors and White civic leaders. Jonathan Walton recounted how colonialism's ideology of White supremacy still permeated modern-day discourse. He suggested pastors who felt ill-equipped to teach racial justice seek help from church leaders of color. Ending racism in the church and society, he said, "begins with white pastors confessing complicity in racist systems and testifying to God's grace and forgiveness in their own lives; then they can lead others to do the same."[20] He mentioned the Doctrine of Discovery written in 1493 and how that series of Catholic edicts also became fodder for White racist attitudes in the colonies.[21] A few sentences later, he added: "No more statements, panel discussions, conferences, or book clubs; what we need is lament, confession, repentance, and a refusal to conform to the world's racist patterns."[22] If we do this, he concluded, all people in the church would experience a slice of Heaven on Earth.

Author and church planter Michelle Reyes, vice president of the Asian American Christian Collaborative, gave readers four practical ways to build inclusive churches mirroring those in the book of Acts.[23] First, churches need diverse leadership and power sharing. Community members should establish ministries for the poor and disadvantaged in their neighborhoods. Second, pastors should often preach about systemic injustice. Infrequent messages could lead listeners to conclude racial justice was not crucial to church leadership. Third, she claimed, "Congregants can be trained to collectively use their voices, resources, and platforms to effect real change in society. They can be taught about healthy engagement with protests and marches . . . They must understand the necessary balance between calling out and calling in, between critique and engagement."[24] Fourth, she concluded, believers can "listen, lament, and legislate."[25]

Charlie B. Dobson explained that genuine repentance requires behavioral changes and that "Racism in America is a white person's sin issue that can only be resolved by white America."[26] She led readers through events in recent American history when the word of a White woman, even if it was a lie, carried unchallenged credibility. She cited examples of the words of a White woman leading to the 1955 murder of Emmett Till and the 1920 wholesale massacre of Blacks in Tulsa, Oklahoma. She said that the unquestioned voice of a White woman is an example of White privilege, and that people of color cannot do anything to stop this privilege from leading to oppression—and even death—for people of color.[27]

Other articles included a suggestion that White Christians tackle racial injustice with the same vigor and advocacy they exhibited in their opposition to abortion.[28] Another claimed White evangelicals who voted for Trump condoned violence against people of color.[29] Another claimed Whites were reluctant to worship with Black believers or submit to Black pastors because they see African Americans "as less educated, hence socially and culturally inferior to whites, compelling most white Christians to reject the idea of submitting to African American spiritual leadership."[30]

A few of the articles criticized evangelicals for ignoring, and therefore contributing to, racism in America. Not content to just recount the history of racism in America, practical suggestions are peppered throughout.

The editors of *Christianity Today* made two other strategic editorial decisions following the George Floyd murder. During the summer and fall of 2020, Portland, Oregon, became the epicenter of continual clashes between protestors and the police. The city suffered from more than 75 straight nights of violence. Writer Andrew Shaughnessy authored an article titled "Portland is Still Protesting: Where is the Church?"[31] The article assumes that the church should be at the center of reconciliation and relief efforts in civil unrest. But Shaughnessy implied they were not. It also quoted some pastors expressing ambivalence about the aims of many protestors, particularly their involvement in the Black Lives Matter movement.

In fall 2020, the magazine published four articles about the churches of Atlanta, Georgia, involved in political, cultural, and economic activism.[32] In introducing the package, news editor Kate Shellnutt said the story's spark was her search to understand how the city responded to civil rights abuses in the past. She observed that "Across the generations, Atlanta—with the black church as its heartbeat—has worked to honor its hard-won progress as well as to lament the cost of the ongoing fight for justice."[33]

The stories acknowledged that racial reconciliation was still a dream, but the Black church was a prominent community organizer. Additionally, Black entrepreneurs started and sustained businesses to reduce the economic divide between the city's residents. The insight and in-depth reporting in the Portland and the Atlanta stories stress the complexities of fighting for racial justice and how Christians could make a difference.

Lest it appeared to be anti-police in its coverage, the magazine asked in its September 2020 edition, "What are Police For?"[34] In the first essay, Esau McCaulley set forth a theology of policing in the New Testament. In the Roman world, soldiers performed the policing role. McCauley claimed that while Romans 13 says obeying those in authority was necessary, Paul's admonition is a two-way street. Authority figures and those carrying out orders must also heed the law. Paul's words apply to both the police of that time and the rulers who directed the police.

McCaulley argued that the application to today's world is straightforward. He said: "Over the course of centuries, not decades, our government has crafted laws that were designed to disenfranchise black people. These laws were then enforced by the state's sword."[35] He added then that it is the responsibility of citizens to hold these authority figures and institutions responsible for righting the injustices created in the past.[36] McCaulley concluded with a call for a policing system emphasizing freedom from fear for all citizens, one that would no longer be a source of anxiety for many African Americans.

Author and pastor Michael Lefebvre presented an Old Testament consideration of policing in the same issue. He wrote of two ways Jewish communities ensured peace and safety, both tied to the concept of justice. As no police departments existed in biblical times, the people used two methods of providing justice. The hue and cry method expected the victim to "raise the alarm" (Deut. 22:23–27) so those within hearing distance could respond. In other words, "public security is the duty of all members of the community."[37]

The second Old Testament practice was the custom called the "kinsman redeemer." An injustice against a relative called for a response from an adult male. If a family member was hurt, the relative sought redress on his aggrieved relative's behalf. This kinsman was expected to be the investigator and arresting officer and to either dispense justice or hold a trial with witnesses so the community could decide guilt or innocence.[38] If the accused felt the kinsman redeemer had wronged them, they could flee to a refuge city. There, the city's elders would decide on the fair course of action or hold a trial to determine the truth.

Christianity Today excelled at putting the George Floyd murder into a biblical context. Their extensive series of essays and articles rarely mentioned mega-church pastors and Christian leaders' comments pointing fingers at protestors' violence in the streets. Instead, readers received a well-reasoned and biblically based analysis of what evangelicals should (and should not) do about many of the issues of racism raised by Floyd's death.

Sojourners

Sojourners pulled no punches in condemning the death of Floyd. President Adam Russell Taylor wrote:

> As a father of two black sons, I can't breathe today because I refuse to accept a law enforcement system that so often treats black bodies as being presumed guilty or immediate danger. Will George Floyd's death finally be a tipping point in the public consciousness and outrage that has been so elusive when enough of us demand police accountability and declare definitely that black lives matter?[39]

Taylor encouraged Christians to take action to ensure Floyd's murder led to a more positive relationship between the Black community and the police. He wrote, "I can't breathe today because none of us should feel able to breathe fully or easily in our nation until all of us are able to breathe free from the evils of racism and police brutality."[40]

Dante Stewart expressed anger in his *Sojourners* column, noting that sometimes it takes rage within humans to trigger change. He said that rage was evident in the public cry for Black dignity and the need to assert that Black lives matter to God. Stewart, a Black pastor at a predominantly White church, condemned Christians whose primary focus after Floyd's death was on the protesters and rioters present on the streets of Minneapolis and other major U.S. cities. He argued, "If you're more concerned about the responses of black rage than you are about the system that justifies and rewards black death, you love black people—you just love when they stay in their place. And that's not love, that's hate."[41]

Marc Antoine Lavarin wrote that the problem of racism was a theological challenge for the church: "Every church that preached, 'We don't have a race problem; we have a sin problem,' needs to apologize to their congregation for their failure to name systemic racism as the sin."[42] For those in churches yearning to protest racism, he cautioned: "Consider protesting your own theology that continues to intentionally and unintentionally do harm to black and brown bodies."[43] He added that there is "no substantive difference between a racist holding a Bible in front of a church [a reference to President Trump's holding up of a Bible in front of St. John's Episcopal Church in DC] and a Christian holding up a #BlackLivesMatter sign with no plans to parse out the practical implementation of the holy truth of justice."[44]

Following the publication of measured outrage from its writers, *Sojourners* pivoted to longer-term reflections on institutional racism. The message? Racism is an individual and structural sin problem, and Christians need to pray with introspection before deciding how to respond. Writer Matthew L. Watley acknowledged his anger at Floyd's murder and that of many other innocent Black citizens. He condemned the violent protests taking place across the country. However, as a pastor, he (and all the rest of us) needed to follow the example of Jesus, who would have encouraged us to pray and engage in "courageous conversations with those in your sphere of influence."[45]

Columnist Thao Thi Nguyen said she left the church because of her local congregation's oblivion to the role of Christians in perpetuating racism. She argued that the sin of racism is both an individual sin and a collective sin and that White Christians need to help people of color shape the narratives of the church today. That, she said, will expose blatant racism and structural racism.[46]

An article by Taylor and Wallis presents some optimism. They noted the presence of honest police officers working long hours but observed that real change in racial relations needed more than just police reform. Instead, the death of George Floyd could serve as a "Kairos moment, one in which the sheer brokenness and depravity of the status quo generate an awakening and reckoning that makes radical transformation possible."[47] A week later, Wallis used the Kairos moment metaphor to reinforce his feeling that perhaps the death of Floyd really would awaken the church and society to their own destructive beliefs regarding race.[48]

Chanequa Walker-Barnes, a professor at Mercer University, countered Wallis's guarded optimism by asserting that the Defund the Police movement must continue because the police would not reform themselves. Christians needed to be at the forefront of this advocacy.[49]

A final piece in *Sojourners* following Floyd's death raised the issue of reparations. Kelly Brown Douglas, dean of the Episcopal Divinity School at

Union Theological Seminary, gave readers a history of slavery and White supremacy, adding: "Choosing whiteness—even when it is simply a passive refusal to confront what it means to be a beneficiary of white supremacy and its legacy—is immoral."[50]

Citing recent decisions by institutions such as Princeton Theological Seminary to provide tuition assistance for descendants of enslaved people, she encouraged faith communities to "repair the breach" between the present injustice and a just future, concluding that "Reparations must not simply look back, but most importantly must push forward."[51]

WORLD

World's editorial content wove the biblical journalism idea into dozens of articles focused on the aftermath of Floyd's death. Both evangelical ideology and the publication's views on the culture wars were evident in its content decisions and framing of those articles. The first news piece focused on Derek Chauvin and the other officers involved in Floyd's death. It appeared on May 26, a day after Floyd's death and the officer's termination. The roughly 200-word article took a dispassionate, factual approach: "A video taken by a bystander showed a white Minneapolis police officer pressing his knee on an African American man's neck for several minutes during an arrest on Monday night."[52]

A second paragraph began with bold typeface and the words, "Why did officers arrest and restrain Floyd?" The answer is that "he matched the description of a forgery suspect at a grocery store and resisted arrest."[53] Two days later, the news focused on violent protests in Minneapolis and an appeal by the mayor for the state to call out the National Guard.[54] Three days later, *World* emphasized the strong condemnation of Chauvin emanating from police across the U.S.[55]

Concern for Floyd appeared a few days after his death. In a sympathetic piece, Sharon Dierberger chronicled his troubled life.[56] She, too, interviewed some of Floyd's friends and pastors who spoke of Floyd's devotion to Christ. After summarizing Floyd's complicated life and his coming to faith, she ended with three paragraphs focused on the continued violent protests in Minneapolis.

The next day, editor Olasky wrote a short explanation of *World*'s ongoing coverage, hinting at what the publication would highlight and downplay. He noted that pastors encouraged Christ's followers to "put aside torches and weapons."[57] He added that *World's* staff would report on the unfolding crisis in the streets of America as journalists and "show what that may mean for the future."[58] There is no mention of helping readers understand the angst of protestors or any acknowledgment of structural racism.

Olasky also speculated on the economic damage of violent protests that summer and what they might portend for capitalism's future. "While we report, please mourn with the friends and family of George Floyd, please cry for our beloved country, and please pray for God's mercy."[59]

In a follow-up article, Dierberger described a gathering at the site of Floyd's death of people from four area churches who prayed for healing and an end to the violence.[60] The theme of law and order is also mentioned that day in articles about citizens cleaning up after looters in Dallas[61] and comments from protesters in Los Angeles bemoaning the continual looting in that city.[62]

As protests continued, President Trump ordered protestors to be forcibly cleared from Lafayette Park across the street from the White House. He then walked to St. John's Church and held aloft a Bible. One of his supporters, Dallas pastor Robert Jeffress told the *Atlantic*, "By holding up the Bible, he was showing us that it teaches that, yes, God hates racism, it's despicable—but God also hates lawlessness."[63] A column by Mindy Belz a day later began by announcing the President's executive order calling for the spending of at least $50 million per year to support international religious freedom, "redirecting funding along with diplomatic priorities and foreign aid to protect religious groups overseas."[64] The majority of her column, however, focused on Trump's photo at St. John's Church across from the White House, noting that some religious leaders were outraged at Trump's publicity stunt and its imagery.[65]

While peaceful protests punctuated with violent incidents swept up America and *World's* reporting, the publication wondered how the country's allies and foes were processing the situation. Three articles asking that question appeared in early June. One mentioned other protests internationally.[66] The other two highlighted potential acts by American foes taking advantage of the country's distraction with Floyd's death and its aftermath.[67]

Pentecost Sunday followed soon after Floyd's death, and writer Katie Gaultney interviewed White and African American pastors from various churches. While calling for healing and reconciliation, pastors recommended that White people listen to their Black brothers and sisters. The Los Angeles president of the Baptist Ministers Conference said he helped organize a peaceful march of faith leaders because, at times, "the appalling silence of the church is sometimes why the community boils over."[68] The article added that a 14-year-old boy thanked Rev. K.W. Tulloss for "showing us how to do it right."[69]

While its framing of national protests against Floyd's death questioned the mainstream press narrative of police violence and structural racism, *World* commentator Ryan Bomberger clarified the publication's stance. Interviewed on a *World*-produced radio segment called "The World and Everything in It," he said he understood that people were upset at watching a helpless George Floyd dying before their eyes. Bomberger admitted that Floyd had been treated "unjustly" by the police. But he strongly criticized society's lack of attention to more than just Floyd's death at the hands of the police. As a Black man, he said he was "11 times more likely to be killed by another person of my complexion" rather than a White policeman.[70] He bashed the Black Lives Matter movement as "deeply un-Christian. They're pro-LGBT. They're anti-capitalist. They're anti-fatherhood. There's no reconciliation."[71]

The publication's editorial content debunked the "defund police" movement. A well-researched news article by Jenny Rough established that people of color are arrested more often than Whites for suspected crimes. But more police are present in minority communities, so it followed that they would make more arrests. "It's a matter of putting police in certain neighborhoods that are 'high crime,' and it becomes a self-fulfilling prophecy."[72]

At the end of June, an Olasky column admitted that Blacks are more likely to be profiled by police. He agreed with those asserting that Derek Chauvin's record of misconduct as a policeman should have disqualified him from the profession years before he "confronted" Floyd. "But," Olasky reminded, "it's hard to fire a police officer, given union rules."[73]

Olasky encouraged his readers to look for opportunities to "work side by side to solve problems."[74] At the same time, he pointed out that the other side—admittedly a relative few—on the left and right act "with horror in their hearts."[75] The takeaway? Both Bomberger and Olasky entreat readers to rise above the rhetoric of the moment and look for larger narratives that serve as a counterpoint to leftist voices presenting one-sided views about racism, privilege, and the possibility of reconciliation.

Finally, Janie Cheaney wrote, "Trying to address a broad canvas of historic and persistent racism with broad-brush 'solutions' (like defunding the police or trashing America) is worse than futile—it's destructive. As Paul explained in Romans 7, the law can't reform the human heart."[76] She added that in the Floyd case, law and procedures failed while "overzealous vigilantes went scot-free."[77] She encouraged readers to follow God's word, "Love your neighbor, not your cause or tribe. This is where we can all do better, and we must."[78]

Conclusion

In 2019, a year before Floyd's death, an extensive Barna study commissioned by The Reimagine Group noted that half of practicing Christians believed the history of racism still impacted daily life for Black Americans. Breaking those numbers down more, 80% of Black Christians said racism still negatively impacted their livelihoods, safety, educational opportunities, and economic realities. Only 42% of White Christians agreed. Yet all Christians felt the church could play a part in addressing racial injustice. That included two-thirds of White Christians. Only 19% of those polled said the church could do nothing to impact racial inequality. Respondents said hearing sermons about racial justice "are more likely to affirm the reality of racial injustice and to see a role for the church in addressing it."[79] Conversely, those who didn't hear sermons about racial injustice said they hadn't considered the church's role in combatting ongoing racism.

A second poll a year later, right before Floyd's death, found similar results with a continued disparity in the experiences and opinions of Black and White believers. That study found that 39% of White evangelicals (versus 62% of Black Protestants) felt it was vital for churches to address political issues, especially race relations.[80] More telling, though, 59% of White evangelicals said pastors did not need to preach about political problems like race and immigration from the pulpit.

A June 2020 poll, just after Floyd's death, found pastors open to preaching more about racism, a suggestion made by all four of the evangelical publications. A Barna poll found that 94% of pastors felt the church needed to speak out against racism, and 62% said they had done so in sermons following Floyd's death. Additionally, three-fourths said the "church should support peaceful protests occurring in response to Floyd's killing."[81] Barna Group President David Kinnaman noted: "There are a couple of indications that pastors are as open as they've ever been" to making racial inequity a topic of their sermons.[82]

The George Floyd trauma and the dialogue on racism quickly faded from the public consciousness. A more existential threat arose, threatening people's lives worldwide. How to negotiate the threat of COVID-19 became a hot topic on the pages of evangelical publications trying to make sense of government missteps and church leaders' concerns about individual and religious freedom.

Chapter 7

COVID-19: Science, Politics, and Personal Freedom

IN THE SPRING OF 2020, the world shut down. Over the next two years, the deadly SARs-2 virus, commonly known as the coronavirus or COVID-19, killed millions worldwide. North America did not escape the virus's wrath, as scientists scrambled to understand its seemingly random choice of victims.

The disputed origins of the virus, alongside the confusing and, at times, contradictory public health advice and mandates on how to survive its ravages, created multiple lines of debate, denial, and pushback among evangelicals. A minority of churches declined to move their in-person Sunday worship services to an online format as recommended—and sometimes mandated—by local and state government agencies. Once a vaccine arrived, some refused to get the jab. Several pastors died after debunking the use of masks, social distancing, and vaccinations.[1]

The four evangelical publications faced the challenge of encouraging Christians in this distrustful environment. Three major themes emerge from the thousands of articles published from early 2020 until the end of 2022. These were:

1. Educating readers while countering misinformation;
2. Explaining the intersection of America's First Amendment freedoms with the equally compelling need to obey short-term government efforts to keep people safe; and
3. Suggesting how churches and individuals could exhibit creative compassion toward others.

The Christian Post

In January 2020, *The Christian Post* first alerted readers to a dangerous new virus.[2] The article also noted speculation in *The Washington Post* that the virus originated in Wuhan, China, home of the Wuhan Institute of Virology.

A few days later, an infectious disease expert told *The Christian Post* readers that as the virus's effects grew, they should "stock up on supplies; cover those coughs and sneezes; wash hands frequently for at least 20 seconds; avoid crowds; and stay aware, as the situation could change rapidly."[3] A few days later, the publication quoted a Centers for Disease Control official telling Americans the virus "could be bad."[4] Thus, from the earliest days of our awareness of COVID-19, the *Post* alerted readers of a potential pandemic and how to stay safe.

Editor Richard Land's first of several articles on COVID-19 gave readers four tips for responding to the pandemic. Don't panic, he advised, as God is our refuge and strength; pray for those infected and their families while asking for wisdom for our leaders; take precautions by listening to the medical experts; and don't do anything that puts someone else at risk.[5]

Two aspects of his article stand out. In advising readers to listen to medical experts, Land cautioned that God didn't promise protection just because you did the Lord's work. If experts recommend smaller or no meetings, follow that advice. Second, he quoted Mark 12:31 and Luke 6:31. Both passages command us to love our neighbors. He wrote, "Let's all pray that when we look back on this crisis, our fellow Americans will see this episode in our history as one that reflects credit on the Lord we serve as they see His work in us as we serve them."[6]

During the next few years, the publication ran over 150 articles on the coronavirus. Except for a few opinion pieces casting doubt on health experts' recommendations and mandates, the *Post* encouraged its readers to trust health authorities.

A few articles questioned the often-conflicting advice from health officials as a lockdown began in the spring of 2020. "Simply put, it would be hysterical to say don't travel, absent any specific facts and science to the contrary," columnist Dennis Lennox claimed.[7] That same day, the *Post* noted six ways megachurch pastors dealt with the burgeoning pandemic.[8] Greg Laurie announced that his Harvest Christian Fellowship in California would temporarily move to online-only services. He encouraged parishioners to invite their friends to watch, as fear among Americans was high, and people needed hope. Robert Jeffress, the pastor of First Baptist Church in Dallas, said worship would continue in-person while taking steps to comply with guidance issued by his county. Jeffress's church was in the minority, as most other big churches opted to meet only online.

The publication also created news articles based on tweets from noted evangelicals. In one of those articles, Eugene Cho, president of Bread for the World, criticized President Trump directly. Trump referred to COVID-19 as the "China Virus" at a White House press briefing. Cho responded: "Mr. President: This is not acceptable. Calling it the 'Chinese virus' only instigates blame, racism, and hatred against Asians—here and abroad. We need leadership that speaks clearly against racism: Leadership that brings the nation and world together."[9]

Other reports included speculation about God's involvement with COVID-19, ranging from the return of an ancient Egyptian curse to God's curse on the world for its acceptance of homosexuality and other abominations. Those were promptly debunked.[10] Additional essays presented fact-based ways readers could stay healthy,[11] while others quoted prominent Christians encouraging readers to take the disease seriously.[12]

Pastors defying government mandates to hold services online tapped into a well of conservative and libertarian ideology that Christians could defy those mandates in the interests of religious freedom. Dozens of articles in *The Christian Post* quoted pastors defiantly keeping their churches open (and facing lawsuits and eventually court decisions that further muddied the waters).[13] Other articles contained announcements of the deaths of prominent Christians and *mea culpa* from pastors whose churches became super-spreader sites, resulting in the deaths of members. Still, others reported on hundreds of people falling ill after attending camps and conferences while not always wearing masks or social distancing.[14] *The Christian Post* also published articles highlighting pushback from Christian leaders opposed to rallies staged by others in defiance of state and local mandates limiting large gatherings, even if held outside.[15]

The Christian Post's paucity of original reporting meant it did not provide its readers with examples of how churches responded to the needs of their communities. The other publications, however, highlighted an array of good works.

Christianity Today

One of the publication's earliest articles discussed virus misinformation and who might likely reject government recommendations and mandates for social distancing, masking, and closing non-essential businesses. Ryan Burge summarized recent opinion polling that foretold one of the central narratives of the pandemic. Republicans were "far less likely" than

Democrats to fear the effects of the virus. Republicans were also more likely to be churchgoers whose faith informed their belief that God would care for them. That helped explain why some religious advisers to President Trump urged caution about canceling in-person worship. Burge quoted an Arkansas pastor who explained to *The Washington Post*: "In your more politically conservative regions, closing is not interpreted as caring for you. It's interpreted as liberalism, or buying into the hype."[16]

Another contributor, Jim Denison, debunked those who said the coronavirus was God's judgment on a fallen world, citing logic and biblical precedence.[17] Soon after, missions professor Todd Mangum asserted that God allowed COVID-19 to bring Christians to their knees in repentance. He noted that our repentance allowed us to mourn with those who wept, and believers should "receive any discipline God may intend as coming from the hand of my loving father."[18]

Can government dictate to churches when and where they can meet for corporate worship? *CT* writers explained that a small minority of church leaders argued that God commanded his people to assemble face-to-face to worship him corporately—no excuses accepted. In refusing to move worship services online, churches adhering to this interpretation of Scripture encountered lawsuits and other legal repercussions.[19] A significant bone of contention was that "essential" businesses remained open. Churches were not considered essential businesses in most state and local mandates.

One article pointed out that some churches could not move to online worship because people living in rural areas or poor neighborhoods didn't have internet access. But rather than call for blanket freedom for churches, the article noted: "Candidly, we see downsides when churches assert their rights aggressively by pointing to other activities that the government has allowed. Such assertions can intensify an unhealthy sense of grievance among Christians. They can play into the 'what-about' that often makes it difficult to establish any agreement in public debate today."[20]

Another article about public worship summarized research showing heightened infection rates among racial minorities. Thus, pastors of minority churches urged caution lest churches open too soon and become super-spreaders among one of the most vulnerable groups.[21]

Amidst the controversy over social distancing and mask use, *Christianity Today* widened its lens to report on the effect of the pandemic on international aid organizations that canceled face-to-face fundraising events during the early months of 2020.[22]

The first of a series of vaccines became available in December 2020. Should Christians "get the jab?" *CT* began an education campaign in early 2021. Daniel Chin, a pulmonary and critical care physician, urged Christians to rely on what scientists knew at the time and to get vaccinated.[23]

After moving classes online for the remainder of the 2019–2020 school year, *Christianity Today* noted that most Christian colleges and universities mandated or strongly encouraged students to get vaccinated before the beginning of the next school year, which began in the fall of 2021. In addition to promoting vaccination, several schools sent student ambassadors into their local communities to educate people about the vaccine's safety and to quell fears among undocumented workers who feared that if they sought a vaccination, local authorities would report them to federal officials for deportation.[24] Other articles also included advice for individuals on how to pray during the pandemic and why people should pray for President Trump during his siege with the virus.[25]

Sojourners

Sojourners's educational articles attempted to counter false information they claimed originated from President Trump. Jim Wallis first addressed the rise of COVID-19 with a plea for truth, unity, and solidarity. He noted that essential workers, many of whom were low-income, died at a higher rate than others exposed to the virus. He also reminded readers that race and poverty are pre-existing conditions for COVID-19. Wallis then blasted the Trump administration for lying and staging "despicable reality TV shows disguised as health briefing."[26]

Wallis added that besides older people and the immunocompromised, the most vulnerable include those living in urban communities, neighborhoods with high air pollution, and people who must use public transportation to work essential jobs. He also reminded readers of 1 Corinthians 12:26, when "one part [of the body] suffers . . . every part suffers with it." He alleged that right wing interest groups sowed doubts about the actions of governors in Democratic Party strongholds.[27]

The publication countered President Trump's suggestion that bleach and Lysol could treat COVID-19. While he later said he was joking, author Christina Colon told readers New York City's poison control received 30 calls from people who took the President's words seriously and were even sicker.[28] She suggested rather than trust Trump, readers consult fact-based websites and should be at the forefront of setting the record straight with friends, family, and the larger community.[29]

The publication's frustration with the President was echoed in editor Adam Russell Taylor's provocatively titled editorial "For Heaven's Sake, 'Wear a Damn Mask.'" Quoting Florida Sen. Marco Rubio, he used that title to condemn the political leadership in states such as Florida, Texas, and Arizona, where Republican leaders denigrated masking mandates. He wrote, "I have been growing increasingly exasperated by the selfish individualism and hubris that defines the behavior of far too many Americans who refuse to regularly wear a mask and practice social distancing . . . ."[30] President Trump is "Culprit No. 1," Taylor asserted.[31] Taylor then pivoted to plead with pastors to debunk the many existing conspiracy theories and educate parishioners about the importance of wearing masks and practicing social distancing.[32]

The publication doubled down on its educational role once vaccines arrived. It quoted doctors and ethicists supporting vaccination on the first day of the Pfizer vaccine rollout. In deciding whether to get vaccinated, ethicist Nancy Berlinger noted that people should ask, "What are my responsibilities concerning how we live together as a society?"[33] This plea for community-based ethical behavior often clashed with the individualistic nature of the evangelical response to vaccine mandates.

Those wary of the vaccine also expressed concern that aborted fetal tissue was used in manufacturing or testing the vaccines. Author Lexi McMenamin quoted from a U.S. Conference of Catholic Bishops memo, "Some are asserting that if a vaccine is connected in any way with tainted cell lines, then it is immoral to be vaccinated with them. This is an inaccurate portrayal of Catholic moral teaching."[34]

Sojourners strongly supported vaccinations. Sociologists Andrew L. Whitehead and Samuel L. Perry noted that Christian nationalists were most likely to advance narratives saying vaccines caused autism and that people should not trust doctors and drug companies.[35] Several months later, the publication presented a lengthy historical analysis of vaccine mandates. It said a religious objection to vaccinating was not allowed until 1960.[36] Christians willingly received vaccinations against polio and other diseases before that time, they noted.

The publication reported "progress on the willingness of black adults getting vaccines" in late 2020.[37] It appealed to Black churches to continue advocating for vaccinations by educating their church members while acknowledging the ethical wrongs of healthcare researchers in the past.[38]

Commentaries in *Sojourners* challenged the notion that believers possessed a Constitutional freedom to act in a manner consistent with their interpretation of Scripture and this individualism superseded responsibility to the community. A few weeks after coronavirus hit national headlines, Russell Meek railed against pastors and politicians who seemed willing to sacrifice lives to keep the American economy up and running.[39] These people included TV personality and eventual administrator of The Centers for Medicare and Medicaid Services Dr. Mehmet Oz, who said reopening schools would only result in 2% to 3% of Americans dying. The lieutenant governor of Texas said grandparents like him should be willing to sacrifice their lives for the economy's good. Meeks asked: "What does it mean to love one's neighbor?"[40] His lengthy exposition of the Old Testament Law made it abundantly clear letting the old and weak die of COVID-19 violated biblical principles.[41]

Churches claiming the right to worship in person in defiance of health mandates also dismayed *Sojourners*'s writers.[42] Jim Wallis criticized President Trump for failing to create a comprehensive pandemic strategy while pushing for an early opening of public schools, writing, "Just as he turned mask-wearing into a political litmus test, he's using our children's futures as a political tactic to try and put the pandemic behind us, get the economy going again, and help him win reelection."[43]

In another essay, Wallis praised Congress in April 2020 for passing COVID-19 relief legislation. He also urged leaders to do more by passing another relief package targeting those in prisons, Native Americans, people without housing, and those "affected by the deeply intertwined scourges of racism and/or poverty . . . ."[44]

Sojourners relayed to its readers some comments from George Nicholas, co-convener of the African American Health Equity Task Force, urging churches to take responsibility for helping others. He argued, "We have a moral imperative as Christian clergy that are assigned to work in the African American community. We have to do more than just preach and pray; we have to begin to address really difficult problems that exist within the Black community."[45]

The publication highlighted a campaign by San Antonio pastors taking selfies as they received COVID-19 shots.[46] In Washington, DC, churches hosted vaccination days at their churches.[47] A director of the Christian Alliance for Orphans urged believers to adopt children orphaned by the death of their parents.[48]

Even after the pandemic's death toll eased in 2022, *Sojourners* continued its focus on the COVID-19 virus, asking in a news article how believers should care for neighbors suffering from long COVID.[49]

WORLD

World's first mention of coronavirus appeared in two early February 2020 feature articles on deaths in Wuhan. In the first piece, writer June Chang relayed an anecdote about a pastor holding an online memorial service for a woman. That service went viral on social media. Thousands watched, and several of the woman's friends became Christians through the pastor's preaching.[50]

Cheng also described the Chinese government's attempts to control communication about the spread of COVID-19 and citizens' anger at the complete lockdown of cities. As the virus raged across the city, she gave readers a chilling look at its impact. Cheng also described how local Christians obtained and distributed face masks, found hospital beds for infected people and used social media to help find whatever resources people might need. Those acts of love stood in contrast to the "government's slow response and initial cover-up of the outbreak, as well as incompetency that led to additional deaths."[51]

Those excellent articles opened the floodgates for *World*'s reporting on the coronavirus in the United States and worldwide. Using just the search word "COVID-19," uncovered just over 3,000 articles focused on the disease and debates over masks, vaccines, and the conspiracy theories swirling around the pandemic. Writer Mindy Belz noted in early May 2020 that the print publication had already devoted five covers to the virus.[52] *World*'s consistency in its reporting served as prophetic and visionary as the pandemic spread worldwide.

In its early reporting, *World* occasionally chastised pastors who ignored or defied government health recommendations to move worship services online.[53] Early in the pandemic, Jamie Dean reported on a Tampa, Florida, pastor who told parishioners he would never cancel in-person worship. "This Bible school is open because we're raising up revivalists, not pansies," he asserted.[54] Dean noted that President Trump urged all Americans to avoid gatherings of more than ten individuals so as to lessen the possibility of mass infections. Tampa pastor Howard-Browne was arrested for two misdemeanor violations and canceled on-site meetings a few days later. Dean added that most Christians were content to put the needs of others before their own, stating, "They're not pansies."[55]

In August 2020, Sophia Lee reported from Orange County, California, where outdoor worship attracted hundreds of people. She then wrote about other areas of the country where Christians debated whether to heed various state mandates that included bans on indoor worship and singing. At the same time, "essential businesses" such as gyms, bowling alleys, and other businesses were allowed to open in some states, a sore point with several outspoken pastors and Christian leaders.[56]

Another article in the August series focused on creative ways schools, churches, and businesses were continuing their mission and ministry while adhering to safety protocols.[57] Reports showed Christians around the country struggling to make their way amidst confusing and sometimes conflicting information.

Jamie Dean noted in a news article that Pastor John MacArthur said his Grace Community Church in California would remain open, he said, "to protect our church against unreasonable, unconstitutional restrictions."[58]

The addition of *World*'s politically conservative Opinions section fueled several essays criticizing vaccine mandates and other government mandated restrictions such as shelter-in-place, school and business closures, and travel bans.[59] Christiana Kiefer slammed President Joe Biden's statement that he had "thin patience" for federal employees and employees of businesses with more than 100 employees refusing to get vaccinated.[60] This, she inferred, might mean more government encroachment on individual freedoms.

World publisher Joel Belz wrote a reflective challenge to readers based on his conversations with friends.[61] Christians must reprioritize their time and resources once the pandemic finally subsided, he said. Churches and schools would need emergency aid, and Christians must rethink how they spend leisure and entertainment dollars. He added a personal note that he and his wife were still discussing what their part might be in helping with the recovery process, concluding "none of us dare fall back to what we did last year. The devastation is just too extensive."[62]

Another Olasky column highlighted the generosity and faith of others. This column contrasted the bottom-up response of Americans to the top-down directives of the authoritarian Chinese government.[63] The good works in America included a New York union finding emergency child care for essential health workers; parents canceling a Bar Mitzvah and sending the food for the celebration to friends in quarantine; a grocery store opening early to accommodate seniors; and a Washington school district sending out their bus drivers to deliver meals to poor children on their regular route.[64]

World also reported on the emotional toll of COVID-19 on pastors and church leaders.[65] Church leaders described themselves as exhausted and uncertain about the pressures they faced to preserve church unity. Pastor Chuck Bower said a few people complained about everything the church tried: masking, social distancing, and outdoor in-person worship. He said one parishioner wore a Trump 2020 mask to church, while another said everyone needed to vote for Trump. He confessed, "What weighs on me most is, I just wonder . . . did they miss what we tried to teach over the years about being a disciple of Jesus? How do people get sucked [into politics] so easily?"[66]

Conclusion

Hundreds of articles and opinion essays dissecting the COVID-19 pandemic from every conceivable angle appeared in the evangelical publications. Did attitudes and actions of evangelicals caught up in legitimate and ill-informed doubts about masking, social distancing, getting vaccinated, and attending potential super-spreader events like in-person church change based on those articles and essays? Hopefully, but the evidence is slim.

Christians prayed more during the pandemic, but some did not heed the encouragement of evangelical publications to get vaccinated.[67] Twenty-eight percent of White evangelicals said in the spring of 2021 that they would not get vaccinated, according to a Kaiser Family Foundation poll.[68] Vaccine hesitancy was prevalent in pockets of the South where evangelicals lived. Samuel Perry, the author of several evangelical studies, told *CNN*, "We're going to see consequences in those regions of the country. And that they will be felt by the vulnerable and the elderly."[69] While vaccine hesitancy was not the only factor, a Georgetown University study found that between January 2020 and September 2021, the southern U.S. accounted for 48% of all U.S. COVID-19 deaths, while representing only 38% of the population.[70]

Not only did COVID-19 upend the economic, religious, and cultural landscapes of 2020 and 2021, but it also factored strongly into the contentious 2020 Presidential election.

Chapter 8

The 2020 Election: The Evangelical Dilemma

IN DECEMBER 2019, nearly a year before the 2020 election, the U.S. House of Representatives voted to impeach President Donald Trump for abuse of power. Mark Galli, editor of *Christianity Today*, called for the Senate to remove Trump from office after calling the president's actions immoral. Galli's opinion piece made major headlines across the nation. It resulted in a strong rebuke from the president, who called *CT* a "far-left magazine."[1] Trump claimed the publication preferred a nonbeliever (Joe Biden) to himself, a president who had overwhelming support from evangelicals.[2]

Galli's editorial shocked the evangelical world and led to heated push-back. Richard Land, executive editor of *The Christian Post*, called Galli's op-ed "lofty," alleging that secular media had seized on *CT*'s remarks as signaling a long-awaited evangelical schism: "In reality, nothing could be further from the truth . . . ."[3] Land noted that 200 evangelical leaders had already signed a letter opposing Galli's op-ed (the next day, an equal number of evangelical leaders praised Galli's editorial) claiming that the magazine "is a shell of its former self and that *CT* speaks to, and for, fewer evangelicals with each passing year."[4]

Land also reprinted a long paragraph allegedly written by Galli. In the excerpt, Galli said he knew few people who voted for Trump in 2016.[5] Galli added that he was an evangelical "elitist," unlike many Trump voters who lacked a college degree (evidently necessary to separate Trump's lies from other political speech), and "they don't attend conferences of evangelicals for social justice or evangelicals for immigration reform."[6]

Land's editorial made it clear that "*CT*'s op-ed does not represent evangelical Christianity today, yesterday, or in the future," further adding, "*CT*'s disdainful, dismissive, elitist posture toward their fellow Christians may well do far more long-term damage to American Christianity and its witness than any current prudential support for President Trump will ever cause."[7] Land's rebuttal to Galli's opinion signaled that almost a year before the 2020 election, at least two evangelical magazines held vastly divergent viewpoints on Trump's re-election bid.

In 2020, President Donald Trump's character shortcomings and occasional policies that ignored biblical values were no secret to evangelicals. The hope expressed by some that he would curtail his hostile and uncivil rhetoric did not materialize. But for most evangelicals, including *The Christian Post* and *World*, Trump's opposition to abortion and appointment of conservative judges outweighed his failings. Here's how each of the publications approached the 2020 Presidential election.

The Christian Post

The Christian Post's selection of articles about events, opinion leader comments, and sermon excerpts favored Donald Trump. Early in 2020, an opinion article by Sheldon Roth, a retired Harvard medical psychiatrist, claimed Donald Trump was indeed a Christian.[8] Best-selling author and pastor Norman Vincent Peale pastored the church Trump once attended and Trump occasionally mentioned Peale as an influential person in his life.[9] "In this religious struggle of the faithful, his empathic talent to excite contagious witnessing captures the hearts of believers. How could it not? He aids and abets the salvation of their souls. Donald J. Trump has Christian charisma," Roth said.[10]

Editor Land spoke of his support for Trump to Judy Woodruff, host of the PBS News Hour. He admitted to having difficulty accepting Trump in 2016. However, four years later, he praised Trump as "the most pro-life president in the modern era" and also noted that the President had acted to preserve religious liberty by appointing conservative judges.[11]

Southern Baptist leader Albert Mohler likewise indicated his support for Trump despite not voting for him in 2016.[12] Meanwhile, the *Post* used its pages to feature commentary criticizing evangelicals who supported Biden. One commentary accused author Beth Moore of hypocrisy for criticizing Trump's infidelities while not condemning Biden, who had been accused of sexual harassment (but never charged) in the past.[13]

In June 2020, though, the *Post* published articles pointing out the spiritual danger of Donald Trump because his rhetoric and actions occasionally hurt the Christian witness. Worse, though, would be a Biden win ushering in anarchy nationwide.[14] Another article said Trump's friend and spiritual mentor Paula White had declared that a "demonic network" opposed Trump's re-election.[15]

Even articles that may have reflected positively on Biden pointed out his support for abortion. For instance, the *Post* profiled Josh Dickson, National Faith Engagement Director for the Biden campaign. Dickson emphasized Biden's concern for fighting for civil rights and for the poor, values that arose from his Catholic faith. Writer Michael Gryboski quickly reminded readers that for many Catholics and evangelicals, liberal stances on abortion and religious liberty were "deal-breakers."[16] Gryboski wrote of Pastor Robert Jeffress telling Fox Business that evangelicals who supported Biden "have sold their soul to the devil and accepted the Democrats' barbaric position on abortion."[17]

Others piled on the anti-Biden bandwagon. Frequent contributor Michael Brown called the 2020 Democratic nominating convention "hopeless," quoting President Trump as he called the gathering "the darkest, angriest and gloomiest convention in American history."[18] Brown said the candidate providing voters with hope (presumably Trump) would score better than someone peddling pessimism.[19] A few days later, an article quoted pastor John MacArthur alleging that no honest Christian could vote for a Democrat. "There is no way that a Christian can affirm the slaughter of babies, homosexual activity, homosexual marriage, or any kind of gross immorality," MacArthur said while visiting Liberty University.[20]

By September, though, the *Post* reported on new data from American swing states showing Biden with as much as an 11-point margin of victory over Trump. Vote Common Good Executive Director Doug Pagitt summarized the poll results: "Four years ago, many religious voters decided to look the other way and give Trump a chance, but after witnessing his cruelty and corruption, some of them are searching for an off-ramp."[21] Columnist Robin Schumacher admitted Trump's shortcomings were many but also said of Biden: "When it comes to creating meaningful moral legislation, [he] couldn't hit water if he fell out of a boat."[22]

During the final run-up to the election, the publication printed far more anti-Biden articles than pro-Trump pieces.[23] Brown rhetorically asked Biden if he supported sterilizing children, a reference to the candidate's support for a child's right to begin sex reassignment protocols.[24]

To its credit, the *Post* published an essay by candidate Biden near election day. His op-ed focused on Matthew 22:36–40, where Jesus tells his followers that the greatest commandment in the law is to love God and your neighbor as yourself.[25] According to those commandments, Biden said he had tried to live as a Catholic. He promised to deal with issues of public health, poverty, and immigration.

The day before the election, the publication summarized Franklin Graham's comments on Biden from a *Newsmax* interview: "I'm afraid there will be an attack against Christian businesses like we saw during the Obama administration."[26] Ryan Foley ended this piece by returning to past comments from Graham, including the evangelist's warnings on Twitter that a Biden victory would usher in "all-out socialism" and result in the political left closing down churches.[27]

The *Post* published more pro-Trump articles as the election loomed. Asserting that a vote for Trump was a vote for biblical truth, Derek Rogers, pastor of Cowboy Church in Texas, warned believers of the "evil agenda of the Democratic party" and that Biden would "fight to take away every religious freedom and every right we have as Christians."[28] Admitting that Trump "ain't the greatest dude in the world," Rogers still insisted that Trump would fight for Christianity rather than attempt to squash it.[29]

The only anti-Trump article leading up to the election came from a *Post* summary of author and pastor John Piper's blog. Piper warned Christians not to vote for sinful people who refused to repent of sexual immorality and vulgarity while condemning pro-choice individuals who supported transgender rights (for the record, Piper said he would not be voting for either Trump or Biden).[30] To its credit, the *Post* published a follow-up article of tweets supporting Piper's position.[31]

While lacking many staff-generated articles, the *Post* provided readers with a dizzying array of viewpoints and opinions to digest. The volume of pro-Trump articles made their presidential choice crystal clear.

Christianity Today

Christianity Today's writers gave context, background, and further information. They did not, however, cheerlead for either candidate. Early in 2020, the publication ran several articles on President Trump's campaigning. Kate Shellnutt visited an Evangelicals for Trump rally in Florida. She noted that Hispanics represented a growing segment of conservative Protestantism, especially within the Pentecostal or New Apostolic Reformation Movement. Within these groups, 41% voted for Trump in 2016, and more were likely to favor him in 2020. She quoted Samuel Rodriguez, head of the National Hispanic Christian Leadership Conference, asserting that Democrats had taken a "hard left turn" and were out of step with evangelicals on issues like abortion.[32] A month later, an article featured pro-life Democrats in South Carolina hoping the party would remember their opposition to abortion.[33]

The first confirmation of evangelicals' continued loyalty to Trump arrived in a Pew survey in March 2020. While White evangelicals approved of Trump, Black Protestants held fewer positive opinions about his character or policies. Pew researchers noted, "Trump's election must be part of God's overall plan, but doesn't necessarily mean God approved of Trump's policies."[34]

A few articles dissected Biden's faith during the campaign's final months. One contained quotes from former Fuller Seminary president Richard Mouw, a Biden supporter, who said "He may not be the conservative Catholic that many evangelicals would like him to be, but when he talks about his faith, it rings true."[35]

The issue of abortion dominated evangelical discourse during the campaign as much as Trump's occasionally contradictory actions and statements about COVID-19.[36] In a few articles, disappointment and disapproval of Trump's personality characteristics are illuminated by anecdotes of pro-life leaders saying they could not support the President's re-election.[37]

One sound of caution came from Ryan P. Burge's polling analysis on the Catholic vote. He said if just a few Catholics in swing states switched to Biden in 2020, Trump might lose swing states like Pennsylvania.[38] The publication also highlighted Hispanic and Chinese American voting preferences.[39]

In 2016, *CT* asked Ed Stetzer to feature endorsements for candidates on his blog site. The 2020 version featured fewer prominent evangelical celebrities than in 2016.[40] Trump's endorsement came from his spiritual adviser, Paula White, who argued that Trump deserved re-election partly because elections aren't about personalities but policies. To that end, she listed ten reasons Trump had succeeded and would continue to do so. In addition to the appointment of conservative judges and his opposition to abortion, he also moved the American embassy to Jerusalem. For Pentecostals like White, moving the embassy is part of what is necessary to fulfill divine prophecy about the second coming of Christ. Trump, she added, was never ashamed of America.[41]

A second endorsement of Trump came from Skip Heitzig of Trump's Christian advisory team. He reiterated White's arguments and added, "In a perfect world, I would want a candidate who is warm, winsome, polite, respectful, deferential, as well as one who gets things done. That world doesn't exist, so I will be firmly settling for one who gets things done."[42]

Josh Dixon endorsed Biden, saying his worldview adhered to biblical norms, especially his promise to seek justice for the marginalized.[43] A day later, John C. Richards Jr., a pastor and activist, said his support for Biden stemmed from Trump's unacceptable actions against women and people of color.[44]

Karen Swallow-Prior, an author and professor at Southeastern Baptist Theological Seminary, argued against the election of either candidate.[45] Neither candidate met her criteria as someone vowing to protect life and human dignity. She cited Trump's anti-abortion stance as questionable, called his lifestyle disgusting, and condemned his unacceptable exploitation of racial divisions. Biden was "complicit in abortion on a mass scale."[46] She thus encouraged Christians to write in a more suitable candidate.

The last word (literally) a day before the election came from *Christianity Today* President and Publisher Timothy Dalrymple, who summarized the publication's negative opinions about President Trump. At the same time, he reflected on the feedback he received after Mark Galli's editorial calling for Trump's conviction during the first impeachment trial. Some readers, Dalrymple said, were heartbroken that the publication supported the removal of a president who fought to end abortion and protect the Christian way of life.

To answer the critics, Dalrymple employed a wide-angle viewpoint. Those expressing heartbreak, he asserted, grew up in environments in which Christianity had been the dominant cultural force. Today, however, they saw their freedom and the "common good of the community deteriorating."[47] This group he called the Church Regnant. Facing a weakening of their hegemony over culture, these Christians favored increasing political power to preserve Christian culture.

The Church Remnant is a differing mindset, he asserted. Members of this group are younger, more diverse, and more urban than those in the Church Regnant. In this worldview, the church is not the dominant cultural force, but rather he argued, "The kingdom of heaven is among us when we speak the gospel in word and deed, serve the homeless and the refugee, and come alongside our suffering neighbors."[48] Church purity is more important than political power to this group; thus, they are more comfortable living in a multicultural and complex world.[49]

Dalrymple noted that evangelicals fall into both groups and are now so divided that they fail to understand each other's hearts. But, he said, "I believe the evangelical alignment with the Trump administration has advanced the kingdoms of men but not the kingdom of God. I worry it has damaged the culture and tarnished our witness for generations."[50]

Dalrymple did not say he would automatically vote for Church Remnant-favored candidate Joe Biden, only that Donald Trump was a poor choice for Christians—including many of his friends and colleagues. Dalrymple's explanation of these two evangelical worldviews and his support for a Church Remnant viewpoint showed that *Christianity Today* fell comfortably within the "Never Trump" voting group.

Sojourners

Founder and publisher Jim Wallis wrote most of *Sojourners*'s commentaries on the election. In April 2020, he said America's history of racism should be a particular prayer target during the election year, writing "The movement toward fascism and white nationalism, which we see around the world, is led by one of the most effective marketers of America's worst instincts and demons, Donald Trump."[51]

In May, long-time senior editor Rose Marie Berger lashed out at Trump. Noting that White evangelicals and Catholics often supported him, she said, "As a Catholic, I'm deeply troubled by this president. Trump stands against everything I've been taught to believe."[52] She added, "Let's be clear: There is nothing 'pro-life' about President Trump. His weaponization of whiteness, 'pussy-grabbing' tendencies, vicious racism, and an all-out assault on America's working poor stand in stark contradiction to the 'culture of life' that Catholics embrace."[53]

On the day of noted civil rights pioneer John Lewis's funeral, President Trump began his campaign to discredit the 2020 election results if he were to lose. He tweeted his disapproval of universal mail-in voting, saying that the 2020 election "will be the most INACCURATE & FRAUDULENT Election in history."[54] He suggested that the election be delayed "until people can properly, securely and safely vote???"[55]

The tweet's timing drew the ire of *Sojourners*'s editors.[56] They said it was appalling because it appeared simultaneously with a celebration of the life of Rep. Lewis, who strongly supported voting rights. Noting that Trump could not change the election date without congressional approval, they called the president's suggestion illegal and immoral. Likewise immoral, they continued, were Trump's attempts to suppress voting rights and intimidate specific populations into not voting for Biden.[57]

On the eve of the election, Wallis issued an altar call, encouraging Christians to protect the image of God in 2020. In the election, mistreating others by, among other things, trying to stop people from voting was "an offense to the image of God, an assault on *imago dei*."[58] He added, "Now it is up to you. I am asking you to step up, speak up, and stand up for the image of God at our polling places and early voting sites and for the safety of mail-in ballots."[59]

Sojourners published poll results in October showing most Christians believed climate change should be a higher priority for Congress and the next president. The article noted that President Trump has been unwilling to accept climate science, and Vice President Biden had put forth various pro-environmental measures he would implement if elected.[60]

In that same issue, editor Jim Rice urged people not to squander their voting privilege by entering a "protest vote."[61] Calling this vote a national referendum on racism, he also reviewed other issues. He condemned robocalls by "right-wing operatives" telling voters in Democratic-leaning cities that if they voted, their "information from mail-in ballots would be used by police and collection agencies to track down anyone with outstanding warrants or debts."[62] Rice clarified that a choice for Christians existed without encouraging a vote for Biden by name.[63]

Finally, anticipating an attempt by President Trump to hijack the election if he lost, the publication encouraged its readers to resist such attempts—peacefully, writing, "As people of faith and as Americans, we have a profound religious and civic duty to ensure that any attempt to subvert a free, fair, and safe election or to dishonor the electoral outcome is met with the full force of bold and sustained moral resistance."[64]

The majority of *Sojourners*'s content continued a four-year pattern of pointing out President Trump's failings (from their perspective) on issues such as immigration, care for the poor, voting rights, the environment, and other social and cultural flashpoints. While much fewer articles extolled the virtues of Biden, the publication's preferences were easily discernible.

WORLD

Given Donald Trump's anti-abortion stance, one would expect *World* to reflect favorably on his policies and accomplishments, even while criticizing his personal life and inflammatory rhetoric. While that's the case, the endorsement one finds in the articles and op-eds is a tepid endorsement at best.

The unprecedented nature of campaigning for President amidst a killer pandemic was not lost on Jamie Dean. She reported on the slick campaign videos released nearly every evening on YouTube, extolling President Trump's accomplishments. In contrast, the Biden campaign—conducted from a corner of his bedroom in Delaware—got off to a bad digital start. Dean reported, "Less than six months before Election Day, Biden narrowly leads Trump in a handful of presidential polls, but he widely lags in the digital race that may prove critical for reaching voters sequestered from political gatherings and cut off from the usual rhythms of a traditional campaign ahead of November."[65]

While not signaling out a presidential candidate, editor Olasky tackled the use of a term he coined for then-Texas Governor George W. Bush, "compassionate conservatism."[66] "In 2020, we are two nations," he declared; "Power, money, and compassion abide, but the greatest of these is compassion, which neither major party candidate promotes."[67]

Olasky commented on the choices before voters: "Some *World* readers continue to praise Donald Trump. Others will grudgingly vote for him. Some may vote Democratic, dancing to the music of Joe and the Radicals."[68] That turn of phrase (Joe and the Radicals) makes his preference clear. Olasky pointed out areas of policy where the warring factions were working together. Abortion, unfortunately, did not appear to be a bipartisan concern. Ultimately, he reminded readers we serve an awesome God, and if we remember that fact, "we won't wake up depressed on Nov. 4 no matter who wins."[69]

In the 2016 election, *World* convened a group of evangelical leaders to provide insight into how evangelicals perceived the Republican presidential candidates. With President Trump already the Republican nominee for 2020, the publication took a different approach: helping readers when a biblical position seemed unclear. They professed, "We will help sharpen you by presenting contrasting views. If we don't sharpen you, we're doing you a disservice."[70]

To shed truth on the election conundrum, Olasky interviewed two prominent evangelical leaders. Wayne Grudem, a professor of theology and biblical studies at Phoenix Seminary, told Olasky that character mattered, but policy and accomplishments mattered more. These included actions that lowered Black unemployment at home and tried to advance school choice initiatives in impoverished neighborhoods.[71] Grudem also asserted that a more robust economy, defense, and border security were "evidence of God's blessing on the nation with President Trump."[72] With Biden, he added, America could expect more crime, judges who legislated instead of interpreted the law, and weaker religious freedoms, signs that God's blessing has been withdrawn.[73]

Conservative commentator David French, then senior editor of *The Dispatch*, made the case against Trump. French said that during COVID-19 and other crises, Trump had divided the nation to fulfill his ends.[74] French downplayed most of Trump's accomplishments, praising only the 2017 tax cut. Despite not supporting Biden, French said he hoped a resounding Biden victory would prevent the very result that did eventually occur—that of Trump's charges of election fraud. Finally, French asserted that any president's power to stop abortion was limited and that the number of abortions in the nation had decreased in the past few decades regardless of who was in the White House.

Founder and publisher Joel Belz best summarized *World*'s implicit position. He began his analysis by noting that of the hundreds of thousands of *World*'s readers, more than half would vote for Trump, while 25% would vote for Biden (and even that high percentage would be a surprise). But he added, "Those *who fervently wish they had a third choice*—Something approaching 100 percent"[75] (italics in original).

For Belz, voting for Biden was a non-starter: "The reasons stretch from his comprehensive commitment to the pro-abortion movement to his selection of demonstrably leftist Kamala Harris as his running mate."[76] He acknowledged Trump's accomplishments in appointing "right-thinking" judges and other government leaders, "But we were stressed—again and again—at the president's utter carelessness with facts, his rudeness and crudeness, and his mocking disdain for his opponents and sometimes even for his friends."[77] Ultimately, Belz realized he could not vote for either candidate.

World did not include a positive endorsement of Biden because he supported abortion. In the stories and columns the publication presented to readers, neither presidential choice met its standards. With the vice-presidential candidates, the choice was clear. Jamie Dean's analysis of the two clarified that Mike Pence presented a better character and policy potential than candidate Kamala Harris.[78]

Conclusion

Given the nearly unanimous support for Trump among rank-and-file evangelicals, their publications faced a dilemma: endorse Trump to keep up readership and subscriptions or state why Biden's overall platform and personality made him a better candidate. That latter choice became one that several publications embraced despite the potential pushback.

The 2020 election did not end on election day. The nation held its breath until the January 2021 inaugural ceremony when Biden officially took office. November 2020 to January 2021 was one of the most tumultuous months in American history. The evangelical publications had much to say about the election's aftermath.

Chapter 9

Joe Biden and the
End of Evangelicalism?

AT 11:20 P.M. EASTERN TIME on November 3, 2020, Fox News analyst Bill Hemmer stood by a massive map of the U.S. showing the popular and electoral vote for the 2020 presidential elections. Staring at the map, he saw that his pro-Trump news agency predicted a Joe Biden win in Arizona, a state Trump won easily in 2016. "What is happening here?" he asked, "Why is Arizona blue? Did we just call it? Did we just make a call in Arizona?"[1] Indeed, Fox News surprisingly predicted a Biden win in that critical state before other news agencies made the call.[2] A win in Arizona virtually assured Joe Biden the presidency.

Thus began the aftermath of the hard-fought campaign filled with delayed voting counts, lawsuits, and President Trump's continued claims of victory taken from him by fraud. The repercussions of the election's aftermath reached its climax when angry Trump supporters stormed the U.S. Capitol. Congress had assembled on January 6, 2021, to certify the decision of America's voters. Trump's speech earlier that day seemed to encourage the Capitol's storming, resulting in violence and deaths.

For the record, Joe Biden received 306 electoral votes to Trump's 232. The largest voting turnout ever saw Biden receive 81.2 million popular votes, while Trump tallied 74.2 million. Democrats won the majority of seats in the U.S. House of Representatives. The U.S. Senate held an equal number of Democrats and Republicans, allowing newly elected Vice President Kamala Harris to cast the tie-breaking vote. The anger unleashed at Fox News by Trump supporters for accurately predicting a Biden win in Arizona cost Digital Politics Editor Chris Stirewalt his job.[3] As expected, the publications' reactions varied depending on their pre-election reporting and advocacy.

The Christian Post

As the publication most devoted to Trump, *The Christian Post* continued to denounce Biden even after the polls closed. On election day, an article reported that Franklin Graham told conservative TV network Newsmax that a Biden victory meant more attacks against Christian businesses. He referenced past court decisions forcing business owners to provide services for gay weddings. Graham also asserted, without evidence, that the left would "want to try to come after churches and tax churches and tax-exempt organizations that are doing humanitarian work, social work throughout the country."[4]

A few days later, as final votes trickled in and Biden's victory seemed imminent, the publication noted that Biden had declared himself the victor, ignoring that most media outlets had also declared him the victor. Melissa Barnhart's article on the vote offered a counterpoint to Biden's claim, noting that the Trump campaign said the election was "far from over."[5] In his victory speech the next day, Biden, the "presumptive president-elect," quoted the hymn "On Eagles Wings" and Ecclesiastes 3:1–8, adding that now was a season for America to heal.[6]

The following day's update to the Biden story noted that former President George Bush said that Trump had the right to ask for a recount in states where the voting was close. Not until the fourth paragraph does the article mention that Bush had already congratulated Biden and Vice President-elect Kamala Harris. Further, Bush called Biden "a good man who has won his opportunity to lead and unify our country."[7] That article also quoted Sen. Lindsey Graham, who encouraged President Trump to demand recounts: "Do not concede, Mr. President. Fight Hard."[8]

In addition to Biden's potential impact on small business autonomy (and religious freedom in general), three other issues dominated news coverage: the future of abortion, evangelical voting patterns in the election, and evangelical leaders' reactions regarding the vote's legitimacy.[9]

January 6, 2021, is likely to be a day historians refer to as significant in the history of the United States. The storming of the U.S. Capitol by angry mobs that day changed American politics in ways still unfolding years after the event; likewise, regardless of the outcome of the various legal allegations that day, Donald Trump encouraged his followers to march to the Capitol and stop Congress from discharging its pro-forma duty to certify the election.[10] (The full extent of Trump's culpability, if any, in encouraging violence that day is still to be determined, especially after the Special

Counsel established to investigate his actions that day terminated its work after Trump's return to the White House in 2025.)

The Christian Post's first article that day focused on the peaceful assembly of Trump supporters at the Save America March, sponsored by Women for America First. Not until the story's fourth paragraph does reporter Ryan Foley tell readers that violence broke out as "hundreds of Trump supporters and others stormed the United States Capitol while members of Congress were debating the certification of electoral votes."[11] The remainder of the article focused on interviews with people assembled in DC that day, most asserting that Trump won while condemning the violence that later erupted. Foley's article also extensively quoted Trump excoriating Republicans who disagreed with him, including Rep. Liz Cheney, Georgia Gov. Brian Kemp, and even Vice President Mike Pence. Foley also reminded voters of the alleged corruption in the voting systems that Democrats had allegedly exploited to deny Trump a second term.[12]

While Foley's article early on January 6 gave voice to some Trump supporters disillusioned by his loss and believing the election was stolen, subsequent reporting focused on the reaction of evangelical leaders. Jim Denison condemned the violence in his column, calling believers to pray that God would use the incident as a "turning point for our nation."[13]

Leonardo Blair's news article listed four critical takeaways from January 6. He noted that finally, two weeks before the inauguration, Trump had conceded; that Education Secretary Betsy DeVos resigned her position after blaming Trump's rhetoric for the attacks; that politicians had urged Trump's remaining cabinet members to invoke a seldom-used clause in the 25th Amendment to the Constitution to remove Trump from office; and that rioters potentially stole national security secrets by breaking into lawmakers' offices.[14]

After Biden's victory, what came next for Republicans and evangelicals? Columnist Jack Hibbs lauded President Trump for fulfilling his promises to protect the unborn, strengthen the military, appoint conservative justices to the Supreme Court, and move the American Embassy to Jerusalem. Hibbs wrote, "Unfortunately, this is not something we expect in the foreseeable future under President Biden."[15] Finally, he signaled to evangelicals that it was time to consider the 2024 Presidential election: "And while we must always remember that the Messiah will never arrive on Air Force One, we need to look to 2024 with an eye towards finding the next president whose policies will be in line with our values."[16]

Christianity Today

After the election, *Christianity Today* noted that Trump said, "We'll win," while Biden said, "Keep the faith."[17] Whoever wins, the publication noted, had a tough challenge ahead to bring unity to the nation.

Four days after the election, *Christianity Today* acknowledged Biden's victory, noting he won battleground states during a record-breaking turnout of voters.[18] Demographic voting data showed that Biden received strong support from Black Protestants, Catholics (including two-thirds of Hispanic Catholics), and "Never Trump" evangelicals. At that point, however, Trump still insisted, "This election is far from over."[19]

Editor-in-chief Daniel Harrell wrote after the election that he hoped the large turnout and peaceful conduct marked a hopeful sign and that "a Biden presidency may portend the end of religion as a political weapon and free it for serving the common good."[20] As had others who commented on the election's results, Harrell discussed biblical instances of conflict and unity but noted: "The historically high voter turnout does not guarantee meaningful change. The enormous numbers may only intensify division and stiffen resolve. Social media is sure to keep resentment simmering until the next conflict."[21]

Christianity Today also published an opinion piece from Daniel Bennett, an associate professor of political science at John Brown University. He condemned Christians perpetuating the myth of voting fraud: "Speaking as a political scientist and as a Christian who did not vote for Joe Biden in November, I think it is important to say that these allegations are baseless nonsense. They are grounded in selectively presented half-truths, ambiguous and out-of-context videos, and outright falsehoods. They fall apart under the slightest scrutiny."[22]

Of the January 6 Capitol storming, the publication said Pastor Rick Warren called the riot "domestic terrorism."[23] Russell Moore said it was "immoral, unjust, dangerous, and inexcusable."[24] He called on Trump to tell his supporters to "stop this dangerous and anti-constitutional anarchy."[25] Later in the article, Trump supporter Al Mohler said, "President Trump is responsible now for unleashing mayhem."[26] Frequent columnist at *The Christian Post* Michael Brown said, "More than evangelicals bringing out the best in Trump, he has brought out the worst in us. Face it."[27]

The publication's editorial director of ideas and books, Bonnie Kristian, denounced Trump's supporters. Several Republican leaders said in November that Trump would quickly acknowledge defeat and retreat to one of his golf courses. Instead, she said, Christians who tolerated Trump's lies helped create the turmoil by going along with his tendency to call evil good and good evil to enhance political power, concluding that "It is what happens when warnings about the importance of character are ignored."[28]

In another column, she bemoaned those Christians who accepted fake news and conspiracy theories by QAnon.[29] She called on churches to conduct conversations to train and encourage members to discern truth from lies.

In the weeks following the January 6 storming of the Capitol, *Christianity Today* published several forward-looking articles. One considered the political future of Vice President Mike Pence (and lauded his commitment to both Trump and the Constitution). However, he was "thrown under the bus" by Trump.[30] Another addressed the failure of prophets who predicted a Trump victory, those who repented of the false prophecy, and those who continued to believe a miracle would occur. The article gave an excellent historical perspective on the charismatic movement and noted that these failed prophecies lessened society's respect for evangelicals.[31] In short, the election had ended for *Christianity Today*'s editors and columnists, and it was time to move on.

Sojourners

Sojourners, of course, was pleased with the election's outcome. While most of the early reporting from other Christian publications focused on reactions from evangelical leaders, *Sojourners* took a different approach. That approach was best summarized in an undated news release on its site. It partially reads, "But what Donald Trump won't accept does not and should not matter. Our democracy is not determined by him, it is determined by the people—and *Sojourners*, along with other faith groups across the country, stands ready to fight to ensure that the will of the people, the will of our democracy, is carried out."[32]

That statement frames the themes of the reporting and opinion pieces written after the 2020 election. An initial piece appeared after Biden officially won Pennsylvania and crossed the necessary electoral college vote. Biden's commitment to his Catholic faith dominated this article and noted that his policy proposals reflected his belief. Author Mitchell Atencio focused the remainder of the article on Biden's history with the Catholic Church and the controversy over his pro-abortion stance.[33]

While *The Christian Post, Christianity Today,* and *World* featured statements from evangelicals calling on their flocks to pray for the president, regardless of his politics, a *Sojourners* article told readers that Democrats Nancy Pelosi and Alexandria Ocasio-Cortez had prayed for Donald Trump during his tumultuous tenure as President. It's doubtful the other publications sought reactions from liberal Catholics who adhered to Jesus's call for all believers to pray for their political leaders.

A month later, Atencio turned his attention to how Biden won the election. He quoted Rep. Jim Clyburn of South Carolina who observed, "Traditionally, Democrats have taken the separation of church and state to an extreme. When you have a candidate who doesn't mind expressing his faith and demonstrating it, you get a much better connection with the faith community, and Joe is that kind of a candidate."[34] The analysis credited Josh Dixon, Biden's outreach director for religious groups, for successfully rallying non-evangelicals and some people who were undecided before the election.

The January 2021 print edition, published before the storming of the Capitol, contained several articles responding to the theme of "Finding Our Way in a Post-Trump America."[35] Short essays by Christian leaders addressed what President Biden should do to improve the lives of Americans and immigrants. Leana Wen, an emergency room physician in the DC area and frequent guest on MSNBC, summed up the authors' advice with this statement: "The single biggest challenge facing President-elect Joe Biden is how to win the hearts and minds of the American people. He can pass and even implement great policies, but unless he can get the American people to follow his moral authority, he will not be successful."[36] She suggested more frequent health briefings to restore faith in agencies like the Centers for Disease Control.

On the afternoon of January 6, *Sojourners* president Adam Russell Taylor blamed the violence on Donald Trump, Republicans who enabled him, and "too many Christians."[37] The toxic presidency led to deadly consequences. Instead, Taylor admonished "Let us build bridges over the troubled waters of hate, fear, and grievance to create the beloved community, to yank down some pieces of heaven, and help make God's kingdom come onto earth—come onto the United States of America—as it is in heaven."[38]

The next day, he teamed with founder Jim Wallis on another advocacy essay calling for Trump's premature removal from office. They argued that he incited the insurrection with his lies. Two moral conclusions emerged, they said. One was that silence was unacceptable, and faith leaders should condemn the violence. Second, in advocating for Trump's removal, they called him "a morally deranged president" and that "Republicans who voted to overturn the election results be held accountable for their own sedition."[39] The duo advised their readers to pray because "faithful action must always follow prayer."[40]

That same day, pollster Robert P. Jones told *Sojourners*'s reporters that the majority of those storming the Capitol were White Christians, some of them "carrying Confederate flags."[41] Later, he said, "I think the biggest thing we're still missing is a facing of our history, particularly by white Christians."[42]

A further round-up of reactions from prominent Christians quoted Kelsey Herbert, national campaigns director for Faith in Public Life. "One more day of Trump is too many," she said.[43] Russell Moore is quoted as directly addressing the president: "Mr. President, people are dead. The Capitol is ransacked. There are 12 dangerous days for our country left. Could you please step down and let our country heal?"[44]

Could Biden help unite and heal the nation? This question dominated articles appearing at the time of his inauguration. Editor Adam Taylor asserted that accountability by Trump and his enablers would be a prerequisite for any healing.[45] A group of *Sojourners*'s contributors wrote short essays listing their hopes for economic justice, lessening racial tensions, improving climate, reforming immigration policies, and pushing for gender equity. "It's Time to be the Conscience of American Politics," these writers asserted.[46] Christians needed to stand up and hold their leaders accountable for their actions, a theme as relevant on inauguration day 2021 as when Jim Wallis and his fellow students founded the *Sojourners* movement in 1971.

Biden's ascension to the Oval Office still rankled Trump supporters three years after the events of January 6, 2021. *Sojourners* president Adam Russell Taylor reminded readers that recent polls showed Republicans were "more sympathetic to those who stormed the U.S. Capitol and more likely to absolve Donald Trump of responsibility for the attack than they were in 2021."[47] Taylor encouraged his readers to continue to cite the well-documented fact that Biden won the election and that 58% of Americans felt the rioters "threatened democracy," while only 12% still held to the belief that those attacking the Capitol were defending democracy.[48]

WORLD

World's election day coverage asked Washington, DC, Ohio, rural Mississippi, and Minnesota voters for their views and voting preferences.[49] Harvest Prude detailed how DC city officials worked to build barricades against possible demonstrators protesting the election. In Mississippi, Kim Henderson interviewed a woman who listed her concerns as "Abortion, how we treat our elderly. It's unacceptable. God would not approve killing a baby up to birth."[50]

In Ohio, Leah Hickman quoted a registered Republican who said, "Trump's a menace," and he had not brought people together during his four years in office.[51] In Minnesota, the scene of violence after George Floyd's death, Sharon Dierberger talked to a Muslim man who didn't feel safe with Trump as President.[52]

Over the next week, the publication found good news that Republicans had increased their representation in Congress and that seven Democrats lost seats (but not the majority). Other articles blasted late-night TV hosts for criticizing President Trump's refusal to concede.[53]

More than a month after the election, long after mainstream media declared Biden the winner, the publication reported briefly that the Electoral College had affirmed Biden as president-elect.[54]

On January 6, Emily Belz wrote about the "unprecedented domestic attack, noting that "historians believe Capitol Police have never been overwhelmed by a mob like the one on Wednesday."[55] She quoted Senate Majority Leader Mitch McConnell denouncing the rioters and commenting on President Trump's delay in asking them to go home.[56] Sen. Mitt Romney called the event "insurrection incited by the president."[57] At the same time, Southern Seminary President Al Mohler (whom Belz was quick to note was a *World* board member who supported Trump in 2020) said, "President Trump is responsible now for unleashing mayhem."[58]

Three articles appeared online the day after the Capitol breach. In one, world leaders weighed in on the violence.[59] The second article summarized the day's events and mentioned Trump's complaints about suspending his Twitter (X) account.[60] A final piece that day asked why the violence. One eyewitness told *World*'s Joshua Raimundo that the people he saw entering the Capitol were not dressed like Antifa protestors. Why would someone bring up Antifa? Just hours after the rioters left the Capitol, social media pundits began speculating that the rioters weren't Trump supporters but Antifa members trying to embarrass the President.[61]

Fittingly, Marvin Olasky penned the last significant commentary on January 6, titled "Sack of the Capitol."[62] He recounted his "addiction" to Communism early in life and how he lived in an alternate reality because of his blind obedience to the ideology. He likened his media consumption during that time to the present when political conservatives and many evangelicals shunned mainstream media as too leftist and instead consumed Fox News and Salem Broadcasting radio programs. "Some recent Trump voters know no one who voted for Joe Biden," Olasky wrote, "So when I or other Worldlings described his victory factually, it's not surprising that some said, *Stop my World subscription. I want to get off.*"[63]

Olasky asked all readers to pray that "Joe Biden will be more patriotic than partisan."[64] He also repeated a refrain from other evangelical pundits that the current crisis in America was not a political problem but a theological one, reminding them, "Biblical objectivity exists. God is sovereign. Praise His plan, not mine or yours."[65]

While Trump's loss discouraged many evangelicals and conservatives, his appointment of conservative Supreme Court justices was directly responsible for laying the groundwork for their most significant political victory in over 50 years: overturning Roe v. Wade.

Chapter 10

The End of Roe v. Wade: A Pyrrhic Victory?

DONALD TRUMP LOST the 2020 Presidential election, but his most significant achievement as president occurred 17 months after his defeat. That's when his three U.S. Supreme Court nominees joined with three others on the court to strike down its 50-year-old decision guaranteeing an abortion nationwide to almost any woman seeking one during her first trimester of pregnancy. Announced on June 24, 2022, the ruling overturned Roe v. Wade of 1973 and a 1992 ruling in Planned Parenthood v. Casey.

Immediately after its Dobbs v. Jackson Women's Health Organization ruling, more than a dozen states invoked trigger laws banning abortion should *Roe* ever be overturned. Other states passed new anti-abortion laws. Some laws banned abortion at conception; others banned it after a certain point in the pregnancy; others made provisions for allowing the procedure if a woman's life was endangered or she had been raped. Others held that women must give birth regardless of the circumstances leading to the pregnancy. Each state's subsequent decisions, lawsuits, and attempts to make sense of the *Dobbs* ruling continued to captivate the public discourse for years afterward.[1] Most evangelical publications, with *Sojourners* as the outlier, hailed the decision.

The Christian Post

In high school, a classmate of editor Richard Land brought a 12-to-14-week embryo to share as a class project. Land recalled, "It was clearly a human being. That sensitized me to the issue."[2] Even though many of his Southern Baptist friends and the Southern Baptist Convention (SBC) felt abortion should be legal, he vigorously campaigned against the practice since that shocking presentation. It's difficult to underestimate his influence on turning the SBC from pro-abortion rights to anti-abortion rights during the 1970s and after.[3]

Thus, it would be expected that Land penned the most extensive response to the *Dobbs* decision in *The Christian Post*. At 1,500 words (that's a lot for the *Post*), the article covered theology, history, and ethics related to abortion. Part of his intent, he said, was to present a better understanding of the Supreme Court's decision and rationale than the "truly hysterical" reaction of mainstream media.[4] After that 1992 *Casey* decision, he claimed the United States had been one of only seven nations allowing abortion on demand after 20 weeks of pregnancy.

Land took to task a *Journal of Clinical Ethics* study claiming that 44% of the women interviewed regretted their abortion decision. He said that having counseled numerous young women, he felt the 44% figure was an understatement.[5] As a result of the guilt felt by women post-abortion, he said that when preaching against the procedure, he also emphasized God's love, grace, and forgiveness for those who regretted their decision.

He also criticized politicians and pro-life advocates desiring to pass new anti-abortion laws that included criminalizing women who received an abortion. He said this would lead to very few laws against abortion receiving approval, especially from voters.[6]

Land wrote another commentary on abortion early in 2023. This piece discussed how Christians should act in a post-*Roe* world. He said a sanctity of life ethos should replace the culture of death (for the unborn). This required revisiting the question, "Who and what is a human being?"[7] As for Christians, the task was to do "everything we can in word and deed to refute the libel that the pro-life movement is only pro-life from conception to birth. We should make it clear that we are pro-life from conception to natural death and everywhere in between."[8]

The first *Post* story after the Supreme Court *Dobbs* decision included excerpts from Judge Samuel Alito's explanation of the Court's opinion, emphasizing the error of the 1972 decision of Roe v. Wade. The court sent the decision regarding abortion "to the people's elected representatives."[9] The article also summarized the highlights of the bill the court considered, Mississippi's Gestational Age Act, that banned most abortions performed after 15 weeks of pregnancy.

Following the facts of the ruling, Michael Gryboski summarized reactions: The president of the Susan B. Anthony Pro-Life America group said the decision was a "historic human rights victory for unborn children and their mothers and a bright pro-life future for our nation."[10] Planned Parenthood, on the other hand, said the decision was "as dangerous as it is shocking."[11] The organization's statement added: "The consequences of this devastating decision will fall largely on people who already face the greatest barriers to health care due to this country's legacy of racism and discrimination, including Black, Latino, and Indigenous communities, people with low incomes, LGBTQ+ people, immigrants, and people living in rural areas."[12]

Another article that day gave readers reactions from seven Christian leaders, both pro and con.[13] While the *Post* remained staunchly anti-abortion in the tone and the framing of most of its articles before and after the *Dobbs* decision, they quote both Planned Parenthood and Christians favoring abortion (under limited circumstances and during a limited period). Most of the articles celebrated the end of Roe v. Wade.

Christianity Today

Christianity Today seized on the potential demise of Roe v. Wade once Justice Samuel Alito's draft statement leaked to the media in May of 2022. Four articles in May speculated on different scenarios if the leak was confirmed.

Kate Shellnutt reported on a March 2022 Pew study showing American opinions on abortion remaining legal was "it depends." That report noted that 75% of White evangelicals favored making abortion illegal. Around 21% of those people wanted to ban abortion in all cases—regardless of circumstances leading to the pregnancy or the dangers of continuing to full-term birth.[14]

Then columnist Russell Moore (soon to become *CT*'s editor) used the leak to address the future of the pro-life movement once Roe v. Wade ended. He lamented the widespread divide in the nation, leading to extreme viewpoints, saying "Whether the world agrees or disagrees with us on abortion or any other matter, they need to see us love vulnerable children—whether in the womb, in abusive homes, in foster care, or in our own pews."[15]

Complementing Moore's column, columnist Chelsea Sobolik noted that rumors and fearmongering reached a fever pitch after the Supreme Court leak. She appealed to zealous anti-abortion advocates aiming to institute state abortion bans to exercise caution and provide "the utmost care and concern for both a woman and her preborn child."[16] The crux of her argument was that 10 to 20% of pregnancies ended in a miscarriage, and up to 2% were ectopic. These situations needed to be excluded from attempts to outlaw abortion, especially given the sometimes-confusing medical terminology labeling some miscarriages as "spontaneous" or "missed" abortions. Additionally, when miscarriages occur, doctors sometimes prescribe mifepristone and misoprostol as abortifacients to end the pregnancy safely. This practice should continue to be allowed. Thousands of pro-life hospitals that don't perform abortions do treat women with these unfortunate health crises, she added, and this must continue to ensure the health of all women.[17] Meanwhile, a consortium of pro-life obstetricians and gynecologists said they would continue to treat women suffering from miscarriages or ectopic pregnancies because those situations differed from treating abortion on demand.[18]

Daniel Silliman's article announcing the death of *Roe* reminded readers that all three new judges appointed by President Trump voted to overturn the court's former ruling. Matthew Lee Anderson, an ethicist and religion professor at Baylor University, summed up well the reaction of those who had worked so hard to end abortion on demand as a national law: "This day belongs to the many people who have labored long and hard to make it happen—and to President Trump, who deserves our thanks for keeping a promise I did not think he would keep."[19] In addition to noting the triumphant reaction of groups like the Assemblies of God and Focus on the Family, Silliman provided an excellent, detailed history of the past 50 years of advocacy by pro-life groups.

CT's educational articles about the end of Roe v. Wade included a four-part series of excerpts from former *World* editor Marvin Olasky's co-authored book, *The Story of Abortion in America: A Street-Level History, 1652–2022*.[20] Among other historical highlights, the excerpts focused on the beginning of pro-life laws in America, the use of ultrasound in visualizing pregnancy, how abortions were performed before Roe v. Wade, and the doctors who performed abortions before they were legalized.[21]

While most evangelicals took well-deserved victory laps, many Black Protestants did not. *Christianity Today*'s reporting gave them a voice. That's because the issue of being pro-life encompasses far more to African Americans than just banning abortion. Author Amethyst Holmes noted that Black women are three times more likely to die from pregnancy-related causes, and Black babies are twice as likely as White babies to die before age one. Holmes reported that "Racial disparities persist across nearly every measure, from income for covering childcare to quality of education."[22] Holmes added that a recent Pew Research survey found that 67% of Black Protestants favored keeping abortion legal.[23] And even if opposed to an outright ban on all abortions, Holmes noted that African American leaders "are eager for those who have rallied so passionately for the unborn to join whole-life causes to support women too: pay equity, childcare, affordable housing, mental health support, and health care."[24]

In 2024, in his new role as a contributor to *CT*, former *World* editor Marvin Olasky cautioned anti-abortion advocates not to become complacent. The number of abortions rose since the *Dobbs* decision and some state politicians talked as if "pro-lifers might treat miscarriages as crime scenes."[25] He argued that the pro-life movement needed to adopt a position of convincing society of the reasons to oppose abortion rather than legislating against it. He also noted that since Donald Trump moderated his anti-abortion stance during the presidential campaign of 2024, neither political party could be trusted to carry a positive pro-life message. Hence the title of his article, "Triumphalism After Dobbs Was a Mistake." Overall, the reporting and opinions expressed in *Christianity Today* included well-researched and persuasive arguments for compassion while celebrating the Supreme Court's verdict.

Sojourners

Through most of its history, *Sojourners* characterized the abortion debate as one of justice for the unborn child and for the mother potentially bringing that child into a world of poverty and oppression. The magazine thus developed a position that abortion under certain circumstances should be legal, but discouraged. It always registered opposition to so-called "late term" or "partial birth" abortions.[26] During the late twentieth century and the early twenty-first century, as the national debate over abortion created strong opinions and divisions within society, the publication asked its readers if a common ground existed. In a number of articles and opinion pieces, the magazine called for dialogue that would create a way to make abortion a rare procedure and not a form of birth control.[27]

When the *Dobbs* decision draft leaked in 2022, *Sojourners* president Adam Russell Taylor quickly reacted. He called the possible ending of abortion "deeply flawed and alarming."[28] If states proceeded to enact their laws, he said as many as 28 would ban or limit abortion. Those most negatively affected would be low-income people, especially women of color. He said that as a Christian, he felt women should be free to make their own healthcare decisions. He also favored providing services to women such as holistic health care and economic support, so women did not need to choose abortion because of their circumstances.[29]

Taylor's advocacy for the continuance of abortion, he tried to say, was not a callous and dispassionate consideration but one rooted in an understanding and appreciation for the joys and difficulties of bringing new life into the world. In this context, he continued to advocate for allowing the option to terminate a pregnancy for people unable to successfully and joyfully bring a healthy new life into the world.

A few weeks later, Taylor criticized the Court's official declaration, making *Sojourners* one of the few evangelical media advocating for the continuance of "the full range of reproductive healthcare services, including safe and legal abortion."[30] He predicted the decision would be counterproductive to ending abortion "given that many of the countries with the most restrictive abortion laws are among those with the highest rates of abortion."[31] He also called on all Christians to adopt a pastoral approach to serve women facing unwanted pregnancies: "It is my hope and prayer that the majority of Americans who hold a both/and view can help bridge our growing divide by resisting extreme positions and working to ensure that abortion is kept legal, even as we pursue evidence-based ways of making it more rare."[32]

The other articles in May and June 2022 amplified Taylor's columns. After Justice Alito's draft of the decision leaked, Katherine Pater wrote an explanation of Jeremiah 1:5, a passage often quoted as condemning abortion: "Before I formed you in the womb, I knew you, and before you were born, I consecrated you; I appointed you a prophet to the nations." Citing Jewish commentaries and a Southern Baptist wire service report on the 1973 *Roe* decision, she said the verse was meant to encourage Jeremiah that God would empower him to preach the prophetic message even if he felt inadequate. The message from God was directed to Jeremiah and his current circumstances, not a blanket statement that we became human beings at conception. "Jesus hated it when people used scripture to put people in chains instead of liberating them from bondage," she wrote.[33]

Also in May, writer Mitchell Atencio spoke with several Christian leaders about the potential impact of the overturning of Roe v. Wade.[34] More than half his sources were women, and almost all expressed dismay that the option of abortion might be taken away. If this occurred, those interviewed said, there was a need for churches to protest the decision and at the same time provide more assistance for impoverished women who would be harmed the most.

Sojourners uploaded three articles after the Supreme Court's decision appeared on June 24. The first reprinted a Reuters wire service article providing the basic facts.[35] Atencio followed with an article reporting on the joyous response of conservative evangelicals and that a few believers had reacted with sadness. Noting that 54% of women receiving abortions identified as Protestant or Catholic, the article added that mainline Protestants, Black Protestants, Jews, Muslims, Buddhists, and Hindus supported some form of legal abortion.[36] The Rev. Katey Zeh, CEO of the Religious Coalition for Reproductive Choice, told the publication she hoped that people of faith would now be willing to speak up and "disrupt . . . the dominant narrative" that all believers oppose abortion.[37]

Atencio's article also interviewed African American and Roman Catholic advocates who called on Christians to support federal aid programs for minority women and to rally together to find ways to help women facing difficult decisions regarding their pregnancies.

In this brief review, it's evident that *Sojourners* maintained a position supporting some abortions, a position guaranteed to displease the majority of White evangelicals. It did, however, endear itself to mainline Protestants and moderate to progressive Catholics. Finally, for *Sojourners*, a pro-life worldview also encompassed any action that improved the quality of life for all people. Christians should do everything possible to improve the climate, end systemic injustice and racism, and provide needed services for the poor, incarcerated, and communities facing unprecedented gun violence. That's the true definition of "pro-life."

WORLD

World's reporting and opinion columns reveal a vastly different stance than *Sojourners*. Since its inception, *World* has tirelessly advocated an anti-abortion stance. The year the Supreme Court overturned the federal right to an abortion, 785 articles mentioned the word "abortion." Typing the search word "Dobbs" returned 249 hits, while typing in the word "Roe" netted 428 mentions. Each year on the anniversary of the 1973 Roe v. Wade decision, *World* devoted a January issue to updating readers about the "pro-life progress and regress over the previous year."[38] The thousands of articles appearing in those issues educated readers on every aspect of abortion, from the scientific and medical facts to the latest political developments in the U.S. and the world. Every conceivable reason to oppose abortion also found itself in print.

Marvin Olasky led the onslaught of anti-abortion articles during his years as editor. He wrote at least one column per year on abortion beginning in 1999 and ending with 21 columns in 2021. Two pieces in 2022 marked his final oversight of *World's* annual abortion issue. In one article, he noted that before the 1850s, most Americans thought life inside the womb did not begin until "quickening."[39] That's when the mother could feel the child's movement in the uterus, usually about halfway through a pregnancy. However, influencers after the Civil War began to change minds and hearts. One doctor, later elected to the U.S. Congress, called abortion, like slavery, a rejection of God's laws: "The fertilized human ovum is not like the seed that has been wrapped in some old mummy and left to await for ages the conditions for its development. Its growth is steady and progressive, physiological and positive."[40]

Olasky's second abortion-related article told the story of an active pro-life doctor, Rudolph Holmes, who practiced medicine early in the twentieth century. Drawing on Holmes's experiences, Olasky asked today's Christians: "How much time will Christians who are pro-life at suite level spend in street-level volunteering at pregnancy resource centers, praying in front of abortion businesses, and helping young women facing crises?"[41] His question echoed his decades-long quest to see the phrase "compassionate conservatism" become a real-world practice. Over the years, much of *World's* coverage advocated that the church become active in ensuring abortion became unnecessary.

World's founder and publisher Joel Belz raged against abortion almost as often as Olasky. For instance, in a 1998 column republished in 2020, he speculated that the battle against abortion would not end even if a majority of the U.S. Supreme Court did vote to overturn *Roe*. He wrote, "My guess is that, as a society, we'd rather give up garbage disposals than our right to abortion on demand."[42] He called on politicians to oppose the majority viewpoint and become moral leaders rather than passive followers of the majority. That, he noted, would be a job for a new generation and would only occur "because God's mercy never quits."[43]

Other columns from Belz included these comments:

". . . We pro-lifers need to engage the actual topic and move the public past the phony issue of choice."[44]

"Abortion is sickeningly different from them all (including death through acts of war) because every individual death is premeditated, calculated, and deliberate. Every such death is personally designed."[45]

"Evangelicals shouldn't be embarrassed to say boldly and clearly: Abortion and same-sex marriage are uniquely heinous sins . . . They take a culture in a dreadful direction. We haven't been wrong to say so. We aren't fanatics."[46]

The publication posted 12 articles and a *World* radio program on June 24, 2022, when the court announced the *Dobbs* decision. The editors likely began writing their June 24 coverage as soon as *Politico* leaked Justice Alito's draft decision a month earlier.

When the decision was announced, Olasky had already retired, and Belz was still recovering from health issues. Therefore, Albert Mohler, head of *World*'s Opinions section and president of The Southern Baptist Theological Seminary, took the editorial lead. He noted that the long-awaited day ended "50 years of judicially sanctioned killing of unborn human beings in the nation."[47] While the federal right to abortion on demand no longer existed, the battle to ultimately end abortion moved on to the state legislatures. In the states, Mohler said, "We will have to redouble our efforts, refine our arguments, stand alongside women in crisis, honor the family, and contend for life for the rest of our lives."[48]

Leah Savas (Olasky's 2023 abortion book co-author) profiled the efforts of Jameson Taylor, a Mississippi lobbyist who co-wrote that state's abortion ban law that became the Dobbs v. Jackson Women's Health Organization lawsuit.[49] In the interview, Taylor cautioned that this was only the first of the victories God planned. Much hard work remained.

A sampling of other *World* headlines that day included:

"Abortion businesses shut down in wake of SCOTUS ruling."[50]

"After *Dobbs*, pregnancy centers brace for more attacks."[51]

"Biden slams *Dobbs* decision."[52]

"*Roe* is dead; babies can live."[53]

"A victory for life and the Constitution."[54]

"Let the little children come to me."[55]

Following the Supreme Court's June decision, dozens more stories appeared in *World* that year and beyond. Many followed the various legal rulings in the states as they passed and litigated laws ranging from banning abortion from conception to banning it up to different stages of pregnancy. To *World*'s leadership, abortion was murder and, therefore, legally and morally wrong. It should not exist. Period.

Conclusion

Each of the publications favored the end of abortion on demand. Yet *Sojourners* blasted the *Dobbs* decision as dangerous for women and for non-believers' opinion of Christians who rejoiced at the end of federal support for abortion. While opinion polls showed that most White self-identified evangelicals opposed abortion, that's not the case for all evangelicals, mainline Protestants, or Catholics. It differs from the monolithic picture of evangelical attitudes prevalent in mainstream and advocacy media on either side of the ideological divide.

With *Roe* no longer in effect, the focus on abortion rights moved to each state. Thus, America's relationship with the practice of abortion became even more contentious and confusing. But then, that's true of many hot button issues conservative Christians discussed early in the twenty-first century.

Chapter 11

Evangelicals and the LGBTQ+ Question

IN JUNE OF 2015, the U.S. Supreme Court ruled 5 to 4 that same-sex couples had a constitutional right to get married. In the majority opinion, Justice Anthony Kennedy emphasized that marriage is a fundamental right inherent in the concept of liberty and protected by the Constitution. He acknowledged that the decision would upset those of "honorable religious or philosophical premises."[1] The Court's ruling in Obergfell v. Hodges was not meant to disparage the beliefs of people who disagreed with its decision. Kennedy further wrote that the First Amendment protected those in society who disagreed with the court and recognized their right to express their opinions vigorously.[2]

They did. The Court's ruling turbocharged the already vigorous debate in evangelical circles over same-sex attraction, same-sex marriage, and a host of other controversies related to the LGBTQ+ (Lesbian, Gay, Bisexual, Transgender, and Queer) conundrum.[3]

Thousands of news and opinion articles on this topic appeared in the four leading evangelical publications. Three took a generally traditionalist approach (sexual activity with a person of the same sex is a sin), while the outlier, *Sojourners*, would be classified as revisionist (God accepts gay and lesbian believers). *The Christian Post, Christianity Today*, and *World* employed a rhetoric that assumes that homosexuality is a choice people make. Further, the publications took the stance that if a person felt attraction to members of the same sex, they should remain celibate.

To set the context for this chapter, it's important to note that evangelical attitudes toward same-sex attraction and relationships slowly changed during the early twenty-first century. In 2007, only 14% approved of gay marriage. A decade later, 35% of evangelicals polled favored same-sex marriage. More telling, perhaps, is that 47% of evangelicals under the age of 40 approved of same-sex marriage near the end of the century's second decade.[4] Among Protestant pastors, a 2024 survey found 75% continued to oppose marriage of gay or lesbian individuals.[5]

The Christian Post

The Christian Post's coverage over the decades focused on the latest news about sermons from pastors and stories containing controversial statements from Christian leaders delivered on X or on Christian TV and radio programs. Some of the opinion pieces it published contained forceful rhetoric, nearly all of it condemning romantic same-sex relationships as a sin.

Writing in 2015, Larry Tomczak warned one way the gay agenda advanced was through the portrayal of gay TV characters. He wrote, "Regularly on TV, celebrities and 'experts' celebrate the 'fact' that probably 25 to 30% of Americans are really gay. Accurate statistics don't bear this out as the actual figure is somewhere between 2 to 3%."[6] Tomczak asserted that millions of unsuspecting viewers saw a steady drumbeat of information depicting what he called an "immoral," "indecent," "shameful," "unnatural action," and a "perversion" (citing Rom. 1:24–27).

Frequent contributor Jim Denison made it clear in his biblical exposition that homosexual conduct displeased God.[7] He focused part of his argument by reaffirming traditional biblical interpretations of Genesis 19, where God destroyed Sodom and Gomorrah. In one part of the story, the men of the area demanded that Lot allow them to rape angels staying at his house. The conventional interpretation is that the men of the cities wanted to have sex with the angels because the men desired same-sex relations and eventually God destroyed them because of this lust.

Another interpretation is that the men of the cities wanted to treat Lot's visitors as women and rape the visitors as a way of humiliating them. Denison sided with the first interpretation while also asserting that homosexuality was not an unpardonable sin. Only rejecting God's forgiveness is unpardonable. Second, Denison asserted, Christians err if they do not speak to homosexuals with tough love, pointing out that God considers homosexual behavior to be a sin. But we should do so gently. "So-called 'gay bashing' is always wrong," he said.[8] If someone has same-sex attraction, Christians should convince them to remain celibate, as difficult as that might be.[9]

In 2019, Mark H. Creech penned a column calling same-sex attraction an "undisciplined desire," and a "disorder that fundamentally countermands and contradicts God's creative will."[10] He added that "Homosexuality is emphatically different than other sins. It poses an enormous threat to family, health, the hope of a bright future for our country, and even the propagation of the Gospel."[11] Creech didn't go as far as to condemn gay conduct as an unpardonable sin, but he came close.[12]

A series of articles on Bible translator Eugene Peterson illustrate the gravity of the topic for *The Christian Post*'s editors. Peterson's 2012 translation of *The Message Bible* left out the word homosexual in its translation of Leviticus 18:22 (in which other translations say "Do not practice homosexuality"). He argued that the word wasn't perceived in modern society as just an "immoral behavior but as an immoral identity which is then attacked as an enemy. The term has been used so frequently in mean, dehumanizing ways that it is difficult to use it in the spirit of Paul and Jesus in our culture."[13]

In 2017, Peterson was asked if he would marry a gay couple, and he said he would.[14] The resulting firestorm led his publisher, LifeWay, to consider removing his books from their catalog and bookstores.[15] Later, Peterson backpedaled, saying "To clarify, I affirm a biblical view of marriage: one man to one woman. I affirm a biblical view of everything."[16]

In addition to the topic of gay attraction and same-sex marriage, *The Christian Post* reported on court decisions on the topic. This included whether small business owners could refuse to provide services such as wedding cakes or event photography for same-sex weddings (the Court ruled that they could).[17]

Denominations continued to grapple with whether they should ordain people who identified as gay. Sometimes, those decisions led to splits within those religious bodies. Numerous articles in the *Post* chronicled denominational conventions discussing the issue and how and where denominations split as disagreements caused churches to withdraw from—or be expelled from—fellowship with those denominations. Others mentioned pastors removed from their posts for supporting gay marriage.[18]

Not all articles in *The Christian Post* focused on condemning same-sex attraction and marriage. Ian M. Giatti wrote about a 2022 documentary titled "1946: The Mistranslation That Shifted Culture."[19] The film claimed that in 1946, translators of the Revised Standard Version erroneously translated two Greek words as "homosexual" rather than "effeminacy," "pervert," or "sexual pervert," words that more closely resembled the Greek meaning.[20] The controversy centered around the translation of 1 Corinthians 6:9. The documentary claimed that researchers had uncovered a letter from the head of the translation committee admitting to a critic that he and his translators "acknowledge their mistake and commit to correcting their grave error."[21]

The translation continues to be published today without any change to that error. "Many conservative religious leaders have used these biblical texts to condemn and marginalize LGBTQ+ Christians," claimed the documentary's director, Rocky Roggio, adding that "society at large has been shaped —at least in part—to believe the idea that sexual and gender minorities must choose between their faith and their identity."[22] While the article gave readers potential food for thought, it's worth noting that the subhead to the article reads, "Dallas Theological Seminary prof. says film is misleading, ignores biblical context, other verses."[23] This helped readers understand that the *Post* did not endorse the viewpoints expressed in the article. On balance, then, *The Christian Post* took a strong stance against certain actions of people who identified as LGBTQ+.

Christianity Today

Throughout its coverage, *Christianity Today* maintained a generally conservative stance on the topic while providing space for a range of evangelical voices. The publication felt the topic important enough to create an online index to its numerous articles.[24]

Since its founding, the publication tried to educate its readers about traditional evangelical interpretations that led to its position on same-sex attraction. After reviewing relevant Bible verses, scholar B. L. Smith noted: "What is manifestly clear from these passages is that homosexuality is not singled out for a separate treatment or given special prominence. It is one sin—one symptom among many, and our alarm at its presence in society ought, perhaps, to be no greater than our alarm over the presence of adultery, drunkenness, covetousness, boastfulness, insolence, gossip, and so on."[25]

A few years later, editor Carl Henry reinforced that viewpoint, criticizing advocates of same-sex relationships as presenting, "ad hominem arguments used in the attempt to validate a practice that Scriptures forbid."[26] A 1999 *Christianity Today* forum convened to discuss gay issues and public policy raised valid questions and insights for evangelicals. None of the attendees, convened by then Fuller Seminary president Richard Mouw, called same-sex relationships an acceptable practice for Christians.[27]

As the nation's dialogue intensified in the early twenty-first century, Andy Crouch penned a helpful editorial for pastors.[28] He argued that if a person accepted homosexuality, then gender differences were irrelevant: "What unites the LGBTQIA coalition is a conviction that human beings are not created male and female in any essential or important way. What matters is not one's body but one's heart—the seat of human will and desire, which only its owner can know."[29] He argued that sexual differentiation is the theological norm and that believers can hold the position that God created male and female while still loving their gay neighbors. He added, somewhat provocatively, that "along the way, we all will be queer, groaning as we await the redemption of our bodies. To the LGBTQIA alliance, add an H—for this is what it is to be fully, incompletely, expectantly Human."[30]

A year later, Ron Sider wrote that evangelicals should take the lead in "condemning and combatting verbal or physical abuse, [and] better teaching on how parents should respond" should their child announce they were gay.[31] Regaining the respect of the LGBTQ+ community, he asserted, would take generations: "But if evangelicals can choose this countercultural, biblical way for several generations, we may regain our credibility to speak to the larger society."[32]

Having educated its readers for several decades to take a firm stance against the same-sex lifestyle, it is no surprise that the publication reacted strongly to the Supreme Court's *Obergefell* decision. Then-editor Mark Galli's piece "Six Things to Do after the Supreme Court Decision on Gay Marriage" urged Christians to rethink their views on marriage and engage in dialogue with the LGBTQ+ community after the court's disappointing ruling.[33] *CT* also published an "Evangelical Declaration on Marriage," reaffirming the belief that marriage is between one man and one woman while calling for respectful and loving engagement with those who disagreed.[34]

After *Obergefell*, the publication ran articles covering every conceivable angle of the continuing dialogue on LGBTQ+ issues. Greg Johnson discussed the shift from attempting to "cure" gay individuals to providing care and support. Johnson highlighted the failures of the ex-gay movement and its history and called for the church to prove wrong the perception that Christians hate gay people.[35]

CT also gave voice to "Side B Christians," those who experience same-sex attraction but choose celibacy.[36] Bekah Mason's 2021 article argued that such individuals are an asset to the church, demonstrating faithfulness to Scripture despite personal challenges: "I stuck it out because of my deep conviction that my life as a celibate gay Christian was just as much a walking picture of the gospel as any of the marriages I encountered at church."[37]

In a 2022 article, *Christianity Today* provided a reality check for its readers. Grove City College professor David Ayers analyzed a subset of a more extensive poll and based on his findings, reported that 17% of evangelical women admitted to at least one sexual encounter with another woman. Around 5% of evangelical men reported a homosexual encounter. More than 1,800 people were in the cohort analyzed by Ayers, who noted: "Among younger people especially, it has been quite a few years since biblical beliefs and practices have been the norm among evangelicals."[38]

Christianity Today also reported on how the LGBTQ+ debate played out within evangelical denominations. As denominations passed measures approving or disapproving fellowship with LGBTQ+ believers and ordaining gays and lesbians to the ministry, church and denominational splits gained attention.[39]

Sojourners

Sojourners encountered their first taste of the difficulties of dealing with the theology and practice of same-sex relationships in 2011. Early that year, a group called Believe Out Loud asked to run a series of ads in the magazine, and it refused. Editor Jim Wallis addressed that refusal and its logic. He noted that his staff disagreed on the Bible's theology of same-sex attraction and relationships and that the issue was not a core concern of the *Sojourners* movement. Wallis said, "Our message has always been that no matter what your theological perspective or biblical interpretation on the issue of homosexuality, every Christian has an obligation to defend the lives, dignity, and civil rights of gay and lesbian people."[40] He also said that churches should welcome LGBTQ+ believers as *Sojourners* had over the years, including hiring staff who identified as gay. After *Obergefell*, *Sojourners* remained true to Wallis's stance. All four articles reporting on the decision were reprinted from Religious News Service and not original to the publication.[41]

In later years, *Sojourners* began reporting on LGBTQ+ issues. Writer Austen Hartke attended a Gay Christian Network conference in Houston in 2016.[42] He reported that transgender people wanted Christians in their church to know that they were human beings deserving of God's love and that they represented a diverse group of people of different races, classes, disabilities, sexuality, citizenship, and age.

Another article focused on alleged homophobia in the Christian music industry, lamenting that gay Christian recording artists rarely found acceptance as they faced "the wrath of CCM [Contemporary Christian Music]."[43] This article quoted gay Christian musician Grace Semler Baldridge, who said: "I wrote a Christian project about my Christian experience. That doesn't mean it's going to be for all Christians, but I'm just saying that it is in that category of contemporary Christian music. You can't gatekeep that just because you disagree with where I'm coming from."[44]

Staff writer Lexi McMenamin profiled Issac Simmons, the first openly gay United Methodist Church ordained minister. Simmons occasionally taught the Bible in church dressed as an alter-ego named Penny Cost.[45] McMenamin presented readers with a short history of men dressing as women. For Simmons, the idea to dress in drag, he said, was inspired by Russian philosopher Mikhail Bakhtin. Among his ideas, Bakhtin stressed that communicators could use the "carnivalesque" and the "grotesque" as a means of turning upside down "systems of oppression to subvert them."[46] Dressing in drag, Simmons said, was a means of subverting the oppression of homophobia and using a new art form to catch the attention of potential audiences. "One of my missions in drag is to show that these two seemingly opposite things—spirituality and queerness—aren't mutually exclusive and that the divine is accessible by all people," he added.[47]

For Pride Month (June) of 2023, *Sojourners* printed a series called "The Joy of Being Queer and Christian."[48] Gay, transgender, and nonbinary authors celebrated their identity. One writer summed up the essence of the series: "At its core, my queer joy is the joy of knowing the Father has created my unique identity and calls it very good that Christ 'queers' or subverts the norms of this world, and that the Holy Spirit is continually forming me to love this world as my full self."[49] The publication also profiled Women's National Basketball Association star Layshia Clarendon, a nonbinary believer in Jesus.[50]

Sojourners thus presented content educating readers about both the traditional and revisionist Christian theology and was the only evangelical voice reporting and celebrating "outliers" such as Baldridge and Simmons. The publication also admitted that it hired staff who identified as gay. Thus, from avoiding the debate in 2011, *Sojourners* slowly included LGBTQ+ concerns into their editorial umbrella.

WORLD

World's reporting consistently questioned those who accepted gayness as biblical. Its opinion columns showed little sympathy for—and no acceptance of—same-sex behavior or marriage. The *World* search engine lists 2,226 articles mentioning "homosexuality" since its founding in 1986. The word "gay" is mentioned in 2,164 articles. Since the two words are often used interchangeably, it is likely that the total number of articles on the subject (which includes gay marriage, churches leaving denominations, wedding cake and photographer lawsuits, and the personal testimonies from gay and formerly gay people) was just over 2,000. The subject clearly animated *World*'s editors as they commented on and defended historic evangelical values.

World published an excerpt from the ESV Study Bible commentary written by theologian Wayne Grudem two years before the *Obergefell* decision. Grudem's article cited numerous scriptural references, giving readers a detailed apologetic for heterosexual marriage. A lengthy section of the essay discussed objections to the traditional biblical viewpoint while noting that moral teachings of the Bible must be the standard for determining right and wrong; Christians must also recognize that behavior is "biologically influenced" and that "no command of God is predicated for its validity on humans first losing all desire to violate the command in question."[51] He acknowledged that many gay men had suffered abuse by other men, including their fathers. In painstaking detail, he presented compelling logic that pushed back against those who argued that the words translated as homosexual refer to deviant behavior with youths or gay prostitution rather than same-sex relations.[52]

Editor Marvin Olasky traveled to San Francisco in 2015 to report extensively on City Church, a congregation that decided to extend membership to gay couples.[53] Olasky said he went to San Francisco to "get answers for the benefit of City Church members but also members of churches across the country that may soon face an LGBT juggernaut."[54] His investigation focused on accountability and fidelity to the Bible as leading the church down a slippery slope. A piece accompanying his San Francisco exploration gave practical advice for church members hoping to avoid what happened at City Church.

Olasky penned several columns reinforcing Grudem's viewpoint that same-sex behavior was a sin, but that Christians should treat gays with the same love they would extend to any other sinner, including themselves.[55] Olasky did note in 2017 that *World* had not ignored the counterargument advanced by homosexual advocates within the church. He said that the publication reviewed (negatively) several books, such as pastor Ken Wilson's *A Letter to My Congregation*, and Matthew Vines's *God and the Gay Christian: The Biblical Case in Support of Same-Sex Relationships*.[56] The publication commented favorably on other books and highlighted testimonies by Christians who overcame same-sex attraction.[57]

The most pointed statement of *World*'s theology came from founder Joel Belz in a 2018 column. Here, he used scandals within the Roman Catholic Church to warn his readers that church leaders who identify as gay but promise to remain celibate usually fail. He said this occurred often to Catholic priests who swore fidelity to their vows but were eventually arrested for pedophilia and homosexual behavior.[58]

Belz cautioned Protestants that extending compassion toward people who "suffer" from same-sex attraction or "allowing positions of church leadership to people who embrace and celebrate sexual disorders, all on the promise they will be chaste is foolhardy."[59] Finally, Belz warned readers that when a candidate for leadership in their church, school, mission, or other institution claims to be "gay, but celibate," beware: "Every single one of the priests who stand guilty of sexual abuse started with a promise of chastity."[60]

Whereas in years past, controversial issues (see Olasky's news piece on City Church of San Francisco) received treatment through features using the lens of biblical journalism, after 2021 the Opinion section published essays containing less journalistic reporting and more negative commentary on any statement from evangelicals that might stray from the accepted viewpoint on LGBTQ+ issues.

For instance, several essays questioned the theology and practices of megachurch pastor Andy Stanley. Denny Burk, president of the Council on Biblical Manhood & Womanhood, charged that Stanley advocated for accepting into fellowship gay Christians. Thus, Stanley appeared to be affirming gay Christians, which Burke found to be a misleading and unbiblical message.[61]

Later that year, Stanley's Atlanta-area church hosted the "Unconditional Conference," a gathering for parents of LGBTQ+ children and youth pastors. The conference literature promised an exploration of the various topics "from the quieter middle space."[62] In the first of two columns, Opinions editor Albert Mohler wrote that there was no middle space and that the event seemed to be a platform for normalizing the homosexual lifestyle.[63] During a Sunday sermon, Stanley responded to Mohler's criticism by preaching about his position. Mohler responded a few days later by declaring, "Christians should find no joy in addressing theological error, but positivity in the face of serious error amounts to complicity."[64] Mohler noted that in the sermon, Stanley may have affirmed that he believed marriage should be between a man and a woman, "but he did not clarify his convictions on LGBTQ issues, nor did he really clarify the position or policy of his church."[65]

The position of *Sojourners* magazine was the target of writer Barton J. Gingerich. He blasted the publication for its series on "The Joys of Being Queer and Christian," saying, "It was yet another attempt to meld the Christian faith with popular sexual licentiousness and liberationist ideologies."[66] Gingerich noted that a time existed when *Sojourners* "expressed some genuine commitment to Biblical sexual morality, even while advocating certain policies of the political left in America."[67] Now, he added the theological has been "twisted to serve progressive agendas and positions."[68]

Conclusion

Sexual behavior is, and always will be, a hot topic in Christian churches and society. As Americans' acceptance of LGBTQ+ individuals grew more tolerant in the twenty-first century, evangelical publications—except for *Sojourners*—attempted to reassure pastors and church leaders that the Bible and evangelical theology stood against the growing permissiveness of some churches, denominations, and society at large. The evidence presented here suggests that most evangelicals and their leaders remain steadfast in promoting traditional sexual values. But opinion polling showing an increased acceptance of LGBTQ+ behavior among evangelical youth could signal another potential fault line for the future of the movement.

Chapter 12

The 2024 Presidential Election

DONALD TRUMP WON the 2024 presidential race in a vote that was nowhere near as close as many pollsters and pundits predicted. Once again, a vast majority of evangelicals voted to put him back in the White House after four years of the presidency of Joe Biden and his vice president and Democratic nominee Kamala Harris.[1]

In the run-up to the election, *The Christian Post* and *World* backed Trump and urged their audience (again) to look past his character failings and re-elect the man who paved the way for the dismantling of Roe v. Wade. Both executive editor Richard Land of the *Post* and Opinions editor Albert Mohler at *World* staked out strong anti-abortion positions throughout their careers in academia, and thus, they preferred Trump. They also framed the election as one pitting Harris, who they claimed would limit Christian speech and religious freedom, against Trump, who on the campaign trail promised to protect "my beautiful Christians" so believers would not need to vote again.[2] *Sojourners* clearly supported Harris. At the same time, *Christianity Today* pointed out various biblical reasons for rejecting Trump without endorsing Harris's candidacy.

The Christian Post

The Christian Post's support for Trump recognized his human failings. Dozens of news and opinion articles discussed his track record as president, the assassination attempts, and his claims and promises while on the campaign trail.[3] Others focused on influential Christian leaders who criticized Trump's waffling on his opposition to abortion.[4] With some trepidation, the reporting on vice presidential candidate J.D. Vance trended favorably. While pro-lifers exhibited mixed enthusiasm for Vance, other commentators praised his work ethic and faith.[5]

News about Kamala Harris often comprised articles focused on criticism of the Democrat and her running mate, Tim Walz.[6] The *Post* also analyzed several of the policies she advocated during the election. These included articles with headlines such as "Kamala Harris is a mean girl," "Kamala Harris and late-term abortion: A cold-blooded abomination," and "6 progressive policies of Kamala Harris that should scare you."[7] Of the hundreds of articles mentioning Harris, only a handful contained a favorable view of her politics or faith.[8]

Executive Editor Richard Land's opinion piece in late October 2024 began with this confession: "I would not want Donald Trump as a father, brother, nephew, brother-in-law, son-in-law, or pastor. I would not want Kamala Harris as a mother, sister, niece, sister-in-law, daughter-in-law, or pastor."[9] Despite his disdain for the candidates, he said he supported Trump, as in 2016 and 2020, as the lesser of two evils. Of Harris, he said: "In addition to the life issue (Ms. Harris is the most radical and aggressively pro-abortion candidate to ever head a presidential ticket), Ms. Harris is also strongly in favor of the transgender agenda and will certainly curtail parental rights to protect their children from transgender propaganda, indoctrination, and potential surgery against their parents' will."[10]

Land concluded by admonishing his readers: "Make no mistake about it. If you do not vote for Donald Trump as at least the lesser of two evils, you will become morally culpable for the triumph of evil by, as Mr. Edmund Burke said, 'doing nothing.'"[11]

The publication skewered Harris on several occasions. A July 2024 article said Harris called her pastor, Rev. Amos C. Brown, the day she decided to run for president after Joe Biden announced he would not seek a second term.[12] In his story, writer Anugrah Kumar's rhetorical choices gave away his viewpoint. He told readers that Harris and Rev. Brown had "reportedly" known each other for two decades.[13] He also quoted from various sources in other publications featuring positive and negative views of Harris. He also noted that Harris "has faced controversies," including an affair with California political kingpin Willie Brown, a former mayor of San Francisco. Brown "helped launch Harris' political career" by selecting her to two state commissions regarding healthcare and unemployment insurance.[14] There's a clear inference in the tone of that article, that Harris slept her way to power.[15]

On election day, Ian Giatti's roundup of Trump's final rallies reported that Trump voiced regret over leaving the White House in 2021, even though he lost the vote to Joe Biden.[16] Giatti's article also reported on Trump's comments to a crowd gathered in Pennsylvania that included references to the assassination attempt on his life and an inference that perhaps the "fake media" —whom he called "bloodsuckers"—should be shot as well.[17] Trump's campaign quickly attempted to clarify that Trump was not advocating violence against mainstream media, Giatti noted.[18]

The Christian Post's support for Trump is evident in its more subtle editorial decisions on election day, decisions revealing where the publication stood on several hot-button cultural issues. One article said seven Roanoke College women's swim team members endorsed the Trump-Vance ticket because the duo had vowed "to keep men out of women's sports," a reference to fears that men who transitioned to become women would dominate female sporting events and teams.[19] A second article on election day featured a plea from actress Candace Cameron Bure to "vote like Jesus."[20] While she did not endorse a candidate, the remainder of the article quotes a Texas pastor who advocated that Christians vote in part because the government had moved its priorities from building roads and issuing driver's licenses to "redefining marriage, erasing gender, reframing abortion as reproductive rights, and then using the government school system to indoctrinate everybody's kids into believing those things . . . ."[21]

Christianity Today

In the 2016 and 2020 elections, *Christianity Today* gave a platform to various evangelical leaders endorsing the major presidential candidates. In the run-up to the 2024 election, the only essay similar to those from the past two elections was penned by Robert Postic, a political scientist. Kamala Harris's positions were "inconsistent with scripture," while Donald Trump "lacks the requisite character to be president."[22] Thus, he could not vote for either candidate.

Columnist Bonnie Kristian commented in a January 2024 piece that, "The Trump Debate is Dead."[23] She acknowledged that in evangelical circles, almost all believers endorsed Trump. The exception was the "evangelical elite," people with seminary degrees who wrote books and articles."[24]

Kristian then provided readers with an elitist analysis of why this is so. One reason is that White evangelicals vote by party and conduct little research into the policies candidates hope to enact. Busy lives preclude research, and thus, evangelicals tend to vote Republican as they have in nearly every election of the twenty-first century. Personal character or what the candidate might do to the nation, the world, and the church is not considered as crucial as this loyalty to the party and friends.[25]

The publication's news section did follow Trump's rise to the nomination in 2024, along with the various outcomes of his legal issues (guilty of sexual abuse, trying to invalidate the 2020 election, stashing and hiding classified government documents, and committing fraud in his real estate investment business).[26]

Several articles quoted Trump's allies and apologists defending him but incorporated a more theological approach. Daniel Bennett noted that the loudest voices demanding justice or retribution should avoid falling "in line with the prevailing partisan sentiments."[27] Instead, he said, we should reject that temptation and "approach the political sphere with consistency, discernment, and a humility not of this world, but from the mind of Christ."[28]

Overall, the editorial emphasis of the 2024 election reflects the prolific writing and speaking of editor Russell Moore. Moore's negative opinion of Donald Trump remained consistent since the reality TV star first announced his attention to seek the presidency in 2016.[29] Moore's anti-Trump statements generated controversy within the Southern Baptist Convention, where Moore had served as head of its Ethics and Religious Liberty Commission.[30] Like Galli, Moore called on President Trump to immediately step down as president after the January 6, 2021 attacks on the Capitol.[31]

As *CT*'s editor, Moore continued to criticize Trump. In a July/August essay, he warned readers not to worship the king of Mar-a-Lago rather than the king of Mount Zion. Noting that the magazine itself would not endorse candidates, Moore wrote that his "views of the former (and possibly future) president's fitness for office and its implications for the American republic are public and emphatic, they are beside the point here."[32] He said the crisis within evangelicalism was not about whom to vote for but about "witness and identity."[33] Loyalty tests based on political considerations threatened the witness of the church and its identity as a religion loyal only to Jesus Christ. He ended with a poignant rhetorical question: "What difference does it make who walks into the tune of 'Hail to the Chief' if our children don't believe us when we say, 'Jesus is Lord'?"[34]

In an essay published right before the 2024 election, he said people had asked him if he held out hope for the 2024 presidential election. "The most hopeful thing I could say in the lead-up to Election Day is to encourage you to *lose* hope in anyone other than the resurrected Christ," he said.[35]

In 2024, *Christianity Today* called evangelicals' attention to eternal truths rather than undue fretting over who would become the next president of the United States. The fact of the risen Christ and eternal salvation for believers should not be shaken.

Sojourners

Sojourners's stance on the 2024 presidential elections is best summed by this quote appearing just after the Associated Press projected that Donald Trump won in 2020: "His campaign was marked by racist and misogynistic rhetoric, promises of authoritarian tactics including a dramatic expansion of executive power and retribution for his political rivals, as well as policies that appealed to the anxieties of conservative religious communities, especially Christians."[36]

The article also quoted faith leaders analyzing the election results. Their comments included a reminder that "significant, radical, course-changing movements for justice" arose from times of difficulty and repression.[37] Others interviewed contrasted Christian nationalism with the gospel, one even noting that nationalists and evangelicals wanted "Jesus to be more like Trump."[38] Another leader said, "... I am full of hope in God's sovereignty and will only use the election results as an added incentive to work harder for peace and justice."[39]

While *The Christian Post* and *World* favored Trump, sometimes downplaying his lies and hateful statements by not adequately fact-checking his assertions, *Sojourners* criticized the former president for his unsubstantiated claims and occasionally fact-checking his assertions. For instance, Trump claimed in his debate with President Joe Biden that all faith leaders opposed the Roe v. Wade Supreme Court verdict when it was decided in 1973. *Sojourners* noted that before the 1960s, five of the largest denominations in the U.S. supported legal abortion.[40] In 1971, the Southern Baptists passed a resolution stating that they would "work for legislation that will allow the possibility of abortion under such conditions as rape, incest, clear evidence of severe fetal deformity, and carefully ascertained evidence of the likelihood of damage to the emotional, mental, and physical health of the mother."[41] Even in 2024, one-third of evangelicals and 61% of mainline Protestants said they supported legal abortion in "all/most cases," while 52% of Black Protestant Christians supported legal abortions.[42]

Articles about the Harris-Walz campaign appeared far more frequently than those about Trump. *Sojourners* introduced readers to Harris's pastor, Rev. Brown and Brown told the publication about a phone conversation with Harris the Sunday she learned that Biden would step down as the Democratic nominee for president. Brown shared Micah 6:8, which reads, in part, "Do justice, love mercy, and walk humbly with your maker." Brown added: "That's what we need in this nation. There's too much arrogance and egocentricity after all this Trumpism."[43]

Other *Sojourners* articles discussed the hiring of a faith and justice organizer for the Harris campaign, how Harris's policies could reduce child poverty and her claim that a person does not need to abandon their faith to support abortion rights.[44] The publication did not blindly praise Harris, however. An article on her immigration actions as vice president and a recently introduced border policy enacted by President Biden received criticism from faith and immigration leaders, who generally said nonetheless that they felt she would support more humane immigration policies than Donald Trump.[45]

In an October opinion article, *Sojourners* reminded its readers that Jesus did not support a particular political party; instead, he was an immigrant. Further, despite the growth of Americans desiring less immigration, the hateful rhetoric toward immigrants did not please God. Trump's declaration that he would institute mass deportation if elected would "usher in a truly hellish chapter in the nation's history."[46] The article also reminded readers that "When people speak poorly of immigrants, they are not talking about some distant other—they are talking about the God we purport to serve."[47]

Following the same reasoning, *Sojourners* president Adam Russell Taylor encouraged readers to speak out against the fascist rhetoric appearing more frequently in Trump's campaign.[48] A few days before the election, *Sojourners* directed readers to prayer resources and non-partisan groups offering mass online prayer opportunities. They also encouraged people to rest and pray after the election.[49]

It's worth noting that the voice of Jim Wallis, so prominent in commenting on the candidates for president in previous elections, was noticeably absent from the 2024 campaign's final months. Nonetheless, the publication's focus on "faith in action for social justice" remained solid and prophetic in its coverage and commentary in 2024.

WORLD

World skewed its reporting and opinion essays to show its support for Donald Trump, despite his waffling on abortion while campaigning in 2024. Harris did not fare so well. The publication questioned her use of rap and hip-hop artists and noted that for Gen Z, abortion rights didn't rank as an important priority. Instead, inflation, gas prices, and climate change were more important.[50]

An opinion piece in mid-August criticized a group called Evangelicals for Harris. Denny Burk, a Southern Baptist Theological Seminary professor said the group distorted Christianity to promote Harris's policies.[51] Burk said Harris was influenced by her affinity for Hinduism and her marriage to a Jew, and thus, she could not be fully committed to Christian values. He ended his analysis by criticizing the evangelical group's push for Harris, saying, "It's barbarism and syncretism in the service of partisan politics. It is wrong for any Christian to portray this kind of message as if it were in any way faithful to the Christian gospel. It is, in fact, a betrayal of the gospel. This isn't evangelical. It's not even Christian. Don't fall for it."[52]

Other pieces criticizing Harris's platform focused on her economic proposals that could "court disaster."[53] An opinion piece by Jordan J. Ballor told readers that Harris's plans to enact price controls and increase government intervention in the economy were "misguided solutions to problems created by government policy and would only prolong the suffering and malaise experienced by so many Americans."[54] Another opinion article criticized the Democratic Party's full-throated embrace of abortion.[55]

A rare news article published just after the Democratic National Convention officially nominated Harris contained quotes from attendees who praised Harris's joy and her policies. The article also included information about her accomplishments and her ill-fated campaign in the 2020 election.[56]

While *World*'s reporting and opinion section continued to lambast Democrats and, by extension, Harris, Trump did not escape criticism. His waffling about abortion and gender issues on the campaign trail concerned *World*'s editors. In September of 2024, for instance, Trump said he would vote for a Florida bill allowing abortion on demand. He had to walk back his statement the next day. In an opinion piece, Burk accused Trump of running from the issue by saying he preferred to let the states decide on abortion and invitro fertilization (IVF). Burk contended that destroying a fertilized embryo constituted murder, just like abortion: "IVF is morally fraught for the same reasons abortion is morally fraught. Human lives are at stake in both procedures and together they have destroyed countless millions of human beings."[57]

Andrew T. Walker opined that Trump was his own worst enemy when it came to the abortion issue, and he encouraged anti-abortion Republicans to make their voices heard by the Trump-Vance ticket.[58] Opinions editor Albert Mohler ventured that Trump didn't know what Trump believed about abortion: "Instead of pointing to the radicalism of the Harris-Walz platform, he has tried to land in some kind of artificial (and apparently moveable) island of fuzzy policy."[59]

Besides the abortion issue, *World* kept readers informed about the candidates' viewpoints on what it called transgender ideology. A news piece began with an anecdote about a liberal Democrat whose viewpoints on gender changed when her 13-year-old daughter announced she was gender fluid. The family endured pressure from school officials, family therapists, and even child protective services. All insisted that the family accept their daughter's sexual identity and her choice of pronouns. The liberal Democrat mother, Amanda Ericsson, said the situation led her to renounce her long-time party affiliation and that she planned to vote for Donald Trump.[60] The morality tale goes on to note that *World* spoke to 10 self-identified Democrats who still supported same-sex marriage and abortion but drew the line with "policies that would permit males to access female-only spaces and allow doctors to prescribe cross-sex hormones to gender-confused youth."[61] While Kamala Harris had not staked out a policy position in 2024, the article said she had supported providing "gender transition surgery" to California inmates when she served as attorney general of California.[62]

An explainer a few days later focused on both candidates' stance on LGBTQ+ issues, noting that one candidate (presumably Trump) "has a record of upholding a correct interpretation of federal law."[63] Harris, on the other hand, "is committed to a federal regime that unburdens little girls from their body parts, female athletes from their medals, and women across America from the safety and dignity of their single-sex spaces—all in the name of 'equality.'"[64] Another opinion piece noted that Harris has made her viewpoint clear: "she views mutilative transgender surgeries as a fundamental human right."[65]

Another explanatory article tackled the issue of how Muslims might vote in the 2024 election. Rather than wade into the Israeli invasion of Gaza and the anger expressed by some Muslims and Hamas sympathizers, readers were told that for decades, Democrats took the Muslim vote for granted. The 2024 election might be different, writer A. S. Ibrahim asserted, "Simply put, American Muslims are walking away from the Democratic Party because they are religiously, culturally, and socially conservative, and the radical left agenda embraced by Democrats is pushing them away."[66]

Other articles and opinion pieces criticizing Harris and Democrats included Burk calling Democrats "the pro-pornography party,"[67] the folly of Democrats calling for an expansion of the U.S. Supreme Court, and Harris's statement that she would not allow religious exemptions for healthcare workers refusing to participate in abortions.[68]

In his final opinion article before the election, Mohler revealed his struggles supporting Donald Trump. Harris, on the other hand, was unacceptable because of her stance on abortion. In choosing Trump, he hoped that Republican leaders would slow down the transgender revolution and push to protect religious liberties.[69]

Amidst the careful and extensive analysis of the options for voters in 2024, John Wilsey's opinion piece put the election into its eternal perspective. He wrote: "The 2024 election is not Armageddon. Democracy is not at stake. Our electoral system has been tried and tested and is supple and resilient. Whatever happens on Election Day and the days, weeks, or months that follow, we can be confident that the losing party will get another shot in 2028. Politics is not ultimate. God is ultimate. Let us live carefully under His gaze."[70]

Conclusion

For evangelicals and the publications aimed at informing them, Donald Trump was a well-known, if unpredictable, presidential candidate in 2024. Thus, fewer articles about his candidacy appeared than in 2016 and 2020. Harris was much less known, and multiple news articles and opinion pieces tried to dissect her character and policies. In the end, the four publications studied here differed widely in their coverage of the 2024 presidential election. *The Christian Post* and *World* supported Trump, albeit with reservations. *Christianity Today* remained neutral while pointing out the myriad ways Trump's character and past actions clashed with Christian values and character. *Sojourners* promoted Harris's candidacy because she often spoke about human rights issues and cared for people experiencing poverty.

In the 2024 election, 82% of White evangelicals voted for Trump while

17% voted for Harris. George Barna's polling for the Cultural Research Center at Arizona Christian University found that among all voters 72% identified as Christian and this made the difference in the race. Overall, though, only 56% of self-identified Christians voted in the election.[71]

Having been elected once again with widespread support from White evangelicals, Trump embarked on a widespread plan to reshape the U.S. government and its policies using the extensive power given to him by the American public and a potentially compliant Congress and Senate. How evangelicals fare in this second Trump administration is yet to be determined.

Conclusion

Evangelical Publications and the Movement's Future

IN EXAMINING ESSENTIAL issues of concern to evangelicals, the shadow of Donald Trump looms large. His policies and priorities, coupled with his tweets and social media posts, make it impossible to consider evangelicals and their future without examining their responses to Trump. Still, Trump's presence on the world stage is fleeting. Christianity and its evangelical movement shall continue into eternity.

During his first presidency, Trump's actions gave Christian publications the opportunity to educate their readers and to advocate for a different view of the world than that expressed by the president and his followers. At times, the publications assumed a prophetic role, raising criticism from the very believers they set out to inform. At other times, their writers and essayists supported the president and his administration.

All four publications studied—*The Christian Post*, *Christianity Today*, *Sojourners*, and *World*—varied in their opinions of the cultural and political events during one of American history's more tumultuous and head-scratching periods. *Christianity Today* and *Sojourners* remained largely critical of Trump, even as evangelicals deemed him the lesser of two evils when compared to abortion advocates Hillary Clinton, Joe Biden, and Kamala Harris. *The Christian Post* and *World* initially condemned his fitness to be president but gradually came around to supporting his candidacy.

All four differed when presenting news and opinions on other important topics in the so-called culture wars. These included abortion, immigration, Christian nationalism, race, and LGBTQ+ issues, among others. Overall, though, the four publications differed in degree, not in their overall theological understanding. The primary difference among them is centered on how evangelicals should live out their beliefs in a hostile world.

Church historian Martin Marty once noted that religious periodicals were "vibrant but invisible."[1] During the first quarter of the twenty-first century, evangelical publications retained their vibrancy, with thousands of articles covering dozens of essential topics of concern to Christians.

Invisible? Not so much anymore. Mark Galli's call for President Trump to be removed from office (and the backlash from Trump and others), *World's* reporting on missteps by government and religious leaders during the editorship of Marvin Olasky, and the speaking and book-writing efforts of *Sojourners's* founder Jim Wallis caused mainstream media to take notice of the efforts of dedicated Christian journalists.

In the Introduction, I asked three questions that guided my examination of the evangelical press. The first was whether the divide between the evangelical press and evangelical voters who embraced Trump would be the pattern for subsequent presidential elections. The answer is yes.

All of the four publications warned against Trump's candidacy in 2016. Two eventually recommended voting for him because the Democratic candidates supported abortion on demand, the "transgender agenda," and a variety of other policies conservative Christians found troubling.

The second question asked if the values underlying the news and opinions expressed in the publications mirrored the findings of opinion polls tapping into the values and beliefs of voters who identified as evangelicals. The answer to that question is complicated.

Regardless of the topic, the content of the publications suggested a Christian response that often contradicted what opinion polls said were the beliefs and actions of people who identified as evangelicals. These evangelicals approved of President Trump's actions initiating a ban on immigrants from certain countries, his desire to build a wall separating the U.S. and Mexico, and his criticism of his own government's COVID-19 recommendations.

We do know that a certain percentage of these people chose to identify themselves as evangelicals because they were White and Protestant. The complicating factor was determining how many of these people met the criteria set forth by the National Association of Evangelicals mentioned in the Introduction. Christian pollster George Barna cautioned believers and the media not to confuse self-reported evangelicals with those who met evangelical theological criteria. This flaw might skew polling results, leading to a conclusion that more evangelicals adhere to certain political and cultural beliefs than is actually the case; therefore the gap between the publications' content and the voting behavior and values of the people interviewed could be less than what has been reported by pollsters.[2]

While Trump's rhetoric on many important issues of the time was troubling for some, his comments often led to articles in evangelical publications that provided valuable information for readers who might not have formed a biblically based response. In practical ways, the president's words and actions led to more evangelical discussions about immigration, racism, abortion, sexual ethics, and other topics that already divided the evangelical elite and the "culture warriors" of the Christian right (e.g., megachurch pastors, traditional media pundits at Fox News, and social media). This helped the magazines' readers to more constructively interact with evangelicals who formed their opinions of the world primarily through Fox News personalities or conservative blogsites (or to counter progressive ideology expressed by pundits at MSNBC and CNN). You'll recall the startling opinion poll conducted in 2015 that found only 12% of evangelicals said their views on immigration came from the Bible. Their opinion about immigrants and immigration, they said, came from interaction with immigrants, media reports, and talking with friends. Hopefully that changed as more and more articles in the publications homed in on the story of the Good Samaritan and Jesus's teachings on helping the poor, even as they grappled with helping readers discern how compassion and the law intersect.

The murder of George Floyd led *Christianity Today* to consider its past reporting on race and civil rights, finding that reporting inadequate. *CT*'s president Timothy Dalrymple wrote after the death of George Floyd: "Neo-evangelicals generally believed it was enough to preach the message of salvation and trust that justice would follow as a matter of course. It hasn't. What we thought righteous was unrighteous. We repent of our sin."[3] Dalrymple suggested tangible ways in which churches could atone for the sin of racism in their history, including the consideration of reparations. These are just two examples of the disconnect between the values of self-identified evangelicals and the biblical values taught through the publications' content.

The final question asked if the publications' coverage of high-profile political and cultural issues discussed from 2015 to 2024 hinted at a more significant split within evangelicalism in the future. That answer is also complex and still unclear. A few trends indicate a split is inevitable, while historical evidence may say otherwise.

Former *Christianity Today* editor Mark Galli has lamented that the divide within evangelicalism, which he attributes to its preoccupation with politics rather than the Gospel, could lead to an eventual split or extinction of the movement. The "evangelical religion has become theologically pluralistic and incoherent; as such, it is too subject to the changing winds of secularism to stand erect in the hurricane of our times."[4] That hurricane, he asserted, is the agenda of conservative politics and evangelicals striving for government power rather than exhibiting a zeal for evangelism and church renewal. That renewal could, if the political landscape in the U.S. becomes even more contentious and vindictive, lead to a resurgence of "Old Time Religion" that splits the evangelical divide even further.[5]

The Educational Divide

Daniel K. Williams wrote about the educational divide within evangelicalism in a *Christianity Today* essay in 2024. About 29% of White evangelicals received a college degree, and he asked his readers (most of whom possessed college degrees), "What should we do when the values we've acquired from our schooling lead us down a political path that many non-college-educated evangelicals view as dangerously wrong.?"[6] College-educated evangelicals might continue to team up with their less-educated brethren on abortion and sexual ethics issues but differ significantly on immigration and climate policy, he noted, adding, "The evangelical groups that historically have been the most suspicious of ecclesiastical and political establishments and the least likely to be college-educated—such as Pentecostals, for instance—have also been Trump's strongest supporters."[7] This could lead to a split among evangelicals along the lines of education.

To avoid widening the split, Williams suggested that evangelicals with a college education learn to practice charity toward those with whom they disagree. "If our education becomes a path to understanding rather than a component of our tribal identity," he wrote, "it can be a valuable gift in the kingdom of God instead of a marker of political division."[8] If the evangelical elite cannot find ways to better communicate with those who sit next to them in the pews, the elites may, as some have done already, break off and start new churches or denominations.

A Changing Audience

Regardless of education level, another factor that will undoubtedly affect evangelicalism's future is the inevitable change in the audience for the Gospel and for publications that speak to the evangelical tribe. Most surveys conducted in the early twenty-first century noted a significant drop-off in evangelical affiliation among younger Americans of all ethnicities.[9] Also, non-White evangelicals are growing much faster than White evangelicals. By 2030, almost half of all Americans will be non-White. Among youths under 18, the percentage of non-White residents is already estimated to be 53% of the population.[10] These demographic realities fuel conspiracy theories such as the Great Replacement Theory. That theory states that conservative White Americans are fearful of what their lives will be like if they are in the minority of U.S. residents. The evangelical publications, for the most part, reminded Christians that diversity should be celebrated as every racial group and ethnicity will be present in heaven. In the future, publications will need to continue to educate their fearful White readers while including more authors and more articles targeted to non-White audiences.

One shortcoming of this study is the omission of publications targeted to Black, Hispanic, and Asian Americans. If the projected demographic changes occur in the future, those magazines and online sites should gain more readers and play a larger role in setting the agenda for conservative Christian believers.

Another challenge facing evangelical publications is the ever-escalating change in technology and how people get their information. Younger people are much less likely to consume printed and online publications. Social media, such as YouTube, TikTok, X, Threads, Bluesky, and other others yet to come are the go-to sources of information for future audiences sought by evangelical publications. To that end, all the publications now produce podcasts and video content for their audiences, and most maintain some form of social media presence. The publications also provide daily and weekly newsletter content to interested readers, some of whom are not paying subscribers. To save money, some struggling community newspapers and smaller magazines are exploring the possibility of having Artificial Intelligence software write news articles. That practice is widely condemned by the journalistic community and the editors and writers of the publications we've studied likely are just as critical. Still, *The Christian Post* is the publication most likely to test the possibility of using AI to write articles that are now written by staff, freelancers, or interns.

Changing Audience Strategies

It's too early to determine how recent changes in editorial personnel will affect the publications' relationship with future audiences. Over the decade from 2015 to 2024, *The Christian Post* changed the least of the four. Richard Land was listed as editor throughout most of its publishing life. Its editorial content consists of articles rewritten from news releases and articles published initially elsewhere, combined with opinion essays contributed by pastors and religious organization executives. This Christian billboard type of function allows the publication to generate an almost endless array of content. Almost all that content appears targeted toward White evangelicals. That can change if management initiates a policy of seeking more diverse voices to contribute to its pages.

Christianity Today moved from Mark Galli's editorship to Russell Moore's. Moore is a refugee from the Southern Baptist Convention and, like Galli, an advocate for keeping alive founder Billy Graham's vision of knitting together the disparate threads of evangelicalism. Its primary audience remains White, although in recent years, the publication featured more non-White voices in its news and opinion coverage. Starting with George Floyd's death, the publication began featuring more authors of color and more of a focus on the challenges and successes of Hispanic, Asian American, and Black churches. Around that same time, the publication inherited a handful of excellent journalists who left *World* and who had already produced well-researched articles including sources and issues of interest to a diverse set of readers.

Sojourners remained true to its focus on social justice, peace, and fighting corporate power even as the movement's leadership moved on from founder Jim Wallis and the long-time editor Jim Rice. Early in its publishing history, it turned to a few African American authors.[11] Today, its president is African American, and its contributing writers and editors are a mixture of racial and ethnic groups. With its focus on issues of concern to younger generations such as climate change and racial equality, *Sojourners* might thrive in the coming decades.

World may have undergone the most significant editorial changes over the past few years. Editor Marvin Olasky and the publication's best journalists resigned after the board of directors instituted an opinion section dedicated to conservative political and religious commentary. The board did this without consulting with its editorial leadership. The death of founder Joel Belz in 2024 further altered the editorial leadership. The masthead of *World* presents a picture of a publication helmed mainly by White men and women. What remains to be discovered is whether its content appeals to the changing Christian demographic of the future.

Donor Pressure

Advertising of products and services of interest to Christians provides some revenue to the evangelical press, but more is needed to meet the budget, even when combined with subscription revenue. All the publications except *The Christian Post* are owned and operated by not-for-profit organizations. Readers and subscribers regularly receive pleas for donations to keep editorial efforts alive. Most donors are likely to be conservative evangelicals who would naturally want to see their donations result in articles and opinion pieces that reflect their values and beliefs. That could and perhaps already has influenced how articles are framed and how strongly they might advocate for biblical values in the face of potential conservative backlash. Thus, the placement of facts and opinions in their articles might be slanted to reflect the social, cultural, and political views of their donors rather than the needs of their readership.

Outside pressure on editorial content from subscribers, advertisers, politicians, and influential power brokers in society is not a new phenomenon in Christian publishing or the mainstream news business. The issue is how well Christian editors balance that pressure with their commitment as Christian journalists to present readers with a biblical viewpoint of the truth, not a political or skewed religious viewpoint forced on them by monied interests.

Economic Viability

To stay economically viable *Christianity Today* and *World* decided over the years to print less often while increasing the number of articles published exclusively online. In 2024, for instance, *CT* moved to a bi-monthly format in its print edition, while greatly expanding its page count. Additionally, *Christianity Today* sold its headquarters in Carol Stream, Illinois, and moved the remaining staff into a smaller office space in nearby Wheaton. Many of its reporters and editors are scattered throughout the country. That same model of distributed working is also practiced in other publications. The heavy rainfall from Hurricane Helene that ravaged North Carolina in 2024 destroyed much of *World*'s headquarters building in Asheville. While the disaster posed a challenge to its existence, the magazine still published on time. *The Christian Post*'s headquarters is in Washington, DC, where it shares space with other business entities associated with the ministries of David Jang.

The challenge to provide readers with new, fresh, and useful content is an everyday reality. For a number of years, most readers accessed the publications online. All but *The Christian Post* require a subscription to read the online content. Despite this, each publication regularly asks readers to contribute donations to support the future of the endeavor. As the technological revolution continues, the viability of publications like these four remains an existential challenge.

In recent years, several mainstream daily newspapers such as *The Washington Post* and the *Los Angeles Times* received lifelines of funding from billionaires interested in keeping alive a thriving press. In recent years, those owners have interjected their political will onto editorial decisions. Christian publications may need to pivot from reliance on donations from their boards of directors and interested citizens to seeking ownership by a deep-pocketed owner. The temptation of that owner to dominate content in the Christian publication would threaten its editorial independence to a degree that the educational function of the publication would be rendered mute.

The Good News

Despite the challenges faced by Christian publications, history provides a hopeful context. Throughout church history, dedicated believers sought to expand their influence to others outside their immediate geographical area through publishing newspapers, magazines, podcasts, TV and video programming, and social media. Over the centuries, new ventures began, and legacy publications failed if they could not engage new generations of readers.[12] The potential audience is still huge, numbering in the millions of evangelicals. These Christians seek more information about how to interact as people in, but not of, the world. The information they crave is more than what is provided at church, by listening to Christian radio, watching Christian talk shows, or reading mainstream press reports. If any of the four publications studied here ceases to exist because it loses its audience in a massive evangelical split, other communication vehicles will arise to take their place.

The other hopeful observation is that despite a period of division and conflict and an evangelical movement primarily dominated by the Republican Party and Donald Trump's politics, numerous articles and essays in the evangelical press remind readers of the ultimate purpose of life. Beyond the disagreements over political and cultural policies lies the indisputable fact of the Gospel of Christ.

Amidst the conflicts within evangelicalism over the political climate of the early twenty-first century, *Christianity Today* editor Russell Moore believed a better climate lay ahead. Moore said, "Those who wish to hold on to the Old Time Religion must recognize that God is doing something new. The old alliances and coalitions are shaking apart. And the sense of disorientation, disillusionment, and political and religious 'homelessness' that many Christians feel is not a problem to be overcome but a key part of the process."[13] That process, he wrote, is God calling Christians back to evangelism rather than conflict and confusion.

> We must refocus our attention on conversion rather than culture wars and actually read the Bible rather than mine it for passages to win arguments. No individual can change the "evangelical movement" alone. Change comes, first, person by person, then congregation by congregation. If enough of us would embrace this sense of homelessness as our new normal—as where we should have been all along—then we can rekindle a longing for a different Kingdom to call home.[14]

For hard-working, underpaid, and oft-criticized journalists and executives of evangelical publications, the fact of eternity with Christ is more important than what they or their readers encounter in the daily challenges of living at the intersection of faith and politics. As they continually remind us of these facts, these will be the "words that shape us."

Endnotes

Foreword

[1] "Elijah P. Lovejoy Monument," Great Rivers & Routes of Southwest Illinois, http://www.riversandroutes.com/directory/elijah-p-lovejoy-monument/.

[2] John P. Ferré, *A Social Gospel for Millions: The Religious Bestsellers of Charles Sheldon, Charles Gordon, and Harold Bell Wright* (Bowling Green, OH: The Popular Press, 1988), 15–42.

[3] "The Aims and Means of the Catholic Worker," Catholic Worker Movement, http://catholicworker.org.

[4] Judith Valente, "The Prophetic Work Reporters Do," Medium, September 27, 2020, https://judithvalente.medium.com/the-prophetic-work-reporters-do-680e8d1a4dea.

[5] Valente, "The Prophetic Work Reporters Do."

[6] Valente, "The Prophetic Work Reporters Do."

[7] Douglas A. Sweeney, "Christianity Today," in *Popular Religious Magazines of the United States*, eds. P. Mark Fackler and Charles H. Lippy (Westport, CT: Greenwood Press, 1995), 215.

[8] Jim Wallis, "Post-American Christianity," *Post-American*, 1:1 (Fall 1971), 2.

[9] *Sojourners*, Editorial Policies and Procedures, https://sojo.net/editorial-policies-and-procedures.

[10] "Who We Are," *World*, https://wng.org/about-world.

[11] *WORLD*, https://wng.org/authors/lynn-vincent.

[12] *The Christian Post*, http://www.christianpost.com; "The Christian Post Bias and Reliability," Ad Fontes Media, http://adfontesmedia.com/the-christian-post-bias-and-reliability.

Author's Preface

[1] David Abrahamson, *Magazine-Made America: The Cultural Transformation of the Postwar Periodical* (New York: Hampton Press, 1996).

[2] See, for instance, Randall Balmer, "The Real Origins of the Religious Right," *Politico*, May 27, 2014, https://www.politico.com/magazine/story/2014/05/religious-right-real-origins-107133/; and Randall Balmer, "The Religious Right and the Abortion Myth," *Politico*, May 5, 2022, https://www.politico.com/news/magazine/2022/05/10/abortion-history-right-white-evangelical-1970s-00031480; and

Randall Balmer, *Bad Faith: Race and the Rise of the Religious Right* (Grand Rapids, MI: Eerdmans, 2021).

[3] Mark A. Noll, *The Scandal of the Evangelical Mind*, 2nd ed. (Grand Rapids, MI, Eerdmans Publishers, 2022); Tim Alberta, *The Kingdom, the Power and the Glory: American Evangelicals in an Age of Extremism* (New York: Harper, 2023); Tim Alberta, *American Carnage: On the Front Lines of the Republican Civil War and the Rise of President Trump* (New York: Harper Paperbacks, 2020); Sarah McCammon, *The Exvangelicals: Loving, Living, and Leaving the White Evangelical Church* (New York: St. Martin's Press, 2024); Russell Moore, *Losing Our Religion: An Altar Call for Evangelical America* (New York: Penguin Random House, 2023); and Kristin Kobes DuMez, *Jesus and John Wayne: How White Evangelicals Corrupted a Faith and Fractured a Nation* (New York: Liveright Publishing Corporation, 2021).

[4] Richard T. Hughes and Christina Littlefield, *Christian America and the Kingdom of God* (Champaign, IL: University of Illinois Press, 2025), 294.

[5] Hughes and Littlefield, *Christian America*, 294.

[6] Hughes and Littlefield, *Christian America*, 294.

Introduction

[1] Jenna Johnson, "Donald Trump: They said I could 'shoot somebody' and still have support," *The Washington Post*, January 23, 2016, https://www.washingtonpost.com/news/post-politics/wp/2016/01/23/donald-trump-i-could-shoot-somebody-and-still-have-support/.

[2] See Galatians 5:22–23.

[3] CP Editors, "Donald Trump is a Scam. Evangelical Voters Should Back Away (CP Editorial)," *The Christian Post*, February 29, 2016, https://www.christianpost.com/news/donald-trump-scam-evangelical-voters-back-away-cp-editorial.html.

[4] CP Editors, "Donald Trump is a Scam."

[5] Jim Wallis, "Donald Trump: Narcissist in Chief," *Sojourners*, July 9, 2015, https://sojo.net/articles/donald-trump-narcissist-chief.

[6] Marvin Olasky, "Donald Trump as Christian and Candidate," *World*, June 30, 2016, https://wng.org/articles/donald-trump-as-christian-and-candidate-1617285470.

[7] Olasky, "Donald Trump as Christian and Candidate."

[8] See Sarah Pulliam Bailey, "White evangelicals voted overwhelmingly for Donald Trump, exit polls show," *The Washington Post*, November 3, 2016, washingtonpost.com/news/acts-of-faith/wp/2016/11/09/exit-polls-show-white-evangelicals-voted-overwhelmingly-for-donald-trump/.

[9] Actual figures are hard to verify. *Christianity Today* has averaged slightly more than 100,000 paid print subscribers with thousands more paying to access their extensive online content. *World* magazine recently had 160,000 annual subscribers with millions more paying to read its content and access past issues online. *Sojourners* does not publish circulation details, but judging by its history numbers, its paid circulation is likely less than 100,000 people, but, again, its website is well populated with articles available for an annual payment. *The Christian Post*, which is only published online, claims 10 million monthly visitors. Thus while firm readership numbers are elusive, the figure of 15 million readers per month is a conservative and informed estimation.

[10] "Evangelicals—Shared Faith in Broad Diversity," National Association of Evangelicals, May 22, 2018, https://www.nae.org/sharedfaith/.

[11] Rachel Kleinfeld, "Polarization, Democracy, and Political Violence in the United States: What the Research Says," Carnegie Endowment for International Peace, September 5, 2023, https://carnegieendowment.org/research/2023/09/polarization-democracy-and-political-violence-in-the-united-states-what-the-research-says?lang=en.

[12] Ken Waters, "Advocacy, Objectivity, Editorial Freedom and Journalistic Quality: A Study of Issues in the Protestant Press," *Christian Scholars Review* (Fall 2001). See also, Douglas J. Trouton, "Professionalization and the Evangelical Press Association," (M.A. thesis, University of Minnesota), 1999.

[13] *Christianity Today* indexes articles and opinion essays in the publication that might be of interest to African American Christians. See https://www.christianitytoday.com/topics/african-americans/.

[14] Terry Mattingly, "Who or What is an Evangelical Christian?" in *Understanding Evangelical Media*, eds. Quentin J. Schultze and Robert H. Woods Jr., (Downers Grove, IL: IVP Academic, 2008), 21.

[15] "The Lausanne Covenant," https://lausanne.org/statement/lausanne-covenant.

[16] National Association of Evangelicals, "What is an Evangelical?" https://www.nae.net/what-is-an-evangelical/.

[17] NAE, "What is an Evangelical?"

[18] Mark A. Noll, *American Evangelical Christianity* (Oxford, UK: Blackwell, 2001), 13.

[19] See, for instance, Amy Black, "Evangelicals and Politics," National Association of Evangelicals, September 19, 2016, https://www.nae.org/evangelicals-and-politics/.

[20] NAE, "What is an Evangelical?"

[21] Many recent books describe aspects of the current evangelical movement and its relationship to politics and culture. Among these are, Anthea Butler, *White Evangelical Racism: The Politics of Morality in America.* (Chapel Hill: University of North Carolina Press, 2021); Andrew L. Whitehead and Samuel L. Perry, *Taking America Back for God: Christian Nationalism in the United States.* (New York: Oxford University Press, 2020); Ryan Burge, *The Nones: Where They Came From, Who They Are, and Where They Are Going,* 2nd ed. (Minneapolis: Fortress Press, 2023); and Kristin Kobes Du Mez, *Jesus and John Wayne: How White Evangelicals Corrupted a Faith and Fractured a Nation.* (New York: Liveright, 2020).

[22] Dennis N. Voskuil, "Reaching Out: Mainline Protestantism and the Media," in *Between the Times: The Travail of the Protestant Establishment in America, 1900–1960,* ed. William R. Hutchison, (Cambridge: Cambridge University Press, 1989), 73.

[23] Roberta Moore, "Development of Protestant Journalism in the United States, 1743–1850," PhD diss. (Syracuse University, 1968), 19.

[24] Moore, "Development of Protestant Journalism," 8.

[25] Moore, "Development of Protestant Journalism," 8.

[26] Teresa Lueck, "Women's Moral Reform Periodicals of the 19th Century: A Cultural Feminist Analysis of the Advocate," *American Journalism* 16 (1999): 37–52.

[27] Richard Hofstadter, *The American Political Tradition: And the Men Who Made It* (New York: Vintage Books, 1989), 185.

[28] An explanation of the various viewpoints present in the fundamentalist-modernist rhetorical battles can be found in Michael Kearney, "Between Fundamentalists

and Funnymonkeyists: Clarence Edward Macartney's Rhetoric of Modern Orthodoxy," *Journal of Communication and Religion*, 46, no. 3 (Fall 2023): 54–73.

[29] See John Perry and Marvin Olasky, *Monkey Business: True Story of the Scopes Trial* (Nashville: B & H Books, 2005); and Edward J. Larson, *Summer for the Gods: The Scopes Trial and America's Continuing Debate Over Science and Religion* (New York: Basic Books, 2006).

[30] Elizabeth C. Nordbeck, *Thunder on the Right: Understanding Conservative Christianity*, (New York: United Church Press, 1990), 1.

[31] Martin Marty, *Modern American Religion: The Noise of Conflict, 1919–1941* (Chicago: University of Chicago Press, 1991), 188.

[32] W. Russell Congleton, "Sword of the Lord," in *Popular Religious Magazines of the United States*, eds. Mark Fackler and Charles Lippy (Westport, CT: Greenwood Press, 1995), 457.

[33] Quentin J. Schultze, *Christianity and the Mass Media in America: Toward a Democratic Accommodation* (East Lansing, MI: Michigan State University Press, 2003), 91.

[34] Lester R. Kurtz, *Gods in the Global Village: The World's Religions in Sociological Perspective*, 2nd edition, Sociology for a New Century Series (Thousand Oaks, CA: Pine Forge Press, 2007), 12.

[35] Schultze, *Christianity and the Mass Media in America*, 100.

[36] Schultze, *Christianity and the Mass Media in America*, 101.

[37] Schultze, *Christianity and the Mass Media in America*, 99.

[38] This idea was first proposed in 1948. A legacy edition of that research is published in Paul F. Lazarsfeld, Bernard Berelson, and Hazel Gaudet, *The People's Choice: How the Vote Makes Up His Mind in a Presidential Campaign* (New York: Columbia University Press, 2021).

[39] Denis McQuail, *McQuail's Mass Communication Theory*, 5th edition, (London: Sage Publications, 2000), 423–428.

[40] Agenda setting was first proposed as a theory in 1972 and has been modified numerous times. See M. E. McCombs and D. L. Shaw, "The Evolution of Agenda-setting Theory: 25 years in the Marketplace of Ideas," *Journal of Communication* 43, no. 2 (February 2006): 58–66.

[41] See E. Goffman, *Frame Analysis: An Essay on the Organization of Experience* (New York: Harper and Row, 1974).

[42] Each of the websites of the four publications contains extensive archives. I began this research by using keyword search terms for the issues studied in the following chapters. Many search terms yielded hundreds of articles and opinion essays. I chose to focus on those addressing significant aspects of the news or theological commentary. Often this meant I chose to analyze those articles covering topics in depth. Occasionally, links within an article led to other important views on the topic. History and context for these issues and more came from my 30 years of research on the role and influence of religious publications, which includes conference papers, journal articles, and book chapters.

[43] Among the most recent of these books and articles are Mark A. Noll, *The Scandal of the Evangelical Mind*, 2nd ed. (Grand Rapids, MI: Eerdmans Publishers, 2022); Tim Alberta, *The Kingdom, the Power and the Glory: American Evangelicals in an Age of Extremism* (New York: Harper, 2023); Tim Alberta, *American Carnage: On the Front Lines of the Republican Civil War and the Rise of President Trump* (New York: Harper

Paperbacks, 2020); Sarah McCammon, *The Exvangelicals: Loving, Living, and Leaving the White Evangelical Church* (New York: St. Martin's Press, 2024); Russell Moore, *Losing Our Religion: An Altar Call for Evangelical America* (New York: Penguin Random House, 2023); and Kristin Kobes DuMez, *Jesus and John Wayne: How White Evangelicals Corrupted a Faith and Fractured a Nation* (New York: Liveright, 2021).

Chapter 1
Journalism through a Biblical Lens

[1] Ben Dooley, "Who's Behind *Newsweek*?" *Mother Jones*, May/June 2014, 30–65, https://www.motherjones.com/media/2014/03/newsweek-ibt-olivet-david-jang/. This investigative piece links Jang's influence, if not funding, to *International Business Times*. It also claims that Asian students enter the United States as students of Olivet University and perform internships working for various Jang-affiliated media. The article also says Jang's funds come from donations by members of his ministry, the so-called Community, and other profitable ministries.

[2] "About CP," *Christian Post*, https://www.christianpost.com/about-us.html.

[3] Ted Olsen and Ken Smith, "The Second Coming Christ Controversy," *Christianity Today*, September 2012, 36–44.

[4] Michelle A. Vu, "Sources in 'Second Coming Christ Controversy' Face Scrutiny," *The Christian Post*, August 17, 2012, https://www.christianpost.com/news/olivet-university-sources-in-second-coming-christ-controversy-face-scrutiny.html.

[5] Vu, "Sources in 'Second Coming.'"

[6] "Tiny Digital Publisher to Put *Newsweek* Back in Print," *The New York Times*, March 2, 2014, https://www.proquest.com/nytimes/docview/2213664267/fulltext/BF2DF5B4B2654C5 BPQ/5?accountid=13159.

[7] Marc Tracy, "A Former Owner of *Newsweek* Pleads Guilty in a Fraud Scheme," *The New York Times*, February 14, 2020, https://www.nytimes.com/2020/02/14/business/media/Etienne-Uzac-newsweek-fraud.html.

[8] Marc Tracy, "A Former Owner of *Newsweek* Pleads Guilty in a Fraud Scheme." See also, Steve Rabey, "Two Plead Guilty in Fraud Scheme Involving Christian Post and Olivet University," *Ministry Watch*, February 29. 2020, https://ministrywatch.com/two-plead-guilty-in-fraud-scheme-involving-christian-post-and-olivet-university/.

[9] Craig Silverman, "A Christian Publisher Was Running the Same Malicious Code That *Newsweek* Media Group Used for An Ad Fraud Scheme," *Buzzfeed News*, March 29, 2018, https://www.buzzfeednews.com/article/craigsilverman/christian-media-corporation-ad-fraud-scheme-newsweek.

[10] Steve Rabey, "IN FRAUD WE TRUST: Did Money-Laundering and Advertising Scam Help '*Christian Post*' Stay Afloat?" *Ministry Watch*, March 11, 2020, https://ministrywatch.com/in-fraud-we-trust-christian-post-used-money-laundering-and-advertising-scam-to-stay-afloat/.

[11] Steve Rabey, "All the News That Fits Its Own Point of View," *Ministry Watch*, March 24, 2020, https://ministrywatch.com/all-the-news-that-fits-its-own-point-of-view/.

[12] Steve Rabey, "The - 'Editorial Advisors' Surprised to Learn of Company's Crimes," *Ministry Watch*, April 13, 2020, https://ministrywatch.com/the-christian-posts-editorial-advisors-surprised-to-learn-of-companys-crimes/.

[13] Colleen Shalby, "California Bible college students claim they were confined, surveilled and made to do unpaid labor," *Los Angeles Times*, September 20, 2024, https://www.latimes.com/california/story/2024-09-20/bible-college-students-claim-they-couldnt-leave-freely-and-were-made-to-do-unpaid-labor.

[14] Graham achieved national and international attention after newspaper mogul William Randolph Hearst told editors of his various publications to "puff Graham." The focus on the then little-known evangelist made him a near household name around the U.S. and abroad. See Ron F. Hale, "'Puff Graham'—Finding the Favor of God," *The Christian Index*, June 25, 2015, https://christianindex.org/stories/puff-graham-finding-the-favor-of-god, 135.

[15] Harold Myra, "A Greater Vision," *Christianity Today*, October 24, 2006, https://www.christianitytoday.com/2006/10/greater-vision/.

[16] Mark G. Toulouse, "*Christianity Today* and American Public Life: A Case Study," *Journal of Church and State*, 35, no. 2 (Spring 1993): 241; See also, J. C. Pollock, *A Foreign Devil in China* (Minneapolis, MN: World Wide Publications, 1971), 238. Another excellent magazine history is Phyllis Alsdurf's "The Founding of *Christianity Today* Magazine and the Construction of an American Evangelical Identity," *Journal of Religious and Theological Information*, 9, no. 1-2 (2010): 20–43.

[17] Memo from Larry Ward to Nelson Bell, March 15, 1956. Nelson Bell collection 318, 53:21. Billy Graham Archives, Wheaton, IL.

[18] See Nelson Bell's February 13, 1956, letter to editor Carl Henry. Nelson Bell Collection 318, 53:21. Billy Graham Archives, Wheaton, IL.

[19] Suggestions for Correspondents, September 1, 1956. Box 19:1 of the Nelson Bell collection.

[20] Jeff Greenfield, "When Richard Nixon Used Billy Graham," *Politico*, February 21, 2018, https://www.politico.com/magazine/story/2018/02/21/billy-graham-death-richard-nixon-217039/.

[21] Sarah Pulliam Bailey, "Q & A: Billy Graham on Aging, Regrets, and Evangelicals," *Christianity Today*, January 21, 2011, https://www.christianitytoday.com/ct/2011/januaryweb-only/qabillygraham.html. As a nonprofit religious publication, *Christianity Today* did not directly advise readers about matters of voting preference. Still, through the framing of articles at times, it did make its position clear enough that readers could infer who the editors, and by extension evangelicals, should vote for.

[22] "Abortion and the Court," *Christianity Today*, February 16, 1973. https://www.christianitytoday.com/ct/1973/february-16/editorials-abortion-and-court.html

[23] When another publication revealed damaging allegations against a pastor, church, or Christian organization, *Christianity Today* didn't hesitate to follow up with its after-the-fact reporting.

[24] Daniel Silliman, "Ravi Zacharias's Ministry Investigates Claims of Sexual Misconduct at Spas," *Christianity Today*, September 29, 2020, https://www.christianitytoday.com/news/2020/september/ravi-zacharias-sexual-harassment-rzim-spa-massage-investiga.html.

[25] The editors, "Why We Report Bad News About Leaders," *Christianity Today*, September 29, 2020, https://www.christianitytoday.com/ct/2020/september-web-only/editors-note-ravi-zacharias-investigation.html.

[26] Daniel Silliman, "Sexual Harassment Went Unchecked at *Christianity Today*," *Christianity Today*, March 15, 2022, https://www.christianitytoday.com/news/2022/march/sexual-harassment-ct-guidepost-assessment-galli-olawoye.html.

[27] Timothy Dalrymple, "We Fell Short in Protecting Our Employees," *Christianity Today*, March 15, 2022, https://www.christianitytoday.com/ct/2022/march-web-only/we-fell-short-in-protecting-our-employees-editorial.html. Dalrymple's explanation contains a link to a PDF copy of the entire report conducted by Guidepost Solutions.

[28] Jim Wallis, "Post-American Christianity," *The Post-American*, Fall 1971, https://sojo.net/magazine/fall-1971/post-american-christianity.

[29] Wallis, "Post-American Christianity."

[30] William Pannell, a professor at Fuller Theological Seminary, wrote for the *Post-American* several times and was listed on the masthead as a contributing editor. See, for example, William Pannell, "Evangelicals and the Social Crisis," *The Post-American*, October 1974, https://sojo.net/magazine/october-1974/evangelicals-and-social-crisis.

[31] John Howard Yoder, "Why I Don't Pay All My Income Tax," *The Post-American*, March 1977, https://sojo.net/magazine/october-1974/evangelicals-and-social-crisis. Unfortunately, Yoder frequently harassed and sexually abused women, many of them his students. A formal apology was issued by the Mennonite Church USA denomination in 2015, long after his death. An investigation of his actions implicated administrators at the Mennonite Biblical Seminary in confronting Yoder about his behavior. Still, he was not forced to resign until more than ten years later.

[32] Jim Wallis, "A Christian Mistake," *Sojourners*, June 2009, 5, https://sojo.net/magazine/june-2009/christian-mistake.

[33] Frances Kissling, "Sex & the Clergy," *Nation*, 279, no. 20 (December 12, 2004): 10.

[34] Teresa Watanabe, "Gospel for Both Sides of the Aisle," *Los Angeles Times*, March 28, 2005, A-1.

[35] Eric Martin, "The Catholic Church Has a Visible White-Power Faction," *Sojourners*, August 2020, https://sojo.net/magazine/august-2020/catholic-church-has-visible-white-power-faction.

[36] Christopher White, "Sojourners pulls article about Catholic Church and race from website," *National Catholic Reporter*, August 13, 2020, https://www.ncronline.org/culture/sojourners-pulls-article-about-catholic-church-and-race-website.

[37] Jim Wallis, "Repentance—A New Way Forward," *Sojourners*, August 12, 2020, https://sojo.net/past-statements-decision-remove-article.

[38] Hana Kim, "*Sojourners* Magazine, 1971–2005: Peace and Justice, a Voice of American Progressive Evangelism," PhD diss. (The Theological School of Drew University, 2011), iv.

[39] Marvin Olasky, *Telling the Truth: How to Revitalize Christian Journalism* (Wheaton, IL: Crossway Books, 1996), 33.

[40] Olasky, *Telling the Truth*, 25.

[41] Mark A. Kellner, "Marvin Olasky preaches Journalism through the lens of Scripture, Faith," *Deseret News*, September 18, 2014, https://www.deseret.com/2014/9/18/20548678/marvin-olasky-preaches-journalism-through-the-lens-of-scripture-faith.

[42] Mark Oppenheimer, "A Muckraking Magazine Creates a Stir Among Evangelical Christians," *The New York Times*, November 7, 2014, https://www.nytimes.com/2014/11/08/us/a-muckraking-magazine-creates-a-stir-among-evangelical-christians.html; For a more extensive explanation of biblical journalism, see Marvin Olasky, "A View from the Editor's Chair," *World*, September 2, 2017, https://wng.org/roundups/a-view-from-the-editors-chair-1617229493; Marvin Olasky, "Boots on the ground,"

World, September 26, 2019, https://wng.org/articles/boots-on-the-ground-1620590064; and Marvin Olasky, *Reforming Journalism* (Phillipsburg, NJ: P & R Publishing), 2019.

[43] Susan Olasky, "Femme fatale," *World*, March 29, 1997, https://wng.org/articles/femme-fatale-1617340805.

[44] Olasky, "Femme fatale."

[45] "*WORLD*'s response to Zondervan's ethics charges," *World*, June 14, 1997, https://wng.org/articles/WORLDs-response-to-zondervans-ethics-charges-1617645609.

[46] "EPA ad hoc ethics committee report," *World*, July 12, 1997, https://wng.org/articles/epa-ad-hoc-ethics-committee-report-1617340746. The Evangelical Press Association (EPA), founded in 1948, represents the interests of publications targeted at conservative Christian readers. After the EPA issued its ad hoc report, *World* ended its membership with the organization.

[47] *Christianity Today* followed up with several stories focused on the new translation of the New International Version (including Today's New International Version). See Timothy C. Morgan, "Bible Translation: Revised NIV Makes Its Debut," *Christianity Today*, February 4, 2002, https://www.christianitytoday.com/ct/2002/february4/16.19.html; Timothy C. Morgan, "Bible Translation: TNIV Critics Blast Scripture 'Distortions,'" *Christianity Today*, April 1, 2002, https://www.christianitytoday.com/ct/2002/april1/10.30.html; and A *Christianity Today* Editorial, "Battle for the Bible Translation," *Christianity Today*, September 2, 2011, https://www.christianitytoday.com/ct/2011/september/bible-translation-battles.html.

[48] Susan Olasky, "Translation manipulation," *World*, July 1, 2021, https://wng.org/articles/translation-manipulation-1624941058.

[49] William Safire, "Political 'God's World,'" *New York Times*, February 17, 2000, https://archive.nytimes.com/www.nytimes.com/library/opinion/safire/021700safi.html.

[50] Safire was referring to Bob Jones IV, "Explaining McCain," *World*, February 19, 2000, 20–24. It is worth mentioning that four cover stories during the 2000 Presidential campaign featured George W. Bush looking either pensive or smiling. Only one featured McCain; no other Republican candidates gained photo coverage on the magazine's cover. Editor Olasky, an unpaid adviser to Bush when the President was Governor of Texas, said that because of his former affiliation with Bush, he recused himself from influencing or editing articles involving Bush during the election season. He claimed, "I read our McCain cover story for the first time after publication." See Marvin Olasky, "The Conspiracy," *World*, March 4, 2000, https://wng.org/articles/the-conspiracy-1617695513.

[51] Jones, "Explaining McCain."

[52] Safire, "Political 'God's World.'"

[53] Safire, "Political 'God's World.'"

[54] Olasky, "The Conspiracy."

[55] R. Albert Mohler, "Into the battle of ideas," *World*, September 30, 2021, https://wng.org/opinions/into-the-battle-of-ideas-1633023747.

[56] Anne Stych, "*World* Magazine Editor-in-Chief Marvin Olasky Resigning Over Media Nonprofit's New Direction, *Ministry Watch*, November 15, 2021, https://ministrywatch.com/WORLD-magazine-editor-in-chief-marvin-olasky-resigning-over-media-nonprofits-newdirection/.

[57] Sarah Einselen, "Former WORLD Editor Marvin Olasky Questions Magazine's Journalistic Integrity," *The Roys Report*, September 15, 2022, https://julieroys.com/former-world-editor-olasky-questions-magazine-journalistic-integrity/; and Marvin

Olasky, "LONG FORM: A Wrinkle in Journalism History," *Current*, September 14, 2022, https://currentpub.com/2022/09/14/long-form-a-wrinkle-in-journalism-history/.

[58] Mindy Belz, "Season finale," *World*, October 21, 2021, https://wng.org/articles/season-finale-1634764472.

[59] Sophia Lee, "Thank you, readers," *World*, November 17, 2021, https://wng.org/articles/thank-you-readers-1637182258.

[60] Lee, "Thank you, readers."

[61] "World Magazine's Big Shakeup Continues as Numerous Leaders Depart, Citing Political Tension," *Relevant*, November 17, 2021, https://relevantmagazine.com/current/nation/world-magazines-big-shakeup-continues-as-numerous-leaders-depart-citing-political-tension/.

[62] Ben Smith, "His Reasons for Opposing Trump Were Biblical. Now a Top Christian Editor is Out," *The New York Times*, November 14, 2021, https://www.nytimes.com/2021/11/14/business/WORLD-magazine-marvin-olasky-trump.html?searchResultPosition=3.

[63] Ben Smith, "His Reasons for Opposing Trump Were Biblical."

Chapter 2
The 2016 Presidential Election: The Lesser Evil

[1] CP Editors, "Donald Trump is a Scam. Evangelical Voters Should Back Away (CP Editorial)," *The Christian Post*, February 29, 2016, https://www.christianpost.com/news/donald-trump-scam-evangelical-voters-back-away-cp-editorial.html.

[2] CP Editors, "Donald Trump is a Scam."

[3] CP Editors, "Donald Trump is a Scam."

[4] CP Editors, "Donald Trump is a Scam."

[5] CP Editors, "Donald Trump is a Scam."

[6] Michael Brown, "An Open Letter to Donald Trump," *The Christian Post*, August 29, 2015, https://www.christianpost.com/news/an-open-letter-to-donald-trump.html.

[7] Michael Brown, "Donald Trump, Anger, and Violence," *The Christian Post*, March 14, 2016, https://www.christianpost.com/news/donald-trump-rally-chicago-anger-protests-liberal-activists-campaign-election.html.

[8] Brown, "Donald Trump, Anger, and Violence."

[9] Michael Brown, "3 Words That Could Change Donald Trump's Life," *The Christian Post*, May 25, 2016, https://www.christianpost.com/news/words-that-could-change-donald-trumps-life.html.

[10] Michael Brown, "A Great Awakening or a Rude Awakening? What Will It Be?" *The Christian Post*, October 8, 2016, https://www.christianpost.com/news/a-great-awakening-or-a-rude-awakening-what-will-it-be-opinion.html.

[11] Brown, "A Great Awakening or a Rude Awakening?"

[12] Brown, "A Great Awakening or a Rude Awakening?"

[13] Brown, "A Great Awakening or a Rude Awakening?"

[14] Richard Land, "Why I Joined Donald Trump's Evangelical Executive Advisory Board," *The Christian Post*, June 22, 2016, https://www.christianpost.com/news/why-i-joined-donald-trump-evangelical-executive-advisory-board.html.

[15] Richard Land, "Laws Are for the Little People, Not Bill and Hillary Clinton,"

The Christian Post, July 7, 2016, https://www.christianpost.com/news/laws-little-people-not-bill-hillary-clinton-fbi-email-scandal.htm.

[16] Richard Land, "An Open Letter to Donald Trump on Evangelical Voters," *The Christian Post*, July 14, 2016, https://www.christianpost.com/news/an-open-letter-to-donald-trump-on-evangelical-voters.html.

[17] Richard Land, "The Presidential Election: An Excruciating Choice," *The Christian Post*, August 23, 2016, https://www.christianpost.com/news/the-presidential-election-an-excruciating-choice.html.

[18] Land, "The Presidential Election."

[19] Eric Sapp, "Hillary Clinton Is the Best Choice for Voters Against Abortion," *The Christian Post*, October 3, 2016, https://www.christianpost.com/news/hillary-clinton-is-the-best-choice-for-voters-against-abortion.html.

[20] Sapp, "Hillary Clinton Is the Best Choice." Editor Land responded to Sapp's column with one of his own, called "Hillary Clinton Is a Dangerous Choice for Voters Against Abortion (A Response to Eric Sapp)," *The Christian Post*, November 7, 2016, https://www.christianpost.com/news/hillary-clinton-is-a-dangerous-choice-for-voters-against-abortion-a-response-to-eric-sapp-170240/.

[21] Deborah Fikes, "To Evangelicals Who Think Hillary Is Deplorable," *The Christian Post*, September 14, 2016, https://www.christianpost.com/news/to-evangelicals-who-think-hillary-is-deplorable.html.

[22] Fikes, "To Evangelicals Who Think."

[23] Napp Nazworth, "Why Evangelicals Shouldn't Vote for Trump," *The Christian Post*, August 23, 2016, https://www.christianpost.com/news/why-evangelicals-shouldnt-vote-for-donald-trump.html. It is worth noting that Nazworth also wrote an October opinion piece entitled, "3 Reasons Hillary Clinton Is a Pro-Abortion Extremist," *The Christian Post*, October 6, 2016, https://www.christianpost.com/news/3-reasons-hillary-clinton-is-a-pro-abortion-extremist.html.

[24] See, for instance, Michael Gryboski, "Donald Trump Evangelical Adviser Denounces Sex Assault Comments as 'Lecherous and Worthless,'" *The Christian Post*, October 11, 2016, https://www.christianpost.com/news/donald-trump-evangelical-james-macdonald-denounces-sex-assault-comments-lecherous-worthless-170716/.

[25] Michael Gryboski, "John Piper Says Both Donald Trump and Hillary Clinton Should Quit the Race," *The Christian Post*, October 13, 2016, https://www.christianpost.com/news/john-piper-donald-trump-hillary-clinton-should-quit-the-race.html.

[26] Anugrah Kumar, "Franklin Graham: Trump's 'Crude Comments' as Indefensible as Clinton's 'Godless Agenda,'" *The Christian Post*, October 10, 2016, https://www.christianpost.com/news/franklin-graham-trumps-crude-comments-as-indefensible-as-clintons-godless-agenda.html

[27] Christina Cleveland, "The Bias in Our Votes," *Christianity Today*, Jan/Feb 2016, 32.

[28] Kate Shellnutt, "Pew: More Sermons Endorse Clinton," *Christianity Today*, August 8, 2016, https://www.christianitytoday.com/news/2016/august/pew-more-sermons-endorse-clinton.html. An October 2016 poll, conducted by LifeWay Research, found similar results when it polled 1,000 evangelical leaders. See Bob Smietana, "Despite Mike Pence, Most Evangelical Pastors Are Not Ready to Vote Trump," *Christianity Today*, October 6, 2016, https://www.christianitytoday.com/news/2016/october/mike-pence-most-evangelical-pastors-undecided-trump-clinton.html.

[29] As expected, the data confirmed the divide between sermons delivered, and

voting preferences, at churches that were predominantly African American verses those that were majority white. See Shellnutt, "Pew: More Sermons Endorse Clinton."

[30] National Association of Evangelicals, "For the Health of the Nation: An Evangelical Call for Civic Responsibility," October 7, 2004; updated and revised March 8, 2018.

[31] Ron Sider, "Why I Am Voting for Hillary Clinton," *Christianity Today*, September 2016, 54–55.

[32] Sider, "Why I Am Voting for Hillary Clinton," 55.

[33] Interview by CT Editors, "James Dobson: Why I Am Voting for Donald Trump," *Christianity Today*, September 23, 2016, https://www.christianitytoday.com/2016/09/james-dobson-why-i-am-voting-for-donald-trump/.

[34] Editors, "James Dobson."

[35] Editors, "James Dobson."

[36] Editors, "James Dobson."

[37] Editors, "James Dobson."

[38] Sho Baraka, "Sho Baraka: Why I Can't Vote for Either Trump or Clinton," *Christianity Today*, September 2016, 62–64.

[39] Baraka, "Sho Baraka," 64.

[40] Andy Crouch, "Speak Truth to Trump," *Christianity Today*, October 10, 2016, https://www.christianitytoday.com/ct/2016/october-web-only/speak-truth-to-trump.html.

[41] Crouch, "Speak Truth to Trump."

[42] Crouch, "Speak Truth to Trump."

[43] Crouch, "Speak Truth to Trump."

[44] Ed Spivey, "The Jokers are On Us," *Sojourners*, January 2016, https://sojo.net/magazine/january-2016/jokers-are-us.

[45] Jim Wallis, "Donald Trump: Narcissist in Chief," *Sojourners*, July 9, 2015, https://sojo.net/articles/donald-trump-narcissist-chief.

[46] Wallis, "Donald Trump."

[47] Wallis, "Donald Trump."

[48] Jim Wallis, "Iraq, ISIS, and Our Need for Repentance," *Sojourners*, May 28, 2015, https://sojo.net/articles/iraq-isis-and-our-need-repentance.

[49] Jim Wallis, "It's Embarrassing to be an Evangelical This Election," *Sojourners*, February 25, 2016, https://sojo.net/articles/it-s-embarrassing-be-evangelical-election.

[50] Wallis, "It's Embarrassing."

[51] Jim Wallis, "Trump's Brand of Bigotry Isn't Going Away. So Neither Are We," *Sojourners*, May 12, 2016, https://sojo.net/articles/trumps-brand-bigotry-isnt-going-away-so-neither-are-we.

[52] Wallis, "Trump's Brand of Bigotry."

[53] Wallis, "Trump's Brand of Bigotry."

[54] Wallis, "Trump's Brand of Bigotry."

[55] See "A Declaration by American Evangelicals Concerning Donald Trump," Change.org, https://www.change.org/p/donald-trump-a-declaration-by-american-evangelicals-concerning-donald-trump.

[56] "A Declaration by American Evangelicals."

[57] Nish Weiseth, "These Evangelicals Have Long Spoken Out Against Trump. No One Was Listening," *Sojourners*, October 18, 2016, https://sojo.net/articles/these-evangelicals-have-long-spoken-out-against-trump-no-one-was-listening.

[58] Cathy Lynn Grossman, "5 Faith Facts About Hillary Clinton, Social Gospel Methodist to the Core," *Sojourners*, April 10, 2015, https://sojo.net/articles/5-faith-facts-about-hillary-clinton-social-gospel-methodist-core.

[59] Lauren Markoe, "Catholics, the Ultimate Swing Voters, Lean Heavily Toward Clinton," *Sojourners*, November 1, 2016, https://sojo.net/articles/catholics-ultimate-swing-voters-lean-heavily-toward-clinton; and Web Editors, "With New Emails, FBI Continues Investigation of Hillary Clinton," *Sojourners*, October 28, 2016, https://sojo.net/articles/new-emails-fbi-continues-investigation-hillary-clinton.

[60] J. C. Derrick, "Whom do evangelical insiders favor in 2016," *World*, July 30, 2015, https://wng.org/sift/whom-do-evangelical-insiders-favor-in-2016-1617407055.

[61] Derrick, "Whom do evangelical insiders favor."

[62] J. C. Derrick, "Bush rises, Rubio pads lead in *WORLD* survey," *World*, February 18, 2016, https://wng.org/sift/bush-rises-rubio-pads-lead-in-*WORLD*-survey-1617251523.

[63] J. C. Derrick, "Cruz dominates latest *WORLD* survey," *World*, March 22, 2016, https://wng.org/sift/cruz-dominates-latest-*WORLD*-survey-1617251523.

[64] D. C. Innes, "Post-Republican Christian Voting," *World*, May 9, 2016, https://wng.org/articles/post-republican-christian-voting-1617287117.

[65] Innes, "Post-Republican Christian Voting."

[66] Marvin Olasky, "Donald Trump as Christian and Candidate," *World*, June 30, 2016, https://wng.org/articles/donald-trump-as-christian-and-candidate-1617285470.

[67] Olasky, "Donald Trump as Christian."

[68] Olasky, "Donald Trump as Christian."

[69] Joel Belz, "Disappearing Evangelicals," *World*, July 9, 2016, 3.

[70] Belz, "Disappearing Evangelicals."

[71] Mindy Belz, "Choose your taint," *World*, August 6, 2016, 28.

[72] Belz, "Choose your taint."

[73] J. C. Derrick, "Trump improves in new *WORLD* survey," *World*, August 25, 2016, https://wng.org/articles/donald-trump-as-christian-and-candidate-1617285470.

[74] Marvin Olasky, "Unfit for power," *World*, October 11, 2016, https://wng.org/articles/unfit-for-power-1617305343.

[75] Olasky, "Unfit for power."

[76] Olasky, "Unfit for power."

[77] Olasky, "Unfit for power."

[78] Marvin Olasky, "Two Unfit Candidates," *World*, October 13, 2016, https://wng.org/sift/two-unfit-candidates-1617406578.

[79] Olasky, "Two Unfit Candidates."

[80] Stoyan Zaimov, "Donald Trump Victory Speech: 'Win Is for Americans of All Races, Religions, Beliefs,'" *The Christian Post*, November 9, 2016, https://www.christianpost.com/news/donald-trump-victory-speech-win-is-for-americans-of-all-races-religions-beliefs-video-transcript.html.

[81] Carmen Fowler LaBerge, "Evangelicals Should Repent for Putting Politics Ahead of the Gospel," *The Christian Post*, November 13, 2016, https://www.christianpost.com/news/evangelicals-should-repent-for-putting-politics-ahead-of-the-gospel-opinion.html.

[82] LaBerge, "Evangelicals Should Repent."

[83] Kate Shellnutt, "Trump Elected President, Thanks to 4 in 5 White Evangelicals," *Christianity Today*, November 9, 2016, https://www.christianitytoday.com/

news/2016/november/trump-elected-president-thanks-to-4-in-5-white-evangeli-cals.html.

[84] Mark Galli, "After Trump, Should Evangelical Christians Part Ways?" *Christianity Today*, November 10, 2016, https://www.christianitytoday.com/ct/2016/november-web-only/should-evangelicals-part-ways.html.

[85] Galli, "After Trump."

[86] Galli, "After Trump."

[87] Galli, "After Trump."

[88] The Web Editors, "Donald Trump Is The 45th President of the United States," *Sojourners*, November 9, 2016, https://sojo.net/articles/donald-trump-45th-president-united-states.

[89] Jim Wallis, "Time for Healing. And Resistance," *Sojourners*, November 9, 2016, https://sojo.net/articles/time-healing-and-resistance.

[90] Wallis, "Time for Healing."

[91] William Barber II, "Make Babylon Great Again," *Sojourners*, March 2018, 16–20.

[92] Jamie Dean, "Trump routs Clinton, wins presidency," *World*, November 9, 2016, https://wng.org/sift/trump-routs-clinton-wins-presidency-1617406375.

[93] Dean, "Trump routs Clinton."

[94] Dean, "Trump routs Clinton."

[95] J. C. Derrick, "Never Trump-ers face the future," *World*, November 9, 2016, https://wng.org/sift/never-trump-ers-face-the-future-1617251483.

Chapter 3
The Challenge of Immigration

[1] "Evangelicals Say It Is Time for Congress To Tackle Immigration," *Lifeway Research*, March 11, 2015, https://research.lifeway.com/2015/03/11/evangelicals-say-it-is-time-for-congress-to-tackle-immigration/. The report said respondents self-identified as born again, fundamentalist, or evangelical Christian.

[2] "Evangelicals Say It Is Time for Congress."

[3] Homeland Security, "Fact Sheet: Protecting The Nation From Foreign Terrorist Entry To The United States," January 29, 2017, https://www.dhs.gov/archive/news/2017/01/29/fact-sheet-protecting-nation-foreign-terrorist-entry-united-states.

[4] Gregory Smith, "Most white evangelicals approve of Trump travel prohibition and express concerns about extremism," Pew Research Center, February 27, 2017, https://www.pewresearch.org/short-reads/2017/02/27/most-white-evangelicals-approve-of-trump-travel-prohibition-and-express-concerns-about-extremism/.

[5] Adam Liptak and Michael D. Shear, "Trump's Travel Ban Is Upheld by Supreme Court," *The New York Times*, June 26, 2018, https://www.nytimes.com/2018/06/26/us/politics/supreme-court-trump-travel-ban.html.

[6] The Supreme Court ruled in June of 2020 that Trump's termination of DACA should be vacated. See "Supreme Court Overturns Trump Administration's Termination of DACA," National Immigration Law Center, June 22, 2020, https://www.nilc.org/issues/daca/alert-supreme-court-overturns-trump-administrations-termination-of-daca/.

[7] Kristinova Justimbaste, "Donald Trump Mexico Wall News: Democrats Reject Proposals," *The Christian Post*, October 10, 2017, https://www.christianpost.com/trends/donald-trump-mexico-wall-news-democrats-reject-proposals.html. Congress approved most of Trump's requests, but for less money and new judges and prosecutors than he requested.

[8] Sarah Pulliam Bailey, "Trump's 'shithole' comments have enraged many. But some evangelical leaders still back him," *The Washington Post*, January 12, 2018, https://www.washingtonpost.com/news/acts-of-faith/wp/2018/01/12/trumps-shithole-comments-have-enraged-many-but-some-evangelical-leaders-still-back-him/.

[9] Eli Watkins and Abby Phillip, "Trump decries immigrants from 'shithole countries' coming to U.S.," *CNN*, January 12, 2018, https://www.cnn.com/2018/01/11/politics/immigrants-shithole-countries-trump/index.html.

[10] Stoyan Zalmov, "U.S. Catholic Bishops Urge Immediate Immigration Reform Action Before Congress Recesses in August," *The Christian Post*, May 30, 2014, https://www.christianpost.com/news/us-catholic-bishops-urge-immediate-immigration-reform-action-before-congress-recesses-in-august.html.

[11] Zalmov, "U.S. Catholic Bishops."

[12] Benge Nsenduluka, "Obama's Executive Order Will Authorize Work Permits for 5 Million Illegals; Immigration Plan is 'Unconstitutional' Top Republicans Say," *The Christian Post*, November 20, 2014, https://www.christianpost.com/news/obamas-executive-order-will-authorize-work-permits-for-5-million-illegals-immigration-plan-is-unconstitutional-top-republicans-say.html; and Stoyan Zaimov, "Obama Bypasses Congress on Immigration Reform: 5M Illegal Immigrants Given Temp Legal Status But No Pathway to Citizenship," *The Christian Post*, November 21, 2014, https://www.christianpost.com/news/obama-bypasses-congress-on-immigration-reform-5m-illegal-immigrants-given-temp-legal-status-but-no-pathway-to-citizenship.html.

[13] Phyllis Schlafly, "Immigration Handbook for Congressional Republicans: Courtesy of Sen. Jeff Sessions," *The Christian Post*, February 3, 2015, https://www.christianpost.com/news/immigration-handbook-for-congressional-republicans-courtesy-of-sen-jeff-sessions.html.

[14] Dan Delzell, "Immigration Plus Law and Order Make America Great," *The Christian Post*, July 7, 2016, https://www.christianpost.com/news/immigration-plus-law-and-order-made-america-great.html.

[15] Delzell, "Immigration Plus Law and Order."

[16] Delzell, "Immigration Plus Law and Order."

[17] Kristinova Justimbaste, "Immigration Reform: Trump Calls for a Law Restricting Federal Assistance," *The Christian Post*, June 28, 2017, https://www.christianpost.com/trends/immigration-reform-news-2017-trump-calls-for-a-law-restricting-federal-assistance.html.

[18] Samuel Smith, "5 Things You Need to Know About DACA and What Happens Next," *The Christian Post*, September 7, 2017, https://www.christianpost.com/news/5-things-you-need-to-know-about-daca-what-happens-next.html.

[19] Selwyn Duke, "Take DACA? No, Leave I.T.: We Already Granted Amnesty to Illegals," *The Christian Post*, January 10, 2018, https://www.christianpost.com/voice/take-daca-no-leave-it-we-already-granted-amnesty-to-illegals.html.

[20] Duke, "Take DACA? No, Leave I.T."

[21] To learn more about President Trump's various statements about the

Dreamers and *Breitbart News*'s anti-immigration stance, see Callum Borchers, "Why Breitbart's shot at 'Amnesty Don' is Significant," *The Washington Post*, January 25, 2018, https://www.washingtonpost.com/news/the-fix/wp/2018/01/25/why-breitbarts-shot-at-amnesty-don-is-significant/.

[22] Jonathan Wilson-Hargrove, "The Immigration Debate is a Moral Crisis," *The Christian Post*, February 9, 2018, https://www.christianpost.com/voice/the-immigration-debate-is-a-moral-crisis.html.

[23] Wilson-Hargrove, "The Immigration Debate."

[24] Wilson-Hargrove, "The Immigration Debate."

[25] Greg Chen, "The President's Cuts to Legal Immigration are Dangerous," *The Christian Post*, February 9, 2018, https://www.christianpost.com/voice/the-presidents-cuts-to-legal-immigration-are-dangerous.html.

[26] Chen, "The President's Cuts to Legal Immigration."

[27] See, https://www.christianitytoday.com/ct/topics/r/refugees/?start=256.

[28] Timothy C. Morgan, "1,180 Churches Help World Relief Resettle Refugees at Record Rate," *Christianity Today*, October 20, 2016, https://www.christianitytoday.com/news/2016/october/1180-churches-World-relief-resettle-refugees-record-rate.html.

[29] Morgan, "1,180 Churches Help World Relief."

[30] Morgan, "1,180 Churches Help World Relief."

[31] See, for instance, "Obama letting in Muslim immigrants, not Christians," *The Horn News*, December 1, 2015, https://thehornnews.com/obama-letting-in-muslim-immigrants-not-christians/.

[32] Jeremy Weber, "Why Tim Keller, Max Lucado, and Hundreds of Evangelical Leaders Oppose Trump's Refugee Ban," *Christianity Today*, February 10, 2017, https://www.christianitytoday.com/news/2017/february/why-tim-keller-max-lucado-evangelicals-trump-refugee-ban.html.

[33] Kate Shellnutt, "Missionaries Dreamed of This Muslim Moment. Trump's Travel Ban May End It," *Christianity Today*, March 20, 2017, https://www.christianitytoday.com/news/2017/march/missionaries-muslim-moment-trump-travel-ban.html.

[34] Kate Shellnutt, "Trump's Revised Refugee Ban Won't Prioritize Persecuted Christians," *Christianity Today*, March 8, 2017, https://www.christianitytoday.com/news/2017/march/trump-revised-refugee-travel-ban-persecuted-christians.html.

[35] Kate Shellnutt, "Refugee Ban Forces World Relief to Lay Off 140 Staff," *Christianity Today*, February 15, 2017, https://www.christianitytoday.com/news/2017/march/trump-revised-refugee-travel-ban-persecuted-christians.html.

[36] Kate Shellnutt, "Max Lucado, Beth Moore, and Hundreds of Evangelicals Call for Immigration Reform . . . Again," *Christianity Today*, February 7, 2018, https://www.christianitytoday.com/news/2018/february/max-lucado-beth-moore-evangelicals-immigration-dreamers-ref.html.

[37] Shellnutt, "Max Lucado, Beth Moore, and Hundreds of Evangelicals."

[38] Shellnutt, "Max Lucado, Beth Moore, and Hundreds of Evangelicals."

[39] Shellnutt, "Max Lucado, Beth Moore, and Hundreds of Evangelicals."

[40] Kent Annan, "Why We Need to Talk about Trump's Haiti Remarks," *Christianity Today*, January 12, 2018, https://www.christianitytoday.com/ct/2018/january-web-only/trump-remark-immigration-haiti.html.

[41] Annan, "Why We Need to Talk about Trump's Haiti Remarks."

[42] Mark Galli, "The Church's Biggest Challenge in 2017," *Christianity Today*,

June 7, 2017, https://www.christianitytoday.com/ct/2017/june/trump-white-evangelicals-churchs-biggest-challenge-2017.html.

[43] Jim Wallis, "We were Strangers Once, too," *Sojourners*, February 2015, 7.

[44] Jim Wallis, "We've Got a Month Until Inauguration Day. Here's What We Can Do Right Now," *Sojourners*, December 15, 2016, at https://sojo.net/articles/weve-got-month-until-inauguration-day-heres-what-we-can-do-right-now.

[45] Wallis, "We've Got a Month Until Inauguration Day."

[46] Jim Wallis, "Matthew 25 in the Age of Trump," *Red Letter Christians*, January 6, 2017, https://www.redletterchristians.org/matthew-25-in-the-age-of-trump/.

[47] Wallis, "Matthew 25 in the Age of Trump."

[48] Jim Wallis, "The Ban Is Not About National Security," *Sojourners*, January 31, 2017, https://sojo.net/articles/ban-not-about-national-security.

[49] Josephine McKenna, "Christian Refugees Will Suffer from Trump Ban, say Iraqi Catholic Leaders," *Sojourners*, January 31, 2017, https://sojo.net/articles/christian-refugees-will-suffer-trump-ban-say-iraqi-catholic-leaders.

[50] See, for example, Jessica Cobian, "Undocumented and Unashamed: DACA Recipients Share Their Stories," *Sojourners*, September 6, 2017, https://sojo.net/articles/undocumented-and-unashamed-daca-recipients-share-their-stories.

[51] Jon Huckins, "The Wall, the President, and the People," *Sojourners*, March 14, 2018, https://sojo.net/articles/wall-president-and-people.

[52] Huckins, "The Wall, the President, and the People."

[53] Jim Wallis, "Explicit Racism From the Oval Office—And Our Response," *Sojourners*, January 13, 2018, https://sojo.net/articles/explicit-racism-oval-office-and-our-response.

[54] See David Beltran, "I'm From a 'Shithole' Country. Here's What I Wish Americans Knew," *Sojourners*, January 12, 2018, https://sojo.net/articles/im-shithole-country-heres-what-i-wish-americans-knew.

[55] Marvin Olasky, "Back to the Future," *World*, August 18, 2016, https://wng.org/articles/back-to-the-future-1617305568.

[56] Joel Belz, "Using the source material," *World*, February 15, 2017, https://wng.org/articles/using-the-source-material-1617304775.

[57] Belz, "Using the source material."

[58] Belz, "Using the source material."

[59] Mindy Belz, "Making Haste," *World*, posted February 2, 2017. https://wng.org/articles/making-haste-1620610569.

[60] Belz, "Making Haste."

[61] Belz, "Making Haste."

[62] Evan Wilt, "Evangelical Leaders urge Trump to reconsider refugee order," *World*, February 9, 2017, https://wng.org/sift/evangelical-leaders-urge-trump-to-reconsider-refugee-order-1617251438.

[63] Wilt, "Evangelical Leaders urge Trump."

[64] Wilt, "Evangelical Leaders urge Trump."

[65] Wilt, "Evangelical Leaders urge Trump."

[66] Wilt, "Evangelical Leaders urge Trump."

[67] Marvin Olasky, "Here to stay?" *World*, 32:19 October 14, 2017, 8–9.

[68] Olasky, "Here to Stay," 9.

[69] Evan Wilt, "Evangelicals diverge on Trump's Haiti comments," *World*, January 12, 2018, https://.wng.org/content/evangelicals-diverge-on-trumps-haiti-comments.

[70] Wilt, "Evangelicals diverge on Trump's Haiti comments."

[71] Wilt, "Evangelicals diverge on Trump's Haiti comments."

[72] Mindy Belz, "Not Just Noise," *World*, January 17, 2018, https://wng.org/articles/not-just-noise-1617302702.

[73] Belz, "Not Just Noise."

[74] Michael Reneau, "Evangelicals' Immigration Tension," *The Dispatch*, March 3, 2024, https://thedispatch.com/article/evangelicals-immigration-tension/.

[75] Ken Chitwood, "Evangelicals Want Immigration Reform. Here's Why It's Unlikely They'll Get It," *Sojourners*, April 8, 2024, https://sojo.net/articles/evangelicals-want-immigration-reform-here-s-why-its-unlikely-theyll-get-it.

Chapter 4
Build That Wall? Evangelicals, Trump, and
the Southern Border Controversy

[1] Sophia Lee, "Who's Funding the Migrant Caravans?" *World*, April 15, 2019, https://wng.org/articles/whos-funding-the-migrant-caravans-1617298710.

[2] Lee, "Who's Funding the Migrant Caravans?"

[3] Lee, "Who's Funding the Migrant Caravans?"

[4] *The New York Times* presented a helpful timeline of candidate and President Trump's statements about the wall he wanted built to stop illegal immigration. While he insisted that Mexico would pay, they never did reimburse the U.S. for the portions of the wall that were eventually constructed. See Ron Nixon and Linda Qiu, "Trump's Evolving Words on the Wall," *The New York Times*, January 18, 2018, https://www.nytimes.com/2018/01/18/us/politics/trump-border-wall-immigration.html.

[5] *Washington Post* columnist Greg Sargent synthesizes the opinion polling from the Public Religion Research Institute showing increasing support for the wall from April 2016 to September 2018. By that September date, two-thirds of White evangelicals favored the building of the border wall. See Greg Sargent, "The walls around Trump are crumbling. Evangelicals may be his last resort," *The Washington Post*, January 2, 2019, https://www.washingtonpost.com/opiions/2019/01/02/walls-around-trump-are-crumbling-evangelicals-may-be-his-last-resort/.

[6] See Julie Hirschfeld Davis, "Separated at the Border From Their Parents: In Six Weeks, 1,995 Children," *The New York Times*, June 15, 2018, https://www.nytimes.com/2018/06/15/us/politics/trump-immigration-separation-border.html.

[7] Julie Zauzmer and Keith McMillan, "Session cites Bible passage used to defend slavery in defense of separating immigrant families," *The Washington Post*, June 15, 2018, https://www.washingtonpost.com/news/acts-of-faith/wp/2018/06/14/jeff-sessions-points-to-the-bible-in-defense-of-separating-immigrant-families/

[8] Zauzmer and McMillan, "Session cites Bible passage."

[9] Vianne Llagan, "Donald Trump proposes to cut TSA, Coast Guard Budget to Build Mexican Wall," *The Christian Post*, March 8, 2017, https://www.christianpost.com/trends/donald-trump-proposes-to-cut-tsa-coast-guard-budget-to-build-mexican-wall.html.

[10] Edward Leano, "Donald Trump Immigration Reform: President Wants $1billion for 62 miles of Border Wall," *The Christian Post*, March 29, 2017, https://www.christianpost.com/trends/donald-trump-immigration-reform-news-president-wants-1-billion-for-62-miles-of-border-wall.html.

[11] Clarissa Partosa, "Trump's Border Wall News: Proposed Bill Imposes Tax on Remittances to Fund Structure," *The Christian Post*, May 29, 2017, https://www.christianpost.com/trends/trumps-border-wall-news-proposed-bill-imposes-tax-on-remittances-to-fund-structure.html.

[12] Edward Leano, "Donald Trump Border Wall News: Environmental Regula-tions Waived for Project," *The Christian Post*, September 14, 2017, https://www.christianpost.com/trends/donald-trump-border-wall-news-environmental-regulations-waived-for-project.html.

[13] Selwyn Duke "We Need to Repeal the 1965 Immigration Act," *The Christian Post*, Posted Jan. 17, 2017, https://www.christianpost.com/voice/we-need-repeal-the-1965-immigration-act.html. See also, https://www.migrationpolicy.org/article/fifty-years-1965-immigration-and-nationality-act-continues-reshape-united-states.

[14] David Ruzicka, "Top 10 Ways the Bible Opposes Illegal Immigration," *The Christian Post*, December 15, 2017, https://sojo.net/articles/christian-refugees-will-suffer-trump-ban-say-iraqi-catholic-leaders.

[15] Ruzicka, "Top 10 Ways the Bible Opposes Illegal Immigration."

[16] Ruzicka, "Top 10 Ways the Bible Opposes Illegal Immigration."

[17] Marvin G. Thompson, "How the Church Must Respond in the Wake of Sessions' Romans 13 Claim," *The Christian Post*, June 21, 2018, https://www.christianpost.com/voice/how-the-church-must-respond-sessions-romans-13-claim.html.

[18] Brandon Showalter, "AG Sessions: Using Romans 13 to Defend 'Zero Tolerance' Immigration Policy Not 'Extreme,'" *The Christian Post*, June 24, 2018, https://www.christianpos t.com/news/attorney-general-jeff-sessions-romans-13-defend-zero-tolerance-immigration-policy-not-extreme.html.

[19] Showalter, "AG Sessions: Using Romans 13." See also, Jenna Browder, "'I Don't Think It Was an Extreme Position I Took': Jeff Sessions on the Bible, Immigration and His Critics," *CBN News*, June 21, 2018, https://www2.cbn.com/news/politics/i-dont-think-it-was-extreme-position-i-took-jeff-sessions-bible-immigration-and-his.

[20] Tony Perkins, "Trump's Opponents Attack Illegal Immigration Border Policy, but Will They Work to Reform the System?" *The Christian Post*, June 16, 2018, https://www.christianpost.com/voice/trumps-opponents-attack-illegal-immigration-border-policy-but-will-they-work-to-reform-the-system.html.

[21] Perkins, "Trump's Opponents Attack Illegal Immigration."

[22] Perkins, "Trump's Opponents Attack Illegal Immigration."

[23] Michael Brown, "What am I missing when it comes to immigration?" *The Christian Post*, December 31, 2019, https://www.christianpost.com/voice/what-am-i-missing-when-it-comes-to-immigration.html.

[24] Brown, "What am I missing when it comes to immigration?"

[25] Brown, "What am I missing when it comes to immigration?"

[26] Brown, "What am I missing when it comes to immigration?"

[27] Napp Nazworth, "White evangelicals support immigration more when active in church and theologically conservative," *The Christian Post*, January 17, 2019, https://www.christianpost.com/news/white-evangelicals-support-immigration-more-when-active-in-church-theologically-conservative.html. Nazworth's article incorporates the findings from Ruth Melkonian-Hoover and Lyman Kellstedt, *Evangelicals and Immigration: Fault Lines Among the Faithful* (New York: Palgrave Macmillan, 2018).

[28] Samuel Smith, "Evangelical leaders call on Christians to take on 'biblical view' of immigration, love one's neighbor," *The Christian Post*, April 29, 2019, https://www.

christianpost.com/news/evangelical-leaders-call-on-christians-to-take-on-biblical-view-of-immigration-love-ones-neighbor.html.

[29] The Evangelical Immigration Table, "Thinking Biblically About Immigrants & Immigration Reform," 2019, https://evangelicalimmigrationtable.com/wp-content/up-loads/2019/04/Thinking-Biblically-about-Immigrants-Immigration-Reform-E-Book.pdf, V.

[30] The Evangelical Immigration Table, "Thinking Biblically," 6.

[31] Octavio Javier Esqueda, "What's Your Immigration Status? Divine," *Christianity Today*, September 6, 2017, https://www.christianitytoday.com/ct/2017/september-web-only/jesus-divine-immigration-status-daca.html.

[32] Kate Shellnutt, "World Refugee Day 2018: 'Welcoming the Stranger' Meets 'Zero Tolerance,'" *Christianity Today*, June 14, 2018, https://www.christianitytoday.com/news/2018/june/world-refugee-day-2018-us-asylum-border-welcoming-stranger.html.

[33] Shellnutt, "World Refugee Day 2018."

[34] See Hannah Hartig, "Republicans turn more negative toward refugees as number admitted to U.S. plummets," Pew Research Center, May 24, 2018, https://www.pewresearch.org/short-reads/2018/05/24/republicans-turn-more-negative-toward-refugees-as-number-admitted-to-u-s-plummets/.

[35] Griffin Paul Jackson, "The Global Refugee Crisis Hit a Record High. The U.S. Welcome for the Persecuted Is at a Record Low," *Christianity Today*, June 20, 2019, https://www.christianitytoday.com/news/2019/june/WORLD-refugee-day-uscirf-resettlement-persecution-us.html.

[36] Kate Shellnutt, "Evangelical Advocates Feel the Sting of More Trump Refugee Cuts," *Christianity Today*, September 27, 2019, https://www.christianitytoday.com/news/2019/september/evangelical-trump-refugee-resettlement-cuts-2020.html.

[37] Jim Wallis, "Christians Can Stop Trump's Wall," *Sojourners*, April 26, 2017, https://sojo.net/articles/christians-can-stop-trump-s-wall.

[38] Wallis, "Christians Can Stop Trump's Wall."

[39] Wallis, "Christians Can Stop Trump's Wall."

[40] Jim Wallis, "A Combination of Cruelty and Ineptitude," *Sojourners*, September/October 2018, https://sojo.net/magazine/septemberoctober-2018/combination-cruelty-and-ineptitude.

[41] Wallis, "A Combination of Cruelty and Ineptitude."

[42] Marvin Olasky, "View from the Texas borderlands," *World*, December 16, 2016, https://wng.org/articles/view-from-the-texas-borderlands-1620600132.

[43] For more on solutions journalism, see the Solutions Journalism Network website, https://www.solutionsjournalism.org/.

[44] Andrew Hanchett, Sarah Holcomb, Hayley Schoeppler, and Anna Smith, "A Midwest welcome," *World*, August 19, 2017, 50–53.

[45] Hanchett, Holcomb, Schoeppler, and Smith, "A Midwest welcome."

[46] Rob Holmes, "Trump, lawmakers respond to immigration outrage," *World*, June 20, 2018, https://wng.org/roundups/trump-lawmakers-respond-to-immigration-outrage-1618208675. A few days later, editor Marvin Olasky added a context piece acknowledging that the separation policy was "bad," but reminding readers that Christians have advocated for fair immigration for years and blaming mainstream media for using misleading photos and rhetoric in their stories rather than providing readers with the history of immigration in the U.S. He also claimed that Barack Obama's DACA order in 2012 created a backlash against it that led to Donald Trump's election

four years later. See "Every 40 Years," *World*, July 4, 2018, https://wng.org/articles/every-40-years-1617301536.

[47] Holmes, "Trump, lawmakers respond."

[48] Marvin Olasky, "Making immigration work," *World*, November 3, 2018, https://wng.org/roundups/making-immigration-work-1617227090.

[49] Olasky, "Making immigration work."

[50] Harvest Prude, "Left Behind," *World*, March 28, 2019, https://wng.org/articles/left-behind-1617298839.

[51] Prude, "Left Behind."

[52] Michael Gryboski, "4 Christian Reactions to Trump's Executive Order Ending Family Separation Policy," *The Christian Post*, June 21, 2018, https://www.christian-post.com/news/4-christian-reactions-trumps-executive-order-ending-family-separa-tion-policy.html?page=1.

[53] Gryboski, "4 Christian Reactions."

[54] Gryboski, "4 Christian Reactions."

[55] Gryboski, "4 Christian Reactions."

[56] John Stonestreet and Roberto Rivera, "Trump's empty noise on religious freedom and refugees," *The Christian Post*, April 15, 2019, https://www.chris-tianpost.com/voices/trumps-empty-noise-on-religious-freedom-and-refugees.html?clickType=link-related-articles.

[57] Stonestreet and Rivera, "Trump's empty noise."

[58] Stonestreet and Rivera, "Trump's empty noise."

[59] Bekah McNeel, "Evangelicals Can Help at the Border. They Just Can't Do It Alone," *Christianity Today*, July 1, 2019, https://www.christianitytoday.com/news/chan-nel/utilities/print.html?type=article&id=161728.

[60] McNeel, "Evangelicals Can Help at the Border."

[61] Lee, "Who's Funding the Migrant Caravans."

[62] Sophia Lee, "One Christian's Quest to Change the Way We See Immigra-tion," *Christianity Today*, October 23, 2023, https://www.christianitytoday.com/ct/2023/november/sami-dipasquale-change-way-we-see-immigration-el-paso-abara.html.

Chapter 5
Charlottesville and the Problem of Christian Nationalism

[1] More information about chants at the rally can be found in David Neiwert's "When White Nationalists Chant Their Weird Slogans, What Do They Mean?" *Southern Pov-erty Law Center*, October 10, 2017, https://www.splcenter.org/hatewatch/2017/10/10/when-white-nationalists-chant-their-weird-slogans-what-do-they-mean.

[2] Rosie Gray, "Trump Defends White-Nationalist Protesters: 'Some Very Fine People on Both Sides,'" *The Atlantic*, August 15, 2017, https://www.theatlantic.com/politics/archive/2017/08/trump-defends-white-nationalist-protesters-some-very-fine-people-on-both-sides/537012/.

[3] Recent books on Christian nationalism include Andrew L. Whitehead and Sam-uel L. Perry, *Taking America Back for God: Christian Nationalism in the United States* (New York: Oxford University Press, 2020); Phillip S. Gorski and Samuel L. Perry, *The*

Flag and the Cross: White Christian Nationalism and the Threat to American Democracy (New York: Oxford University Press, 2022); Paul D. Miller, *The Religion of American Greatness: What's Wrong with Christian Nationalism* (Westmont, IL: InterVarsity Academic, 2022); Jim Wallis, *The False White Gospel: Rejecting Christian Nationalism, Reclaiming True Faith, and Refounding Democracy* (New York: St. Martin's Essentials, 2024); Richard T. Hughes, *Myths America Lives By*, 2nd ed. (Champaign, IL: University of Illinois Press, 2018); and Richard T. Hughes and Christina Littlefield, *Christian America and the Kingdom of God: White Christian Nationalism from the Puritans through January 6, 2021* (Champaign, IL: University of Illinois Press, 2025).

[4] Michael Gryboski, "5 Reactions to the Violence in Charlottesville," *The Christian Post*, August 14, 2017, at https://www.christianpost.com/news/5-reactions-to-the-violence-in-charlottesville.html?page=5.

[5] About a year after the press conference, Trump allegedly told *Washington Post* reporter Bob Woodward that he regretted condemning the neo-Nazis at the rally. See Michael Gryboski, "Trump Said He Regretted Condemning Neo-Nazis, New Bob Woodward Book Claims," *The Christian Post*, September 4, 2018, https://www.christianpost.com/news/trump-regretted-condemning-neo-nazis-new-bob-woodward-book.html.

[6] Brandon Showalter, "Pastor AR Bernard Leaves Trump's Evangelical Advisory Board Citing 'Deepening Conflict in Values,'" *The Christian Post*, August 19, 2017, https://www.christianpost.com/news/pastor-a-r-bernard-leaves-trumps-evangelical-advisory-board-citing-deepening-conflict-in-values.html.

[7] Stoyan Zaimov, "Tim Keller Warns Christians 'Traditional Values' White Nationalists Could Be in Their Circles," *The Christian Post*, August 16, 2017, https://www.christianpost.com/news/tim-keller-warns-christians-traditional-values-white-nationalists-could-be-in-their-circles.html.

[8] Zaimov, "Tim Keller Warns Christians."

[9] Zaimov, "Tim Keller Warns Christians."

[10] David Barton, *The Myth of Separation* (Aledo, TX: WallBuilder Press, 1992); see also David Barton, *Original Intent: The Courts, the Constitution, & Religion* (Aledo, TX: WallBuilders Press, 2004).

[11] Time Staff, "The 25 Most Influential Evangelicals in America," *Time*, February 7, 2005, https://content.time.com/time/specials/packages/article/0,28804,1993235_1993243_19932 61,00.html.

[12] See Justin Taylor, "Christian History: How David Barton Is Doing It Wrong," The Gospel Coalition (blog), May 12, 2017, https://www.thegospelcoalition.org/blogs/evangelical-history/christian-history-why-david-barton-is-doing-it-wrong/; "David Barton," Southern Poverty Law Center, https://www.splcenter.org/fighting-hate/extremist-files/individual/david-barton; and Thomas S. Kidd, "The David Barton controversy," *World*, August 7, 2012, https://wng.org/articles/the-david-barton-controversy-1617306526.

[13] See, for instance, Samuel Smith, "Robert Jeffress: There Has Been 'Failure' on Part of the Church to Denounce Racism," *The Christian Post*, August 17, 2017, https://www.christianpost.com/news/robert-jeffress-failure-church-denounce-racism.html; and Brandon Showalter, "Greg Laurie Condemns White Supremacy at SoCal Harvest: America Needs 'Spiritual Awakening' After Charlottesville," *The Christian Post*, August 20, 2017, https://www.christianpost.com/news/greg-laurie-condemns-white-supremacy-socal-harvest-america-needs-spiritual-awakening-charlottesville.html.

[14] Richard Cizik, "Reject Anti-Muslim Hate Groups After Charlottesville," *The*

Christian Post, August 29, 2017, https://www.christianpost.com/news/reject-anti-muslim-hate-groups-charlottesville.html.

[15] Cizik, "Reject Anti-Muslim Hate Groups."

[16] CP Editors, "Beware Mr. President: Your Need to Condemn White Supremacy Has Just Begun; They Have Declared War," *The Christian Post*, August 15, 2017, https://www.christianpost.com/news/beware-mr-president-your-need-to-condemn-white-supremacy-has-just-begun-they-have-declared-war.html.

[17] Leonardo Blair, "Franklin Graham Defends Trump, Blames Satan for Charlottesville Unrest," *The Christian Post*, August 14, 2017, https://www.christianpost.com/search?s=Franklin +Graham+Defends+Trump.

[18] Ryan Bomberger, "Charlottesville, Chaos, and Confederate Statues," *The Christian Post*, August 18, 2017, https://www.christianpost.com/news/franklin-graham-defends-trump-blames-satan-for-charlottesville-unrest.html.

[19] Bomberger, "Charlottesville, Chaos, and Confederate Statues."

[20] Rachel Alexander, "Charlottesville: Fueling Race Riots One of the Left's Cleverest Tactics," *The Christian Post*, August 16, 2017, https://www.christianpost.com/news/charlottesville-fueling-race-riots-lefts-cleverest-tactics.html.

[21] Kate Shellnutt, "Evangelical Advisers Condemn Charlottesville Rally More Than Trump," *Christianity Today*, August 13, 2017, https://www.christianitytoday.com/news/2017/august/trump-evangelical-advisers-charlottesville-white-supremacis.html.

[22] Theon E. Hill, "The Centuries-Old Habits of the Heart," *Christianity Today*, August 18, 2017, https://www.christianitytoday.com/ct/2017/august-web-only/centuries-old-habits-of-heart.html.

[23] Clifton Clarke and Jarvis J. Williams, "How Christians Can Combat Racism Theologically After Charlottesville," *Christianity Today*, August 21, 2017, https://www.christianitytoday.com/ct/2017/august-web-only/christians-combat-racism-theologically-charlottesville.html.

[24] Clarke and Williams, "How Christians Can Combat Racism."

[25] Ed Stetzer, "On Christians Unable to Critique President Trump: Loyalty and the Rorschach Test," *Christianity Today*, August 14, 2017, https://www.christianitytoday.com/ed stetzer/2017/august/exposing-loyalty-rorschach-test-of-charlottesville-for-evan.html.

[26] Mark Galli, "Confession of Racism Sin," *Christianity Today*, November 27, 2018, https://www.christianitytoday.com/ct/2018/december/where-we-got-it-wrong-segregation-apology.html.

[27] Galli, "Confession of Racism Sin."

[28] Galli, "Confession of Racism Sin."

[29] Galli, "Confession of Racism Sin."

[30] Paul H. DeVries, "Did CT Fail Its Readers on Civil Rights?" *Christianity Today*, August 19, 2019, https://www.christianitytoday.com/ct/2019/august-web-only/did-ct-fail-its-readers-on-civil-rights.html.

[31] Jim Wallis, "What Your Church Can Do After Charlottesville: 5 Steps Forward," *Sojourners*, August 24, 2017, https://sojo.net/articles/what-your-church-can-do-after-charlottesville-5-steps-forward.

[32] Wallis, "What Your Church Can Do."

[33] Jim Wallis, "Who Are We? Hate and Love in America," *Sojourners*, September 14, 2017, https://sojo.net/articles/who-are-we-hate-and-love-america.

[34] Jacob L. Wright, "What Christian Nationalists Get Wrong About the Bible,"

Sojourners, November 22, 2023, https://sojo.net/articles/what-christian-nationalists-get-wrong-about-bible.

35 Wright, "What Christian Nationalists Get Wrong."

36 Mitchell Atencio, "Are You Accidentally a Christian Nationalist?" *Sojourners*, June 17, 2024, https://sojo.net/articles/reconstruct/are-you-accidentally-christian-nationalist.

37 Marvin Olasky, "We, the People," *World*, August 14, 2017, https://world.wng.org/2017/08/we_the_people.

38 Olasky, "We, the People."

39 Olasky, "We, the People."

40 Olasky, "We, the People."

41 Olasky, "We, the People."

42 Jamie Dean, "Alternative evils," *World*, August 29, 2017, https://world.wng.org/2017/08/alternative_evils.

43 Mitchell Atencio, "What Does 'White Christian Nationalism' Even Mean, Anyway?" *Sojourners*, September 8, 2022, https://sojo.net/articles/what-does-white-christian-nationalism-even-mean-anyway.

44 Atencio, "What Does 'White Christian Nationalism' Even Mean?"

45 "8 in 10 Americans say Religion is Losing Influence in Public Life," Pew Research Center, March 15, 2024, https://www.pewresearch.org/religion/2024/03/15/8-in-10-americans-say-religion-is-losing-influence-in-public-life/.

46 Harvest Prude, "White Evangelicals Want Christian Influence, Not a 'Christian Nation,'" *Christianity Today*, March 15, 2024, https://www.christianitytoday.com/news/2024/march/religion-public-life-evangelicals-pew-research-center.html.

Chapter 6
George Floyd and the Continuing Debate Over
Racism in the United States

1 Richard Land, "Ask Dr. Land: What do you think about George Floyd's murder and the aftermath," *The Christian Post*, June 5, 2020, https://www.christianpost.com/news/ask-dr-land-what-do-you-think-about-george-floyds-murder-and-the-aftermath.html.

2 Land, "Ask Dr. Land."

3 Ron Sider, "White evangelicals, racism, and George Floyd: Our hour of decision," *The Christian Post*, June 6, 2020, https://www.christianpost.com/voices/white-evangelicals-racism-and-george-floyd-our-hour-of-decision.html.

4 Sider, "White evangelicals, racism, and George Floyd."

5 Leonardo Blair, "Why Speaking Out Against the Killing of George Floyd is a Pro-Life Issue," *The Christian Post*, May 29, 2020, https://www.christianpost.com/voices/why-speaking-out-against-the-killing-of-george-floyd-is-a-pro-life-issue.html.

6 Jeannie Ortega Law, "Tony Evans, Joel Osteen, Kari Job join Blackout Tuesday in Solidarity Against Injustice," *The Christian Post*, June 3, 2020, https://www.christianpost.com/news/tony-evans-joel-osteen-kari-jobe-join-blackout-tuesday-in-solidarity-against-injustice.htm.

7 Law, "Tony Evans, Joel Osteen, Kari Job."

8 Michael Brown, "4 Reasons the race riots do far more harm than good," *The*

Christian Post, June 1, 2020, https://www.christianpost.com/voices/4-reasons-the-race-riots-do-far-more-harm-than-good.html.

⁹ Dennis R. Edwards, "The Revolution Will Not Be Videoed," *Christianity Today*, May 29, 2020, https://www.christianitytoday.com/ct/2020/may-web-only/dennis-edwards-george-floyd-revolution-will-not-be-videoed.html.

¹⁰ Edwards, "The Revolution Will Not Be Videoed."

¹¹ Edwards, "The Revolution Will Not Be Videoed."

¹² Kate Shellnutt, "George Floyd Left a Legacy in Houston," *Christianity Today*, May 28, 2020, https://www.christianitytoday.com/news/2020/may/george-floyd-ministry-houston-third-ward-church.html.

¹³ Daniel Silliman, "George Floyd Protests Mark a Turning Point for Minneapolis Evangelicals," *Christianity Today*, June 2, 2020, https://www.christianitytoday.com/news/2020/june/george-floyd-protests-minneapolis-evangelicals-cleanup.html.

¹⁴ Silliman, "George Floyd Protests Mark a Turning Point."

¹⁵ Silliman, "George Floyd Protests Mark a Turning Point."

¹⁶ Timothy Dalrymple, "Justice Too Long Delayed," *Christianity Today*, June 10, 2020, https://www.christianitytoday.com/ct/2020/june-web-only/justice-too-long-delayed.html.

¹⁷ Dalrymple, "Justice Too Long Delayed."

¹⁸ Dalrymple, "Justice Too Long Delayed."

¹⁹ Dalrymple, "Justice Too Long Delayed."

²⁰ Jonathan Walton, "The Perils of White American Folk Religion," *Christianity Today*, July 17, 2020, https://www.christianitytoday.com/ct/2020/july-web-only/perils-of-white-american-folk-religion.html.

²¹ Walton, "The Perils of White American Folk Religion."

²² Walton, "The Perils of White American Folk Religion."

²³ Michelle Reyes, "Scripture Calls Churches to Build a Just Society. Here's How," *Christianity Today*, July 31, 2020, https://www.christianitytoday.com/ct/2020/july-web-only/scripture-calls-churches-to-build-just-society-heres-how.html.

²⁴ Reyes, "Scripture Calls Churches to Build a Just Society."

²⁵ Reyes, "Scripture Calls Churches to Build a Just Society."

²⁶ Charlie Dobson, "Hashtags Hit Too Close to Home," *Christianity Today*, July 1, 2020, https://www.christianitytoday.com/ct/2020/july-web-only/police-shooting-brother-racism-white-person-sin-issue.html.

²⁷ Dobson, "Hashtags Hit Too Close to Home."

²⁸ Justin Giboney, "The Absence of Injustice is Not Justice," *Christianity Today*, September 11, 2020, https://www.christianitytoday.com/ct/2020/september-web-only/preach-what-you-practice.html.

²⁹ Christina Barland Edmondson, "The Shocking Necessity of Racist Violence," *Christianity Today*, October 9, 2020, at https://www.christianitytoday.com/ct/2020/october-web-only/shocking-necessity-of-racist-violence.html.

³⁰ Jamal-Dominique Hopkins, "Preach What You Practice," *Christianity Today*, September 18, 2020, https://www.christianitytoday.com/ct/2020/september-web-only/preach-what-you-practice.html.

³¹ Andrew Shaughnessy, "Portland is Still Protesting: Where Is the Church?" *Christianity Today*, August 12, 2020, https://www.christianitytoday.com/news/2020/august/portland-protests-pastors-church-black-lives-matter-justice.html.

³² Cameron Friend, "A Civil Rights Legacy: Inspired and Burdened by Their

History, Generations of African American Faithful Take Up the Work of Becoming a Beloved Community," *Christianity Today*, October 2020, https://www.christianitytoday.com/ct/2020/october/atlanta-black-church-king-center-legacy-history.html; Kathryn Freeman, "A Political Calling: The Biblical Call for Freedom for the Oppressed Led Atlanta Christians to Social Action," *Christianity Today*, October 2020, 44–47; Jacqueline J. Holness, "A Ministry of Reconciliation: In Continued Pursuit of Racial Justice, Atlanta's Church Leaders Preach and Partner Across Long-Standing Divides," *Christianity Today*, October 2020, 46–51; Terasha Burrell, "A New Economic Narrative: In the Capital of the New South, Faithful Black Entrepreneurs See Business as a Way to Bless Their Communities," *Christianity Today*, October 2020, 52–55.

[33] Kate Shellnutt, "Our October Issue: Atlanta's Black Church," *Christianity Today*, September 21, 2020, https://www.christianitytoday.com/ct/2020/october/our-october-issue-atlantas-black-church.html.

[34] "What are Police For?" *Christianity Today*, September 2020.

[35] Esau McCaulley, "Paul and the Police," *Christianity Today*, September 2020, 39.

[36] McCaulley, "Paul and the Police."

[37] Michael Lefebvre, "To Serve, Protect, and Redeem: An Old Testament Vision for Today's Police Force," *Christianity Today*, September 2020, 44.

[38] Lefebvre, "To Serve, Protect, and Redeem," 45.

[39] Adam Russell Taylor, "George Floyd Deserved to Breathe Free," *Sojourners*, May 27, 2020, https://sojo.net/articles/george-floyd-deserved-breathe-free.

[40] Taylor, "George Floyd Deserved to Breathe Free."

[41] Dante Stewart, "Black Rage in an Anti-Black World is a Spiritual Virtue," *Sojourners*, May 29, 2020, https://sojo.net/articles/black-rage-anti-black-world-spiritual-virtue.

[42] Marc Antoine Lavarin, "Instead of 'We Can No Longer Be Silent,' Try 'We Got It Wrong,'" *Sojourners*, June 10, 2020, https://sojo.net/articles/instead-we-can-no-longer-be-silent-try-we-got-it-wrong.

[43] Lavarin, "Instead of 'We Can No Longer Be Silent.'"

[44] Lavarin, "Instead of 'We Can No Longer Be Silent.'"

[45] Matthew L. Watley, "Don't Let Protest Method Distract from Protest Message," *Sojourners*, June 4, 2020, https://sojo.net/articles/dont-let-protest-method-distract-protest-message.

[46] Nguyên Thao Thi Nguyen, "You Can't Speak Up Now Without Owning Your Racist Past," *Sojourners*, June 10, 2020, https://sojo.net/articles/you-cant-speak-now-without-owning-your-racist-past.

[47] Jim Wallis and Adam Russel Taylor, "'A Change is Gonna Come': Reimagining Public Safety," *Sojourners*, June 11, 2020, https://sojo.net/articles/change-gonna-come-reimagining-public-safety.

[48] Jim Wallis, "A Kairos Moment," *Sojourners*, June 18, 2020, https://sojo.net/articles/kairos-moment.

[49] Chanequa Walker-Barnes, "#DefundthePolice Because They Won't Reform Themselves," *Sojourners*, June 16, 2020, at https://sojo.net/articles/defundthepolice-because-they-wont-reform-themselves.

[50] Kelly Brown Douglas, "A Christian Call for Reparations," *Sojourners*, July 2020, https://sojo.net/magazine/july-2020/christian-call-case-slavery-reparations-kelly-brown-douglas.

[51] Douglas, "A Christian Call for Reparations."

[52] Kyle Ziemnick, "Four Minneapolis police officers fired after man's death," *World*, May 26, 2020, https://wng.org/sift/four-minneapolis-police-officers-fired-after-mans-death-1617394281.

[53] Ziemnick, "Four Minneapolis police officers fired."

[54] Kyle Ziemnick, "Minneapolis man's death sparks violent protests," *World*, May 28, 2020, https://wng.org/sift/minneapolis-mans-death-sparks-violent-protests-1617394309.

[55] Kyle Ziemnick, "Police across America condemn Minneapolis officer," *World*, May 29, 2020, https://wng.org/sift/police-across-america-condemn-minneapolis-officer-1617394315.

[56] Sharon Dierberger, "George Floyd's search for a new start," *World*, May 30, 2020, https://wng.org/articles/george-floyds-search-for-a-new-start-1617297601. Out of the top 25 most-read stories in *World* magazine, Dierberger's piece was the 24th most read. At the same time, articles on the Coronovirus and sexual misconduct charges against the late evangelist Ravi Zacharias comprised the majority of the top 10 most-read articles. Mickey McLean, "*WORLD*'s Top 25 articles for 2020," *World*, https://wng.org/roundups/WORLDs-top-25-articles-for-2020-1617220321.

[57] Marvin Olasky, "Pastors vs. poachers," *World*, May 31, 2020, https://wng.org/articles/pastors-vs-poachers-1617297663.

[58] Olasky, "Pastors vs. poachers."

[59] Olasky, "Pastors vs. poachers."

[60] Sharon Dierberger, "Minneapolis churches pray for healing," *World*, May 31, 2020, https://wng.org/articles/minneapolis-churches-pray-for-healing-1617297609.

[61] Katie Gaultney, "Dallas riots leave volunteers, business to clean up the mess," *World*, May 31, 2020, https://wng.org/articles/dallas-riots-leave-volunteers-businesses-to-clean-up-the-mess-1617297638.

[62] Sophia Lee, "In Los Angeles protests, most want peace and some want fight," *World*, June 2, 2020, https://wng.org/articles/in-los-angeles-protests-most-want-peace-and-some-want-a-fight-1617297618.

[63] McKay Coppins, "The Christians Who Loved Trump's Stunt," *The Atlantic*, June 2, 2020, https://www.theatlantic.com/politics/archive/2020/06/trumps-biblical-spectacle-outside-st-johns-church/612529/.

[64] Mindy Belz "Religious liberty order no walk in the park for Trump," *World*, June 3, 2020, https://wng.org/articles/religious-liberty-order-no-walk-in-the-park-for-trump-1617297488.

[65] Belz, "Religious liberty is no walk in the park."

[66] Onize Ohikere, "Protests continue across the U.S.," *World*, June 1, 2020, https://wng.org/sift/protests-continue-across-the-u-s-1617394167.

[67] Mindy Belz, "A distracted nation," *World*, June 1, 2020, https://wng.org/roundups/a-distracted-nation-1617223345; Harvest Prude, "'Axis of disinformation' lines up against U.S.," *World*, June 4, 2020, https://wng.org/roundups/axis-of-disinformation-lines-up-against-u-s-1617223271.

[68] Katie Gaultney, "The Church is a place for healing," *World*, June 3, 2020, https://wng.org/articles/the-church-is-a-place-for-healing-1617297558.

[69] Gaultney, "The Church is a place for healing."

[70] Ryan Bomberger, "Culture Friday-God's Power for reconciliation," *World Radio*, June 5, 2020, https://wng.org/podcasts/culture-friday-gods-power-for-reconciliation-1617917482.

[71] Bomberger, "Culture Friday-God's Power for reconciliation."

[72] Jenny Rough, "The trouble with traffic stops," *World*, July 2, 2020, https://wng.org/articles/the-trouble-with-traffic-stops-1620617307.

[73] Marvin Olasky, "Both sides, now," *World*, June 11, 2020, https://wng.org/articles/both-sides-now-1620617083.

[74] Olasky, "Both sides, now."

[75] Olasky, "Both sides, now."

[76] Janie B. Cheaney, "Local failure, national tragedy," *World*, June 11, 2020, https://wng.org/articles/local-failure-national-tragedy-1617297352.

[77] Cheaney, "Local failure, national tragedy."

[78] Cheaney, "Local failure, national tragedy."

[79] Barna Group, "Where Do We Go From Here?" Barna Group and Reimagine Group, 2019, 12–13.

[80] Beesher Mohamed and Kiana Cox, "Before protests, black Americans said religious sermons should address race relations," Pew Research Center, June 15, 2020, https://www.pewresearch.org/fact-tank/2020/06/15/before-protests-black-americans-said-sermons-should-address-race-relations/.

[81] David Roach, "Most U.S. Pastors Speak Out in Response to George Floyd's Death," *Christianity Today*, June 16, 2020, https://www.christianitytoday.com/news/2020/june/pastors-george-floyd-racism-church-barna-research.html.

[82] Roach, "Most U.S. Pastors Speak Out."

Chapter 7

COVID-19: Science, Politics, and Personal Freedom

[1] Daniel Silliman, "Died: Marcus Lamb, Daystar Founder Who Believed TV Opened a Window for the Holy Spirit," *Christianity Today*, December 1, 2021, https://www.christianitytoday.com/news/2021/december/obit-marcus-lamb-daystar-tv-success-scandal.html; Michelle Borstein, "Marcus Lamb died of COVID-19 after his network discouraged vaccines. But some Christian leaders don't want to talk about it," *The Washington Post*, December 2, 2021, https://www.washingtonpost.com/religion/2021/12/03/marcus-lamb-daystar-vaccine-televangelist-graham/.

[2] Anugrah Kumar, "Coronavirus: Millions on lockdown in China as the virus spreads worldwide," *The Christian Post*, January 26, 2020, https://www.christianpost.com/news/coronavirus-millions-on-lockdown-in-china-as-virus-spreads-worldwide.html.

[3] Jane M. Orient, "The coronavirus—1918 all over again?" *The Christian Post*, January 29, 2020, https://www.christianpost.com/voice/the-corona-virus-1918-all-over-again.html.

[4] Leonardo Blair, "'This could be bad,' CDC official warns of inevitable coronavirus spread in U.S.," *The Christian Post*, February 26, 2020, https://www.christianpost.com/news/this-could-be-bad-cdc-official-warns-of-inevitable-coronavirus-spread-in-us.html.

[5] Richard D. Land, "How should Christians respond to the coronavirus pandemic?" *The Christian Post*, March 14, 2020, https://www.christianpost.com/news/how-should-christians-respond-to-the-coronavirus-pandemic.html.

[6] Land, "How should Christians respond?"

[7] Dennis Lennox, "Why the coronavirus shouldn't keep you from traveling," *The*

Christian Post, March 15, 2020, https://www.christianpost.com/news/why-the-corona-virus-shouldnt-keep-you-from-traveling.html.

[8] Anugrah Kumar, "6 ways megachurch pastors are addressing coronavirus from the pulpit on Sunday," *Christian Post*, March 15, 2020, https://www.christianpost.com/news/6-ways-megachurch-pastors-are-addressing-coronavirus-from-the-pulpit-on-sunday.html.

[9] Leah MarieAnn Klett, "Trump calling coronavirus 'Chinese virus' 'instigates blame, hatred against Asians:' Eugene Cho," *The Christian Post*, March 18, 2020, https://www.christianpost.com/news/calling-coronavirus-chinese-virus-instigates-blame-hatred-against-asians-eugene-cho-says.html.

[10] See, for instance, Leonardo Blair, "Televangelist Candice Smithyman says coronavirus is 'demonic force' from ancient Egypt," *The Christian Post*, April 16, 2020, https://www.christianpost.com/news/televangelist-candice-smithyman-says-coronavi-rus-is-demonic-force-from-ancient-egypt.html; and columnist Michael Brown's analysis of one radio commentator's proclamation that the coronavirus is "divine judgment against Jews who do not believe in Jesus," and later saying a plague is underway because of gays suing churches. See Michael Brown, "Is the Coronavirus a divine judgment on gays?" *The Christian Post*, April 10, 2020, https://www.christianpost.com/voices/is-the-coronavirus-a-divine-judgment-on-gays.html. For the record, Brown debunks these assertions in his column, noting that Christians, too, are dying from COVID-19.

[11] For an example of advice to readers, see Karl Noten, "How to boost your immune system and fight the coronavirus," *The Christian Post*, March 21, 2020, https://www.christianpost.com/voices/how-to-boost-your-immune-system-and-fight-the-coronavirus.html; and also, for an evaluation of the use of hydroxychloroquine, an anti-malarial drug touted by President Trump, see Brandon Showalter, "Hydroxychlo-roquine: What is being said?" *The Christian Post*, August 3, 2020, https://www.christianpost.com/news/hydroxychloro quine-what-is-being-said.html.

[12] See, for instance, Jeannie Ortega Law, "Sandi Patty tests positive for coronavi-rus: 'This is not fake news; it's everything they say it is,'" *The Christian Post*, March 19, 2020, https://www.christianpost.com/news/sandi-patty-tests-positive-for-coronavirus-this-is-not-fake-news-its-everything-they-say-it-is.html; Leonardo Blair, "'Unbearable tragedy': Christian family loses fourth member to coronavirus," *The Christian Post*, March 20, 2020, https://www.christianpost.com/news/unbearable-tragedy-christian-family-loses-fourth-member-to-coronavirus.html.

[13] Samuel Smith, "Chicago threatens to temporarily close churches that defy gathering restrictions," *The Christian Post*, May 26, 2020, https://www.christianpost.com/news/chicago-threatens-to-temporarily-close-churches-that-defy-gathering-re-strictions.html; and Michael Gryboski, "Supreme Court rejects appeal from church threatened with closure by Chicago gov't," *The Christian Post*, March 29, 2021, https://www.christianpost.com/news/scotus-rejects-appeal-from-chicago-church-threatened-with-closure.html.

[14] Leonardo Blair, "Nearly 100 test positive for COVID-19 after Illinois mega-church camp and conference," *The Christian Post*, June 30, 2021, https://www.chris-tianpost.com/news/over-80-test-positive-for-covid-19-after-megachurch-summer-camp.html.

[15] Leonardo Blair, "Missionary Sean Feucht faces opposition over LA New Year's events," *The Christian Post*, December 21, 2020, https://www.christianpost.com/news/missionary-sean-feucht-faces-opposition-over-la-new-years-events.html.

[16] Ryan Burge, "Faith Over Fear? No, It's Political Ideology that Keeps People Unafraid of COVID-19," *Christianity Today*, March 15, 2020, https://www.christianitytoday.com/news/2020/march/political-ideology-faith-fear-coronavirus-us-polls.html.

[17] Jim Denison, "COVID-19 is Not God's Judgement," *Christianity Today*, April 21, 2020, https://www.christianitytoday.com/ct/2020/april-web-only/covid-19-is-not-gods-judgment.html.

[18] Todd Mangum, "The Pandemic as God's Judgment," *Christianity Today*, May 15, 2020, https://www.christianitytoday.com/ct/2020/may-web-only/pandemic-as-gods-judgment.html.

[19] See, for instance, Alejandra Molina, "John MacArthur's Church to Receive $800K COVID-19 Settlement," *Christianity Today*, September 1, 2021, https://www.christianitytoday.com/news/2021/september/john-macarthur-covid-settlement-california-church-grace-com.html; and Daniel Silliman, "First Pastor to Defy COVID-19 Lockdowns Wins in Court," *Christianity Today*, May 16, 2022, https://www.christianitytoday.com/news/2022/may/tony-spell-pandemic-lockdown-louisiana-freedom-religion.html.

[20] Thomas Berg and Shawna Kosel, "Religious Freedom Lessons from COViD-19 Disputes," *Christianity Today*, June 15, 2020, https://www.christianitytoday.com/ct/2020/june-web-only/religious-freedom-covid-church-restrict-reopening-lawsuits.html.

[21] Rebecca Randall, "Research: Racial Minorities Were More Likely to Contract COVID-19 at Churches," *Christianity Today*, November 24, 2020, https://www.christianitytoday.com/news/2020/november/covid-19-church-racial-minority-nature-mobility-research.html.

[22] Andy Olson, "Who is My Covid-19 Neighbor?" *Christianity Today*, May/June 2020, 38–42.

[23] Daniel P. Chin, "Where Two or More Are Vaccinated: Advice for Churches in 2021," *Christianity Today*, January 27, 2021, https://www.christianitytoday.com/ct/2021/january-web-only/church-reopening-vaccine-coronavirus-covid-advice.html.

[24] Liam Adams, "Evangelical Colleges Consider Vaccine Requirements for Fall," *Christianity Today*, May 20, 2021, https://www.christianitytoday.com/news/2021/may/cccu-evangelical-college-covid-vaccine-requirements.html; and Maria Baer, "Evangelical Colleges Join Effort to Promote Faith in the Vaccine," *Christianity Today*, September 21, 2021, https://www.christianitytoday.com/news/2021/september/christian-college-cccu-faith-covid-vaccine-ifyc.html.

[25] Jen Pollock Michel, "20 Prayers to Pray During This Pandemic," *Christianity Today*, March 6, 2020, https://www.christianitytoday.com/ct/2020/march-web-only/covid-19-coronavirus-20-prayers-to-pray-during-pandemic.html; Kate Shellnutt, "Christians Call for Prayer After Trump Tests Positive for COVID-19," *Christianity Today*, October 2, 2020, https://www.christianitytoday.com/news/2020/october/pray-for-president-trump-tweet-covid-pastor-prayers-1-tim.html.

[26] Jim Wallis, "Reopening Will Require Truth, Unity, and Solidarity," *Sojourners*, April 23, 2020, https://sojo.net/articles/reopening-will-require-truth-unity-and-solidarity.

[27] Wallis, "Reopening Will Require Truth, Unity, and Solidarity."

[28] Christina Colon, "In a Pandemic, we must all be fact-checkers," *Sojourners*, May 5, 2020, https://sojo.net/articles/pandemic-we-must-all-be-fact-checkers.

[29] Colon, "In a Pandemic,."

[30] Adam Russell Taylor, "For Heaven's Sake, 'Wear a Damn Mask,'" *Sojourners*, June 30, 2020, https://sojo.net/articles/heaven-s-sake-wear-damn-mask.

[31] Taylor, "For Heaven's Sake."

[32] Taylor, "For Heaven's Sake."

[33] Lexi McMenamin, "The COVID-19 Vaccine is Here. What Ethics Should Guide Its Rollout?" *Sojourners*, December 14, 2020, https://sojo.net/articles/covid-19-vaccine-here-what-ethics-should-guide-its-rollout.

[34] McMenamin, "The COVID-19 Vaccine is Here."

[35] Stephanie Russell-Kraft, "Christian Nationalists Much More Likely to Reject Vaccine, New Study Finds," *Sojourners*, December 9, 2020, https://sojo.net/articles/christian-nationalists-much-more-likely-reject-vaccine-new-study-finds.

[36] David W. Congdon, "The Christian Case for Vaccine Mandates," *Sojourners*, October 19, 2021, https://sojo.net/articles/christian-case-vaccine-mandates. Congdon also links the arguments of some Christians to refuse vaccination to more significant concepts of religious freedom and concepts such as those taught in Critical Race Theory. His central premise is thus, "Viewed structurally, and thus informed by the needs of the community and the good of the human family, religious freedom could and should be the freedom for the vaccine, a freedom that would never need to wait for a mandate because the community of faith would have these structural goods already in mind."

[37] "Dear Black Churches: We Can Overcome Vaccine Skepticism, Inequality," Sojourners, February 18, 2021, https://sojo.net/articles/dear-black-churches-we-can-overcome-vaccine-skepticism-inequity.

[38] "Dear Black Churches."

[39] Russell Meeks, "The Old Testament Law Valued People Over Property," *Sojourners*, April 23, 2020, https://sojo.net/articles/old-testament-law-valued-people-over-property.

[40] Meeks, "The Old Testament Law."

[41] Meeks, "The Old Testament Law."

[42] Rob Schenck, "Wearing a Mask is Biblical," *Sojourners*, August 6, 2020, https://sojo.net/articles/bible-says-wear-mask-Christians-church-coronavirus.

[43] Jim Wallis, "American Families in Crisis," *Sojourners*, July 16, 2020, https://sojo.net/articles/american-families-crisis.

[44] Jim Wallis, "Unequal Suffering: Here's How Congress Should Help," *Sojourners*, April 30, 2020, https://sojo.net/articles/unequal-suffering-heres-how-congress-should-help.

[45] Gabriel J. Atchison, "The Black Faith Leaders at the Forefront of Public Health Crises," *Sojourners*, June 29, 2020, https://sojo.net/articles/black-faith-leaders-forefront-public-health-crises.

[46] Stephanie Russell-Kraft, "Can Faith Leaders' Vaccine Selfies Rebuild Public Trust?" *Sojourners*, January 27, 2021, https://sojo.net/articles/can-faith-leaders-vaccine-selfies-rebuilt-public-trust-interfaith-covid-san-antonio.

[47] Madison Muller, "D.C.-Area Churches Encourage Community to Have 'Faith in the Vaccine,'" *Sojourners*, February 12, 2021, https://sojo.net/articles/dc-area-churches-encourage-community-have-faith-vaccine.

[48] Gina Ciliberto, "CDC: 1.5 Million Children Orphaned by COVID-19," *Sojourners*, July 22, 2021, https://sojo.net/articles/cdc-15-million-children-orphaned-covid-19.

[49] Ceire Kealty, "The Pandemic is a 'Mass Disabling Event,'" *Sojourners*, July 2022, 15.

[50] June Cheng, "Seeking peace in sickness," *World*, February 6, 2020, https://wng.org/articles/seeking-peace-in-sickness-1617297934.

[51] June Cheng, "Infectious anger," *World*, February 27, 2020, https://wng.org/articles/infectious-anger-1617297736.

[52] Belz provided this insight while discussing the possibility of America mounting a Marshall Plan-type response to help bereaved, unemployed, and needy neighbors once the pandemic's sting had subsided. See Mindy Belz, "A bridge to the post-COVID future," *World*, https://wng.org/articles/a-bridge-to-the-post-covid-future-1620616852.

[53] Jamie Dean, "Gathering storms," *World*, April 6, 2020, https://wng.org/articles/gathering-storms-1617297839.

[54] Dean, "Gathering storms."

[55] Dean, "Gathering storms."

[56] Sophia Lee, "The COVID-19 chasm: Viral division," *World*, July 30, 2020, https://wng.org/articles/the-covid-19-chasm-the-pandemic-hits-the-heartland-1620617369. See also Lynde Langdon, Sara Schweinsberg, and Kyle Ziemnick, "The COVID-19 chasm, The Pandemic hits the heartland," *World*, July 30, 2020, https://wng.org/articles/the-covid-19-chasm-the-pandemic-hits-the-heartland-1620617369.

[57] Leah Savas, "The COVID-19 chasm: Some groups take their work outside," *World*, July 30, 2020, https://wng.org/articles/the-covid-19-chasm-some-groups-take-their-work-outside-1620617388.

[58] Steve West, Mickey McLean, and Rachel Lynn Aldrich, "MacArthur vs. California: The battle continues," *World*, August 18, 2020, https://wng.org/roundups/macarthur-vs-california-the-battle-continues-1617221070.

[59] See Marc LiVecche, "Questioning the wisdom of COVID lockdowns," *World*, February 17, 2022, https://wng.org/opinions/questioning-the-wisdom-of-covid-lockdowns-1645099350; Daniel Huizinga, "Let's actually protect our democracy," *World*, January 20, 2022, https://wng.org/opinions/lets-actually-protect-our-democracy-1642679463; R. Albert Mohler, Jr., "A mandate for constitutional government," *World*, January 14, 2022; https://wng.org/opinions/a-mandate-for-constitutional-government-1642164155; and Erin Hawley, "An unconstitutional mandate," *World*, January 7, 2022, https://wng.org/opinions/an-unconstitutional-mandate-1641559746.

[60] Christiana Kiefer, "A breathtaking expansion of federal power," *World*, December 16, 2021, https://wng.org/opinions/holcomb-on-vaccine-mandate-1639658355. Other news articles focused on vaccine mandates include

[61] Joel Belz, "This is different," *World*, April 8, 2020, https://wng.org/articles/this-is-different-1620616717.

[62] Belz, "This is different."

[63] Marvin Olasky, "Inside the outbreak: Bottom-up solutions," *World*, March 16, 2020, https://wng.org/articles/inside-the-outbreak-bottom-up-solutions-1617297764.

[64] Olasky, "Inside the outbreak." See also Leah Savas, "Inside the outbreak: Creative coronavirus help," *World*, May 29, 2020, https://wng.org/articles/inside-the-outbreak-creative-coronavirus-help-1617297650.

[65] Sophia Lee, "2020's church divide," *World*, December 10, 2020, https://wng.org/articles/2020s-church-divide-1617296676.

[66] Lee, "2020's church divide."

[67] Pew Research Center, "Most Americans Say Coronavirus Outbreak Has Impacted Their Lives," Pew Research Center, March 30, 2020, https://www.pewresearch.org/

social-trends/2020/03/30/most-americans-say-coronavirus-outbreak-has-impacted-their-lives/.

[68] Liz Hamel, Lunna Lopes, Audrey Kearney, and Mollyann Brodie, "KFF COVID-19 Vaccine Monitor: March 2021," Kaiser Family Foundation, March 30, 2021, https://www.kff.org/coronavirus-covid-19/poll-finding/kff-covid-19-vaccine-monitor-march-2021/.

[69] Elle Reeve, Samantha Guff, Theresa Waldrop, and Deborah Brunswick, "Many Evangelicals say they won't be vaccinated against Covid-19. Some experts say distrust and misinformation have played a role," *CNN*, April 15, 2021, https://www.cnn.com/2021/04/14/us/covid-vaccine-evangelicals/index.html.

[70] "Higher COVID-19 Death Rates in the Southern U.S. Due to Behavior Differences," Georgetown University School of Health, April 28, 2022, https://health.georgetown.edu/news-story/higher-covid-19-death-rates-in-the-southern-u-s-due-to-behavior-differences/.

Chapter 8
The 2020 Election: The Evangelical Dilemma

[1] Lia Eustachewich, "Trump slams Mark Galli's Christianity Today editorial calling for his removal," *New York Post*, December 20, 2019, https://nypost.com/2019/12/20/trump-slams-mark-gallis-christianity-today-editorial-calling-for-his-removal/

[2] Eustachewich, "Trump slams Mark Galli's *Christianity Today* editor."; Bill Chappell, "Calling Trump 'Morally Lost,' Christianity Today Editor Calls for His Removal," *National Public Radio*, December 20, 2019, https://www.npr.org/2019/12/20/790130632/christianity-today-editor-discusses-calling-for-trumps-impeachment.

[3] John Grano and Richard Land, "*Christianity Today* and the problem with 'Christian elitism,'" *The Christian Post*, December 23, 2019, https://www.christianpost.com/news/christianity-today-and-the-problem-with-christian-elitism.html.

[4] Grano and Land, "*Christianity Today* and the problem."

[5] I say Galli allegedly wrote the paragraphs attributed to him by Land because the Grano and Land editorial does not cite when and where Galli made those remarks. An extensive internet and database search could not find evidence of that quote in any existing literature.

[6] Quoted from Grano and Land, "*Christianity Today* and the problem."

[7] Grano and Land, "*Christianity Today* and the problem."

[8] Sheldon Roth, "Trump: An unseen Christian," *The Christian Post*, January 28, 2020, https://www.christianpost.com/voice/trump-an-unseen-christian.html.

[9] That admiration is not reciprocal as Peale's son, John, said he winces when he hears Trump invoke his father's name. See, Paul Schwartzman, "How Trump got religion—and why his legendary minister's son now rejects him," *The Washington Post*, January 21, 2016, https://www.washingtonpost.com/lifestyle/how-trump-got-religion--and-why-his-legendary-ministers-son-now-rejects-him/2016/01/21/37bae16e-bb02-11e5-829c-26ffb874a18d_story.html.

[10] Roth, "Trump: An unseen Christian."

[11] "How evangelicals see President Trump," PBS News Hour with Judy Woodruff, January 2, 2020, https://www.pbs.org/newshour/show/after-recent-rift-are-evangelical-christians-still-behind-trump.

[12] Leonardo Blair, "SBC leader Albert Mohler indicates support for Donald Trump in reversal of 2016 position," *The Christian Post*, April 17, 2020, https://www.christianpost.com/news/sbc-leader-albert-mohler-indicates-support-for-donald-trump-in-reversal-of-2016-position.html.

[13] Laura Murphy, "Beth Moore and double standards for Joe Biden?" *The Christian Post*, May 21, 2020, https://www.christianpost.com/voices/beth-moore-and-double-standards-for-joe-biden.html.

[14] See Samuel Smith, "'The Spiritual Danger of Trump:' New book asks evangelicals to rethink their vote in 2020," *The Christian Post*, June 15, 2020, https://www.christianpost.com/news/the-spiritual-danger-of-trump-new-book-asks-evangelicals-to-rethink-their-vote-in-2020.html; Michael Brown, "Will the 2020 elections come down to Trump vs. social anarchy?" *The Christian Post*, June 17, 2020, https://www.christianpost.com/voices/will-the-2020-elections-come-down-to-trump-vs-social-anarchy.html.

[15] Paula White, "'Demonic network' opposes Trump's reelection: 'We secure victory in the name of Jesus,'" *The Christian Post*, June 19, 2020, https://www.christianpost.com/news/paula-white-demonic-network-opposes-trump-reelection-we-secure-victory-in-the-name-of-jesus.html.

[16] Michael Gryboski, "Biden campaign faith director talks Christian beliefs, outreach to evangelicals and systemic racism," *The Christian Post*, August 4, 2020, https://www.christianpost.com/news/biden-campaign-faith-director-talks-christian-beliefs-outreach-to-evangelicals-and-systemic-racism.html.

[17] Gryboski, "Biden campaign faith director."

[18] Michael Brown, "Hope motivates better than pessimism," *The Christian Post*, August 25, 2020, https://www.christianpost.com/voices/hope-motivates-better-than-pessimism.html.

[19] Brown, "Hope motivates better than pessimism."

[20] Michael Gryboski, "John MacArthur says 'true believers' will vote for Trump, can't affirm abortion and trans activism," *The Christian Post*, September 2, 2020, https://www.christianpost.com/news/john-macarthur-says-true-believers-will-vote-for-trump-cant-affirm-abortion-and-trans-activism.html. The same article also quoted Billy Graham's granddaughter who told *USA Today* that evangelical support for Trump damaged her grandfather's legacy, pointing out that as a result of Trump's policies, "My faith and my church have become a laughing stock."

[21] Samuel Smith, "Evangelical, Catholic voters in 5 swing states may shift 11% for Biden over Trump: survey," *The Christian Post*, September 12, 2020, https://www.christianpost.com/news/evangelical-catholic-voters-in-5-swing-states-may-shift-11-for-biden-over-trump-survey.html.

[22] Robin Schumacher, "Right thinking on choosing the lesser of two evils," *The Christian Post*, September 14, 2020, https://www.christianpost.com/news/right-thinking-on-choosing-the-lesser-of-two-evils.html.

[23] Ryan Foley, "Pro-life activists protest outside Biden's Delaware home; 'abortion ground zero,'" *The Christian Post*, October 1, 2020, https://www.christianpost.com/news/pro-lifer-protest-outside-bidens-delaware-home.html; and Ryan Foley, "Pro-lifers slam Biden's promise to codify Roe v. Wade if elected," *The Christian Post*, October 7, 2020, https://www.christianpost.com/news/pro-lifers-slam-bidens-promise-to-codify-roe-v-wade-if-elected.html.

[24] Michael Brown, "Mr. Biden, do you really advocate sterilizing children?"

The Christian Post, October 20, 2020, https://www.christianpost.com/voices/ mr-biden-do-you-really-advocate-sterilizing-children.html.

[25] Joe Biden, "The greatest commandment has guided my politics," *The Christian Post*, October 29, 2020, https://www.christianpost.com/voices/the-greatest-command-ment-has-guided-my-politics.html.

[26] Ryan Foley "Franklin Graham warns of 'attacks against Christian businesses' if Biden wins," *The Christian Post*, November 3, 2020, https://www.christianpost.com/ news/franklin-graham-warns-attacks-christian-businesses-if-biden-wins.html.

[27] Foley "Franklin Graham warns."

[28] Leonardo Blair, "A vote for Trump is a vote for 'biblical truth,' says pastor of Cowboy Church," *The Christian Post*, October 23, 2020, https://www.christianpost.com/ news/voting-donald-trump-is-voting-for-biblical-truth-pastor-says.html.

[29] Blair, "A vote for Trump is a vote for 'biblical truth.'"

[30] Leah MarieAnn Klett, "John Piper warns Trump's 'deadly' behavior will lead to 'destruction' in blistering post," *The Christian Post*, October 23, 2020, https://www. christianpost.com/news/john-piper-slams-trump-in-new-blog-post.html.

[31] Leah MarieAnn Klett, "Christian leaders react to John Piper's condemnation of Trump," *The Christian Post*, October 24, 2020, https://www.christianpost.com/news/ christian-leaders-react-to-pipers-condemnation-of-trump.html.

[32] Kate Shellnutt, "Influential Hispanic Pastor Welcomes 'Evangelicals for Trump,'" *Christianity Today*, January 3, 2020, https://www.christianitytoday.com/news/2020/jan-uary/evangelicals-for-trump-pastor-guillermo-maldonado-miami.html.

[33] Megan Fowler and Kate Shellnutt, "Pro-Life Democrats Remind Candidates They Exist," *Christianity Today*, February 28, 2020, https://www.christianitytoday.com/ news/2020/february/pro-life-democrats-south-carolina-primary-abortion-biden.html.

[34] Kate Shellnutt, "White Christians: Trump May Not Be a Good Person, But He is a Good President," *Christianity Today*, March 13, 2020, https://www.christianity-today.com/news/2020/march/trump-white-christians-evangelicals-presidential-poli-cies-e.html.

[35] Daniel Silliman, "Joe Biden Campaigns on Faith," *Christianity Today*, August 17, 2020, https://www.christianitytoday.com/news/2020/august/joe-biden-catho-lic-evangelical-faith-vote-2020-convention.html.

[36] For a round-up of the GOP nominating convention activities and speaker comments, see Kate Shellnutt, "Trump's Faithful: Franklin Graham, Navajo VP, Freed Pastor Andrew Brunson on GOP Convention Lineup," *Christianity Today*, August 25, 2020, https://www.christianitytoday.com/news/2020/august/republican-national-con-vention-speakers-trump-evangelicals-.html.

[37] Daniel Silliman, "On the Front Lines, Some Pro-Life Activists Think Twice About Supporting Trump," *Christianity Today*, September 1, 2020, www.christianityto-day.com/ct/2020/september/pro-life-politics-2020-election-evangelicals-trump-abor-tion.html.

[38] Ryan P. Burge, "Trump Can Afford to Slip Among White Evangelicals, But Not White Catholics," *Christianity Today*, September 20, 2020, https://www.chris-tianitytoday.com/news/2020/september/trump-biden-white-catholic-swing-vote-evangelical-poll.html.

[39] Alejandra Molina, "Latino Evangelicals Narrowly Favor Trump," *Christianity Today*, October 6, 2020, https://www.christianitytoday.com/news/2020/october/lati-no-evangelical-christian-voters-survey-trump-biden.html; and Dorcas Cheng-Tozun,

"Chinese Americans are Becoming More Politically Engaged—and More Divided," *Christianity Today*, October 27, 2020, https://www.christianitytoday.com/news/2020/october/chinese-american-christian-voters-asian-divided-trump-biden.html.

[40] I've kept the references to White, Heitzig, Dixon, Richards, and Sallow-Prior's endorsements in the following five endnotes, even though those articles have been removed from the *Christianity Today* website and can no longer be accessed even through the internet archive. The removal likely occurred when Ed Stetzer became editor of a *Christianity Today* competitor called *Outreach* magazine in 2021.

[41] Paula White, "Paula White: Of Course Evangelicals Should Vote for Trump," *Christianity Today*, October 28, 2020, https://web.archive.org/web/20201101014652/https://www.christianitytoday.com/edstetzer/2020/october/of-course-evangelicals-should-vote-for-trump.

[42] Skip Heitzig, "Skip Heitzig on Supporting Donald Trump: Promises Made, Promises Kept," *Christianity Today*, October 30, 2020, https://web.archive.org/web/20201101091150/https://www.christianitytoday.com/edstetzer/2020/october/skip-heitzig-promises-made-promises-kept.html.

[43] Josh Dixon, "Josh Dixon: The Christian Case for Joe Biden," *Christianity Today*, October 27, 2020, https://web.archive.org/web/20201118080239/https://www.christianitytoday.com/edstetzer/2020/october/christian-case-for-joe-biden.html.

[44] John C. Richards Jr., "John Richards: Here is Why, as a Pro-Life Black Man, I'm Voting for Biden," *Christianity Today*, October 29, 2020, https://web.archive.org/web/20201101091150/https://www.christianitytoday.com/edstetzer/2020/october/skip-heitzig-promises-made-promises-kept.

[45] Karen Swallow-Prior, "Karen Swallow Prior: Voting for Neither," *Christianity Today*, October 28, 2020, https://web.archive.org/web/20201101002543/https://www.christianitytoday.com/edstetzer/2020/october/karen-swallow-prior-voting-for-neither.html?&display=checkout.

[46] Swallow-Prior, "Karen Swallow Prior: Voting for Neither."

[47] Timothy Dalrymple, "Why Evangelicals Disagree on the President," *Christianity Today*, November 2, 2020, https://www.christianitytoday.com/ct/2020/november-web-only/trump-election-politics-church-kingdom.html.

[48] Dalrymple, "Why Evangelicals Disagree."

[49] Dalrymple, "Why Evangelicals Disagree."

[50] Dalrymple, "Why Evangelicals Disagree."

[51] Jim Wallis, "My Lenten Prayer is for National Repentance," *Sojourners*, April 2020, https://sojo.net/magazine/april-2020/my-lenten-prayer-national-repentance.

[52] Rose Marie Berger, "There's Nothing Pro-life About Trump," *Sojourners*, May 2020, https://sojo.net/magazine/may-2020/theres-nothing-pro-life-about-trump.

[53] Berger, "There's Nothing Pro-life About Trump."

[54] Quoted in Jim Wallis, Adam Russell Taylor, and Terrance M. McKinley, "Trump's Dangerous Election Rhetoric," *Sojourners*, July 30, 2020, https://sojo.net/articles/trumps-dangerous-election-rhetoric.

[55] Quoted in Wallis, Taylor, and McKinley, "Trump's Dangerous Election Rhetoric."

[56] Wallis, Taylor, and McKinley, "Trump's Dangerous Election Rhetoric."

[57] Wallis, Taylor, and McKinley, "Trump's Dangerous Election Rhetoric."

[58] Jim Wallis, "An Altar Call for the Election," *Sojourners*, November 2020, https://sojo.net/magazine/november-2020/altar-call-election.

[59] Wallis, "An Altar Call for the Election."

[60] Lexi McMenamin, "Voters of Faith Largely Support Action on Climate Change, New Survey Shows," *Sojourners*, October 22, 2020, https://sojo.net/articles/voters-faith-largely-support-action-climate-change-new-survey-shows.

[61] Jim Rice, "This is Not the Year for a Protest Vote," *Sojourners*, November 2020, https://sojo.net/magazine/november-2020/not-year-protest-vote.

[62] Rice, "This is Not the Year for a Protest Vote."

[63] Rice, "This is Not the Year for a Protest Vote."

[64] Barbara Williams-Skinner and Adam Russell Taylor, "In the Event of a Tainted Election, the Faith Community must Rise Up," *Sojourners*, November 2020, https://sojo.net/magazine/november-2020/event-tainted-election-faith-community-must-rise.

[65] Jamie Dean, "Off the trail," *World*, May 21, 2020, https://wng.org/articles/off-the-trail-1620588580.

[66] Marvin Olasky, "The demise of compassion," *World*, July 29, 2020, https://wng.org/articles/the-demise-of-compassion-1617297456.

[67] Olasky, "The demise of compassion."

[68] Marvin Olasky, "Rescue teams needed," *World*, August 13, 2020, https://wng.org/articles/rescue-teams-needed-1617297378.

[69] Olasky, "Rescue teams needed."

[70] Marvin Olasky, "Two opposing views of President Trump," *World* Radio transcript, October 8, 2020, https://wng.org/podcasts/two-opposing-views-of-president-trump-1617915083.

[71] Marvin Olasky, "The case for Donald Trump," *World*, September 24, 2020, https://wng.org/articles/the-case-for-donald-trump-1620617513,

[72] Olasky, "The case for Donald Trump."

[73] Olasky, "The case for Donald Trump."

[74] Marvin Olasky, "The case against Donald Trump," *World*, September 24, 2020, https://wng.org/articles/the-case-against-donald-trump-1618208280.

[75] Joel Belz, "Third party?" *World*, October 8, 2020, https://wng.org/articles/third-party-1620617721.

[76] Belz, "Third party?"

[77] Belz, "Third party?"

[78] Jamie Dean, "Following the chain of command," *World*, September 24, 2020, https://wng.org/articles/following-the-chain-of-command-1617297064; Jamie Dean, "Prosecutor and persecutor," *World*, September 24, 2020, https://wng.org/articles/prosecutor-and-persecutor-1620617683.

Chapter 9
Joe Biden and the End of Evangelicalism?

[1] Justin Peters, "Fox News' Arizona Call Drove Fox News Crazy," *Slate*, November 4, 2020, https://slate.com/news-and-politics/2020/11/fox-news-arizona-call-trump.html.

[2] Peters, "Fox News' Arizona Call."

[3] Jack Dutton, "Fox News Editor Fired After Arizona Biden Call Says Audit 'Damage' is Done," *Newsweek*, September 27, 2021, https://www.newsweek.com/fox-news-editor-fired-arizona-biden-call-says-audit-damage-done-1632915.

[4] Ryan Foley, "Franklin Graham warns of 'attacks against Christian businesses' if Biden wins," *The Christian Post*, November 3, 2020, https://www.christianpost.com/news/franklin-graham-warns-attacks-christian-businesses-if-biden-wins.html.

[5] Melissa Barnhart, "Joe Biden declares victory, 'honored' to lead country as media projects him winner of 2020 election," *The Christian Post*, November 7, 2020, https://www.christianpost.com/news/joe-biden-declares-victory-in-2020-presidential-election.html.

[6] Anugrah Kumar, "Joe Biden quotes Bible, hymn 'on Eagles Wings' in victory speech, *The Christian Post*, November 8, 2020, https://www.christianpost.com/news/joe-biden-quotes-bible-hymn-in-victory-speech.html.

[7] Anugrah Kumar, "Bush congratulates Biden, says Trump has right to pursue recount," *The Christian Post*, November 9, 2020, https://www.christianpost.com/news/bush-trump-recount-legal-challenges-confidence-election.html.

[8] Kumar, "Bush congratulates Biden."

[9] Ryan Foley, "Biden planning to reverse Trump's pro-life policies by executive orders," *The Christian Post*, November 10, 2020, https://www.christianpost.com/news/biden-to-reverse-trumps-pro-life-policies-by-executive-orders.html; Ronald Sloan, "Dear President-elect Biden, is unity possible?" *The Christian Post*, December 3, 2020, https://www.christianpost.com/voices/dear-president-elect-biden-is-unity-possible.html; Ryan Foley, "Author: Hundreds of thousands of evangelicals sat out election due to Trump's tweets, 'character problems,'" *The Christian Post*, November 11, 2020, https://www.christianpost.com/news/author-trumps-character-problems-cost-him-evangelical-votes.html; Ryan Foley, "Post-election survey: 97% of conservative Christians backed Trump," *The Christian Post*, December 2, 2020, https://www.christianpost.com/news/post-election-survey-97-of-conservative-christians-backed-trump.html; Samuel Smith, "Robert Jeffress denies calling Biden 'president elect,' refutes media reports," *The Christian Post*, November 11, 2020, https://www.christianpost.com/news/robert-jeffress-denies-calling-biden-president-elect.html; Michael Gryboski, "DOJ says election fraud probes not over after AG Barr says evidence presented won't change election," *The Christian Post*, December 2, 2020, https://www.christianpost.com/news/doj-says-election-fraud-probes-not-over-despite-attorney-general.html; Jim Denison, "How should you respond if you consider the election to be illegitimate? A biblical path forward," *The Christian Post*, December 9, 2020, https://www.christianpost.com/voices/how-to-respond-if-you-consider-the-election-to-be-illegitimate.html; Michael Gryboski, "Trump-supporting evangelical leaders Franklin Graham, Al Mohler recognize Biden as winner," *The Christian Post*, December 15, 2020, https://www.christianpost.com/news/franklin-graham-al-mohler-recognize-biden-as-president-elect.html; Michael Gryboski, "'It's all over': Pat Robertson says Biden won, Trump lives in 'alternative reality,'" *The Christian Post*, December 22, 2020, https://www.christianpost.com/news/pat-robertson-says-biden-won-trump-lives-in-alternate-reality.html; and Anugrah Kumar, "Mike Pence 'welcomes' Republicans' plan to 'raise objections' to Electoral College results, demand audit," *The Christian Post*, January 3, 2021, https://www.christianpost.com/news/mike-pence-welcomes-gop-lawmakers-plan-to-challenge-electoral-college-results.html.

[10] According to *Associated Press*, at the three-year anniversary of the event, 1,265 people had been charged with various crimes committed that day. More than 718 people have pled guilty, while 171 others were found guilty by a trial before a judge or jury. See Alanna Durkin Richer and Michael Kunzelman,

"Hundreds of convictions, but a major mystery is still unsolved 3 years after the Jan. 6 Capitol riot," *Associated Press*, January 5, 2024, https://apnews.com/article/capitol-riot-jan-6-criminal-cases-anniversary-bf436efe760751b1356f937e55bedaa5

[11] Ryan Foley, "Trump supporters gather in DC for peaceful Save America March before some storm Capitol," *The Christian Post*, January 6, 2021, https://www.christian-post.com/news/trump-supporters-gather-in-dc-for-peaceful-save-america-march-be-fore-some-storm-capitol.html.

[12] Foley, "Trump supporters gather in DC."

[13] Jim Denison, "4 biblical responses to the Capitol assault and the promise of redemptive hope," *The Christian Post*, January 8, 2021, https://www.christianpost.com/voices/4-biblical-responses-to-the-capitol-assault.html.

[14] Leonardo Blair, "4 important things to know about fallout from the Capitol attack," *The Christian Post*, January 8, 2021, https://www.christianpost.com/news/4-im-portant-things-that-happened-after-capitol-attack.html.

[15] Jack Hibbs, "What's next for evangelicals post-Trump," *The Christian Post*, January 21, 2021, https://www.christianpost.com/voices/whats-next-for-evangelicals-post-trump.html.

[16] Hibbs, "What's next for evangelicals."

[17] Kate Shellnutt and Daniel Silliman, "Christian Trump and Biden Voters Wait on the Lord . . . and Ballot Counts," *Christianity Today*, November 4, 2020, https://www.christianitytoday.com/news/2020/november/evangelical-election-trump-biden-wait-vote-count-pa.html.

[18] Kate Shellnutt and Daniel Silliman, "On a Mail-In Ballot and a Prayer, Biden Wins White House," *Christianity Today*, November 7, 2020, https://www.christianity-today.com/news/2020/november/joe-biden-wins-president-catholic-faith-outreach-trump-evan.html.

[19] Shellnutt and Silliman, "On a Mail-in Ballot and a Prayer."

[20] Daniel Harrell, "The 144 Million and Counting," *Christianity Today*, November 10, 2020, https://www.christianitytoday.com/ct/2020/november-web-only/144-mil-lion-and-counting.html.

[21] Harrell, "The 144 Million and Counting."

[22] Daniel Bennett, "We Need to Be Better Losers," *Christianity Today*, January 6, 2021, https://www.christianitytoday.com/ct/2021/january-web-only/christian-victo-ry-election-loss.html.

[23] Kate Shellnutt, "Christian Leaders Pray for Peace and Safety Amid Capitol Mob," *Christianity Today*, January 6, 2021, https://www.christianitytoday.com/news/2021/jan-uary/christians-condemn-capitol-protests-pray-trump-dc.html.

[24] Shellnutt, "Christian Leaders Pray for Peace."

[25] Shellnutt, "Christian Leaders Pray for Peace."

[26] Shellnutt, "Christian Leaders Pray for Peace."

[27] Shellnutt, "Christian Leaders Pray for Peace."

[28] Bonnie Kristian, "Humoring the President Was Not Harmless," January 11, 2021, *Christianity Today*, https://www.christianitytoday.com/ct/2021/january-web-on-ly/humoring-president-not-harmless.html.

[29] Bonnie Kristian, "Dispelling the Smog of Falsehood and 'Fake News,'" *Christianity Today*, February 4, 2021, https://www.christianitytoday.com/ct/2021/febru-ary-web-only/dispelling-smog-of-falsehood-and-fake-news.html.

[30] Kate Shellnutt, "Most Evangelical Trump Voters Didn't Turn on Mike

Pence," *Christianity Today*, January 13, 2021, https://www.christianitytoday.com/news/2021/january/mike-pence-evangelicals-trump-election-congress-capitol-bre.html.

[31] Craig Keener, "Failed Trump Prophecies Offer a Lesson in Humility," *Christianity Today*, January 20, 2021, https://www.christianitytoday.com/ct/2021/january-web-only/trump-prophets-apologize-election-prophecies-humility.html.

[32] "The People Have Spoken: They choose Joe Biden and Kamala Harris," *Sojourners*, accessed January 21, 2025, https://sojo.net/about-us/news/people-have-spoken-they-choose-joe-biden-and-kamala-harris.

[33] Mitchell Atencio, "Joe Biden Wins Election, Set to Become Second Catholic U.S. President," *Sojourners*, November 7, 2020, https://sojo.net/articles/joe-biden-wins-election-set-become-second-catholic-us-president.

[34] Mitchell Atencio, "How Joe Biden Won a Diverse Group of Faith Voters," *Sojourners*, November 10, 2020, https://sojo.net/articles/how-joe-biden-won-diverse-group-faith-voters.

[35] "Finding Our Way in a Post-Trump America," *Sojourners*, January 2021, https://sojo.net/interactive/finding-our-way-post-trump-america.

[36] Leana Wen, "Moral Authority in a Pandemic," *Sojourners*, January 2021, https://sojo.net/interactive/finding-our-way-post-trump-america.

[37] Adam Russell Taylor, "The Deadly Consequences of a Toxic Presidency," *Sojourners*, January 6, 2021, https://sojo.net/articles/deadly-consequences-toxic-presidency.

[38] Taylor, "The Deadly Consequences."

[39] Adam Russel Taylor and Jim Wallis, "The President Must Be Removed," *Sojourners*, January 7, 2021, https://sojo.net/articles/president-must-be-removed.

[40] Taylor and Wallis, "The President Must Be Removed."

[41] Augusta Saraiva and Katie Livingstone, "Some Evangelicals Condemn Violence Yet Cling to Election Conspiracies," *Sojourners*, January 7, 2021, https://sojo.net/articles/some-evangelicals-condemn-violence-yet-cling-election-conspiracies-capitol-attack-Trump.

[42] Saraiva and Livingstone, "Some Evangelicals Condemn Violence."

[43] Stephanie Russell-Kraft, "Faith Groups Call for Trump's Removal Following Capitol Attacks," *Sojourners*, January 8, 2021, https://sojo.net/articles/faith-groups-call-trumps-removal-following-capitol-attacks.

[44] Russell-Kraft, "Faith Groups Call for Trump's Removal."

[45] Adam Russell Taylor, "Accountability is a Prerequisite for Healing," *Sojourners*, January 14, 2021, https://sojo.net/articles/accountability-prerequisite-healing.

[46] Adam Russell Taylor, Jim Simpson, Terrance M. McKinley, Melody Zhang, Paola Fuentes Cleghorn, Rose Marie Berger, "It's Time to Be the Conscience of American Politics," *Sojourners*, January 21, 2021, https://sojo.net/articles/it-s-time-be-conscience-american-politics-Biden-integrity-policy-advocate.

[47] Adam Russell Taylor, "Is a 'Revisionist History' of Jan. 6 Alive in Your Church?" *Sojourners*, January 5, 2024, https://sojo.net/articles/revisionist-history-jan-6-alive-your-church.

[48] Taylor, "Is a 'Revisionist History' of Jan. 6 Alive?"

[49] Harvest Prude, Kim Henderson, Leah Savas, and Sharon Dierberger, "Election Day Snapshots," *World*, November 3, 2020, https://wng.org/articles/election-day-snapshots-1617297007.

[50] Prude, Henderson, Savas, and Dierberger, "Election Day Snapshots."

[51] Prude, Henderson, Savas, and Dierberger, "Election Day Snapshots."

⁵² Prude, Henderson, Savas, and Dierberger, "Election Day Snapshots."

⁵³ Harvest Prude, "Republications Exceed Expectations in House," *World*, November 4, 2020, https://wng.org/articles/republicans-exceed-expectations-in-house-1620587522; Sharon Dierberger, "Late-night laments," *World*, November 10, 2020, https://wng.org/roundups/late-night-laments-1617220629; and Lynde Langdon, "More states back Texas election lawsuit," *World*, November 9, 2020, https://wng.org/sift/more-states-back-texas-election-lawsuit-1617250813.

⁵⁴ Lynde Langdon, "Biden wins Electoral College," *World*, December 15, 2020, https://wng.org/sift/biden-wins-electoral-college-1617392567.

⁵⁵ Emily Belz, "An unprecedented breach on the Capitol," *World*, January 6, 2021, https://wng.org/articles/an-unprecedented-breach-on-the-capitol-1620536652.

⁵⁶ Belz, "An unprecedented breach."

⁵⁷ Belz, "An unprecedented breach."

⁵⁸ Belz, "An unprecedented breach."

⁵⁹ Onize Ohikere, "World leaders respond to Capitol riots," *World*, January 7, 2021, https://wng.org/sift/world-leaders-respond-to-capitol-riots-1617717276.

⁶⁰ Rachel Lynn Aldrich, "Police confirm deaths in Capitol riots," *World*, January 7, 2021, https://wng.org/sift/police-confirm-deaths-in-capitol-riots-1617392350.

⁶¹ Joshua Raimundo, "How did it come to this?" *World*, January 7, 2021, https://wng.org/roundups/how-did-it-come-to-this-1617220516. A week later, Emily Belz wrote that a Department of Justice investigation found no evidence that anti-fascist left-wing groups like Antifa instigated the violence. See Emily Belz, "Justice Department: No evidence of antifa instigating Capitol riot," *World*, January 11, 2021, https://wng.org/articles/justice-department-no-evidence-of-antifa-instigating-capitol-riot-1618197547.

⁶² Marvin Olasky, "Alternative universes," *World*, January 28, 2021, https://wng.org/articles/alternate-universes-1617296795.

⁶³ Olasky, "Alternative universes" (italics in original).

⁶⁴ Olasky, "Alternative universes."

⁶⁵ Olasky, "Alternative universes."

Chapter 10
The End of Roe v. Wade: A Pyrrhic Victory?

¹ Amy Schoenfield Walker, "Few Exceptions Are Approved for Abortions," *The New York Times*, January 22, 2023, p. 1–15. *The New York Times* published 59 articles using the phrase "Roe v. Wade" from 1989 to 2023, many speculating on what might happen if the 1973 decision were someday overturned, and what did happen in the year and a half after the Supreme Court's ruling in Dobbs v. Jackson Women's Health Organization.

² Jill Waggoner, "Richard Land on Southern Baptists' history of abortion advocacy and the future of the pro-life movement," The Ethics and Religious Liberty Commission of the Southern Baptist Convention, February 15, 2022, https://erlc.com/resource-library/articles/richard-land-on-southern-baptists-history-of-abortion-advocacy-and-the-future-of-pro-life-movement/.

³ David Roach, "How Southern Baptists became pro-life," Baptist Press, January 16, 2015, https://www.baptistpress.com/resource-library/news/how-southern-baptists-became-pro-life/.

[4] Richard Land, "The mythology surrounding Roe v. Wade and abortion in America," *The Christian Post*, July 15, 2022, https://www.christianpost.com/news/the-mythology-surrounding-roe-v-wade-and-abortion-in-america.html. The only research articles in the *Journal of Clinical Ethics* I could find dated back to 1993. See, Douglas Brown, Thomas E. Elkins, and David B. Larson, "Prolonged Grieving after Abortion: A Descriptive Study," *The Journal of Clinical Ethics* 4, no. 2 (Summer 1993): 118–23. (This study claiming 44% of women regretted their abortion analyzed letters from 45 Protestant women asked by a pastor to discuss their emotions after their abortion. The methods used for the study are not sufficient to claim causality); and Jo Ann Rosenfeld and Tom Townsend, "Doesn't Everyone Grieve in the Abortion Choice?" *The Journal of Clinical Ethics* 4, no. 2 (Summer 1993): 175–7. A more recent meta study of the issue is Corinne H. Rocca, Goeen Samari, Diana G. Foster, Heather Group, and Katrina Kimport, "Emotions and decision rightness over five years following an abortion: An examination of decision difficulty and abortion stigma," *Social Science and Medicine* 248 (2020): 112704. The authors' conclusions note: "The overwhelming majority of women felt that the abortion was the right decision for them at all times." The conclusions also noted that among the individuals who did regret their abortion some may have experienced repeated exposure to anti-abortion discourse. This might indicate that women raised in an evangelical setting may have experienced the feeling of regret and condemnation Land describes.

[5] Land, "The mythology surrounding Roe v. Wade."

[6] Land, "The mythology surrounding Roe v. Wade."

[7] Richard Land, "Roe is finally gone. What must we do now?" *The Christian Post*, January 7, 2023, https://www.christianpost.com/voices/roe-is-finally-gone-what-must-we-do-now.html.

[8] Land, "Roe is finally gone."

[9] Michael Gryboski, "Supreme Court overturns Roe v. Wade in Mississippi abortion ruling," *The Christian Post*, June 24, 2022, https://www.christianpost.com/news/supreme-court-overturns-roe-v-wade-in-abortion-ruling.html.

[10] Gryboski, "Supreme Court overturns Roe v. Wade."

[11] Gryboski, "Supreme Court overturns Roe v. Wade."

[12] Gryboski, "Supreme Court overturns Roe v. Wade."

[13] Michael Gryboski, "'Honor all life': 7 Christian leaders react to Supreme Court overturning Roe," *The Christian Post*, June 24, 2022, https://www.christianpost.com/news/7-christian-leaders-react-to-supreme-court-overturning-roe.html?page=1.

[14] Kate Shellnutt, "White Evangelicals Twice as Likely to Want to Ban Abortion," *Christianity Today*, May 6, 2022, https://www.christianitytoday.com/news/2022/may/abortion-legal-evangelicals-supreme-court-pew-research.html.

[15] Russell Moore, "How to Lose the Abortion Debate While Winning It," *Christianity Today*, May 12, 2022, https://www.christianitytoday.com/ct/2022/may-web-only/russell-moore-abortion-debate-prolife-evangelical-christian.html. A few months later, *Christianity Today* reported on a "vocal minority" of anti-abortion activists seeking to arrest women who receive abortions and to ban all abortions, regardless of reason immediately. See, Ericka Andersen, "When 'Pro-Life' Isn't Enough: Abortion 'Abolitionists' Speak Up," *Christianity Today*, August 1, 2022, https://www.christianitytoday.com/news/2022/august/abortion-abolitionists-pro-life-movement-christian-roe-wade.html.

[16] Chelsea Sobolik, "Abortion Bans Should Ban Abortion," *Christianity Today*, May

20, 2022, https://www.christianitytoday.com/ct/2022/may-web-only/abortion-miscar-riage-ectopic-pregnancy-state-bill-pro-life.html.

[17] Sobolik, "Abortion Bans Should Ban Abortion."

[18] Maria Baer, "Pro-Life Ob-Gyns: Ectopic Pregnancy, Miscarriage Care Will Continue After Roe," *Christianity Today*, May 23, 2022, https://www.christianitytoday.com/news/2022/may/christian-ob-gyn-abortion-law-miscarriage-ectopic-pregnancy.html. It is worth noting that after the Supreme Court's *Dobbs* decision, a few states did try to ban mifepristone and misoprostol. Some communities passed legislation against "abortion trafficking," making it a crime to use the city's streets to drive someone out of state for an abortion. Those bans sparked years-long societal debates and legal wrangling in courts.

[19] Daniel Silliman, "Goodbye Roe v. Wade: Pro-Life Evangelicals Celebrate the Ruing They've Waited For," *Christianity Today*, June 24, 2022, https://www.christianitytoday.com/news/2022/june/roe-v-wade-overturn-abortion-supreme-court-ruling-pro-life.html.

[20] Marvin Olasky and Leah Savas, *The Story of Abortion in America: A Street-Level History, 1652–2022* (Wheaton, IL: Crossway Books, 2023). *Christianity Today's* review of the book appears a few months after its publication. See Alex Ward, "Naming Names in the Abortion Debate," *Christianity Today*, January 3, 2023, https://www.christianitytoday.com/ct/2023/januaryfebruary/marvin-olasky-leah-savas-abortion-street-level-history.html.

[21] See, Marvin Olasky, "These Pastors Fell into Sin. Pro-Life Laws Emerged from It," *Christianity Today*, June 23, 2022, https://www.christianitytoday.com/ct/2022/june-web-only/abortion-dobbs-pastors-fell-into-sin-pro-life-laws-emerged.html; Marvin Olasky, "What Came Before Ultrasound—and What Comes After," *Christianity Today*, June 30, 2022, https://www.christianitytoday.com/ct/2022/june-web-only/dobbs-abortion-before-ultrasound-what-comes-after.html; Marvin Olasky, "The Dark History of Abortion Doctors," *Christianity Today*, July 8, 2022, https://www.christianitytoday.com/ct/2022/july-web-only/olasky-dark-history-of-abortion-doctors.html; and Marvin Olasky, "The Pro-Life Conviction of the Hodge Brothers," *Christianity Today*, July 14, 2022, https://www.christianitytoday.com/ct/2022/july-web-only/olasky-pro-life-conviction-of-charles-hodge-hugh-hodge.html.

[22] Amethyst Holmes, "Pro-Life Black Christians Don't Focus on Abortion Alone," *Christianity Today*, June 29, 2022, https://www.christianitytoday.com/news/2022/june/pro-life-black-church-roe-v-wade-abortion-racism-whole-life.html

[23] "America's Abortion Quandary," Pew Research Center, May 6, 2022, https://www.pewresearch.org/religion/2022/05/06/americas-abortion-quandary/.

[24] "America's Abortion Quandary."

[25] Marvin Olasky, "Triumphalism After Dobbs Was a Mistake," *Christianity Today*, September 3, 2024, https://www.christianitytoday.com/2024/09/triumphalism-after-dobbs-was-mistake-pro-life-abortion/.

[26] Jim Wallis, "Abortion—From Symbol to Substance," Beliefnet blog, April 20, 2007, https://www.beliefnet.com/columnists/godspolitics/2007/04/jim-wallis-abortion-from-symbol-to.html.

[27] See Julie Polter, "Women and Children First," *Sojourners*, May-June 1995, 24:2, 16–20; Julie Polter, "A Civil Discourse," *Sojourners*, May-June 1999, https://sojo.net/magazine/may-june-1999/civil-discourse; Jim Wllis, "Pro-Life Democrats?", *Sojourners*, June

2004, 33:6, 5; Heidi Schlumpf, "No Place to Stand," *Sojourners*, June 2004, 33:6, 12–16; Amy Sullivan, "Abortion: A Way Forward," *Sojourners*, April 2006, 35:4, 12–18; Jim Rice and Jeannie Choi, "The Meaning of 'Life," *Sojourners*, November 2008, https://sojo.net/magazine/november-2008/meaning-life; and Glen Stassen, "What Actually Works?" *Sojourners*, June 2009, 38:6, 18. Typing in the word abortion in Sojourners online search engine produces several thousand articles appearing in the magazine and its online site over the course of its history.

[28] Adam Russell Taylor, "As a Christian, I Want to Reduce Abortion, Not Overturn Roe," *Sojourners*, May 12, 2022, https://sojo.net/articles/christian-i-want-reduce-abortion-not-overturn-roe-supreme-court-leaked-memo.

[29] Taylor, "As a Christian, I Want to Reduce Abortion."

[30] Jessica Felix Romero, "*Sojourners* Opposes Supreme Court's Ruling Ending the Constitutional Right to an Abortion," *Sojourners* news release, June 24, 2022, https://sojo.net/about-us/news/sojourners-opposes-supreme-courts-ruling-ending-constitutional-right-abortion.

[31] Romero, "*Sojourners* Opposes Supreme Court's Ruling."

[32] Romero, "*Sojourners* Opposes Supreme Court's Ruling."

[33] Katherine Pater, "About That Bible Verse You See on Anti-Abortion Signs," *Sojourners*, May 24, 2022, https://sojo.net/articles/about-bible-verse-you-see-anti-abortion-signs-jeremiah.

[34] Mitchell Atencio, "What Would the End of Roe v. Wade Mean? Christian Leaders Respond," *Sojourners*, May 3, 2022, https://sojo.net/articles/what-would-end-roe-v-wade-mean-christian-leaders-respond.

[35] Lawrence Hurley, "U.S. Supreme Court Overturns Roe v. Wade," *Sojourners*, June 24, 2022, https://sojo.net/articles/us-supreme-court-overturns-roe-v-wade.

[36] Mitchell Atencio, "Roe Is Over: Faith Leaders on What That Means for Christians," *Sojourners*, June 24, 2022, https://sojo.net/articles/roe-over-faith-leaders-what-means-christians.

[37] Atencio, "Roe Is Over."

[38] PDF copies of those issues are posted on *World*'s website at https://wng.org/special-sections/pro-life-issue.

[39] Marvin Olasky, "Historically deadly demand," *World*, January 13, 2022, https://wng.org/articles/historically-deadly-demand-1641711143.

[40] Olasky, "Historically deadly demand."

[41] Marvin Olasky, "Decreasing abortion demand," *World*, January 13, 2022, https://wng.org/articles/decreasing-abortion-demand-1641711705. Another focus on compassionate conservatism can be found in a *World* article from Olasky, an excerpt from another book on abortion, "Providing room at the inn," December 2, 2021, https://wng.org/roundups/providing-room-at-the-inn-1638631512. Another excerpt from his book *Abortion at the Crossroads* (Brentwood, TN: Bombardier Books, 2021) discusses mainstream media and the topic of abortion. See, "Investigative journalism and abortion," *World*, November 4, 2021, https://wng.org/roundups/investigative-journalism-and-abortion-1636205881.

[42] Joel Belz, "More than politics," *World*, November 5, 2020, https://wng.org/articles/more-than-politics-1617297146. Belz's 1998 column was reprinted in 2020 because he had recently broken his hip and was not writing during his recovery.

[43] Belz, "More than politics."

[44] Joel Belz, "Who am I to say?" *World*, September 8, 2022, https://wng.org/

articles/who-am-i-to-say-1662516451. The original column was published in the December 21, 2002, issue of the magazine.

[45] Joel Belz, "Professional dishonesty," *World*, May 5, 2007, https://wng.org/articles/professional-dishonesty-1617336478.

[46] Joel Belz, "Stop apologizing," *World*, July 12, 2008, https://wng.org/articles/stop-apologizing-1617335592.

[47] Albert Mohler, "The Supreme Court strikes down *Roe* and *Casey*," *World*, June 24, 2022, https://wng.org/opinions/the-supreme-court-strikes-down-roe-and-casey-1656094990.

[48] Mohler, "The Supreme Court strikes down."

[49] Leah Savas, "*Dobbs v. Jackson* started with these folks in Mississippi," *World*, June 24, 2020,https://wng.org/roundups/mississippi-pro-lifers-celebrate-reversal-of-roe-1656107540.

[50] Josh Schumacher, "Abortion businesses shut down in wake of SCOTUS ruling," *World*, June 24, 2020, https://wng.org/sift/abortion-businesses-shut-down-in-wake-of-scotus-ruling-1656116843.

[51] Leah Savas, "After Dobbs, pregnancy centers brace for more attacks," *World*, June 24, 2022, https://wng.org/roundups/after-dobbs-pregnancy-centers-brace-for-more-attacks-1656102951.

[52] Josh Schumacher, "Biden slams Dobbs decision," *World*, June 24, 2022, https://wng.org/sift/biden-slams-dobbs-decision-1656092802.

[53] Josh Schumacher, "Roe is Dead; babies can live," *World*, June 24, 2022, https://wng.org/sift/roe-is-dead-babies-can-live-1656080256.

[54] Erin Hawley and Kristen Waggoner, "A victory for life and the Constitution," *World*, June 24, 2022, https://wng.org/opinions/a-victory-for-life-and-the-constitution-1656086588.

[55] Kevin DeYoung, "Let the little children come to me," *World*, June 24, 2022, https://wng.org/opinions/let-the-little-children-come-to-me-1656085512.

Chapter 11
Evangelicals and the LGBTQ+ Question

[1] Morgan Lee and Jeremy Weber, "Here's What Supreme Court Says about Same-Sex Marriage and Religious Freedom," *Christianity Today*, June 26, 2015, https://www.christianitytoday.com/news/2015/june/supreme-court-states-cant-ban-same-sex-marriage.html.

[2] Lee and Weber, "Here's What Supreme Court Says." In that same article, Chief Justice John Roberts, writing for the dissent, noted various ways in which the court's decision would cascade down to cause other conflicts and that in the future Christian organizations might face challenges to their tax-exempt status if their advocacy for their beliefs led them to deny on-campus housing for same-sex married couples, or fail to extend adoption rights to gay couples.

[3] The Lesbian, Gay, Bisexual & Transgender Center uses the abbreviation as Lesbian, Gay, Bisexual, Transgender, Queer or Questioning, Intersex, Asexual and More, signified by the plus sign. See https://gaycenter.org/community/lgbtq/. I use LGBTQ+ to refer to people who identify as non-binary (male or female).

[4] Riham Alkousaa, "Evangelical Christians becoming less opposed to gay marriage, poll finds," Reuters, June 27, 2017, https://www.reuters.com/article/idUSKBN19I2MT/.

[5] Aaron Earls, "Most Pastors Still Oppose Same-Sex Marriage," *Christianity Today*, June 10, 2024, https://www.christianitytoday.com/news/2024/june/same-sex-marriage-protestant-pastors-oppose-LGBTQ+-lifeway.html.

[6] Larry Tomczak, "Are You Aware of the Avalanche of Gay Programming Assaulting Your Home?" *The Christian Post*, August 1, 2015, https://www.christianpost.com/news/are-you-aware-of-the-avalanche-of-gay-programming-assaulting-your-home-132277/.

[7] Jim Denison, "What does the Bible teach about homosexuality?" *The Christian Post*, May 8, 2019, https://www.christianpost.com/voices/what-does-the-bible-say-about-homosexuality.html.

[8] Denison, "What does the Bible teach?"

[9] Denison, "What does the Bible teach?"

[10] Mark H. Creech, "Constructive criticism for SBC President JD Greear on homosexual sin," *The Christian Post*, September 17, 2019, https://www.christianpost.com/voices/constructive -criticism-for-sbc-president-jd-greear-on-homosexual-sin.html.

[11] Creech, "Constructive criticism."

[12] See, for instance, Nicole Alcindor, "Megachurch pastor says it's 'very unloving' for Christians to affirm friends' LGBTQ+ lifestyles," *The Christian Post*, June 20, 2022, https://www.christianpost.com/news/megachurch-pastor-says-its-unloving-to-affirm-lgbt-lifestyles.html.

[13] Kelly Williams, "Eugene Peterson, The Message Bible and homosexuality," *The Christian Post*, August 17, 2021, https://www.christianpost.com/voices/eugene-peterson-the-message-bible-and-homosexuality.html.

[14] Brandon Showalter, "Message Bible Author Eugene Peterson: Homosexuality Not Wrong, Megachurches Aren't Real Churches," *The Christian Post*, July 12, 2017, https://www.christianpost.com/news/message-bible-author-eugene-peterson-homo-sexuality-not-wrong-megachurches-arent-real-churches-191753/.

[15] See, Anugrah Kumar, "Vicky Beeching on Eugene Peterson Controversy: 'American Christians' Opposition to LGBT Equality Tied to Money," *The Christian Post*, July 15, 2017, https://www.christianpost.com/news/vicky-beeching-american-christians-gay-marriage-eugene-peterson.html; Stoyan Zaimov, "Albert Mohler Offers 3 Lessons for Christians After 'Agonizing' Eugene Peterson Gay Marriage Ordeal," *The Christian Post*, July 18, 2017, https://www.christianpost.com/news/albert-mohler-offers-3-lessons-for-christians-after-agonizing-eugene-peterson-gay-marriage-ordeal.html; Stoyan Zaimov, "Russell Moore on Eugene Peterson Embracing Gay Marriage: If He Can Make Such an Error, Anyone Can," *The Christian Post*, July 13, 2017, https://www.christianpost.com/news/russell-moore-on-eugene-peterson-embracing-gay-marriage-if-he-can-make-such-an-error-anyone-can.html; and John Stonestreet, "Eugene Peterson and Same-Sex Marriage: It's a Gospel Issue," *The Christian Post*, July 18, 2017, https://www.christianpost.com/news/eugene-peterson-same-sex-marriage-gospel-issue.html.

[16] Brandon Showalter, "Eugene Peterson Retracts Support for Gay Marriage, Says He Was 'Put on the Spot,'" *The Christian Post*, July 13, 2017, https://www.christianpost.com/news/eugene-peterson-retracts-support-for-gay-marriage-says-he-was-put-on-the-spot.html.

[17] See, for instance, Anugrah Kumar, "Christian baker who refused to bake cake for lesbian wedding prevails in court," *The Christian Post*, October 23, 2022, https://www.christianpost.com/news/christian-baker-who-refused-to-bake-cake-for-lesbi-an-wedding-wins.html; and Michael Gryboski, "Colo. can't punish Christian website designer for refusing to create sites against her beliefs: Supreme Court," *The Christian*

Post, June 30, 2023, https://www.christianpost.com/news/supreme-court-says-colorado-cannot-punish-christian-website-designer.html; and Michael Gryboski, "Supreme Court vacates ruling against Christian bakers punished for not making lesbian wedding cake," *The Christian Post*, June 30, 2023, https://www.christianpost.com/news/scotus-vacates-lower-court-ruling-against-aaron-and-melissa-klein.html.

[18] Michael Gryboski, "Church of the Nazarene pastor faces removal over gay marriage support," *The Christian Post*, August 23, 2023, https://www.christianpost.com/news/nazarene-pastor-faces-removal-over-gay-marriage-support.html.

[19] Ian M. Giatti, "Documentary filmmaker claims word translated as 'homosexual' in the Bible is a mistake," *The Christian Post*, November 11, 2022, https://www.christianpost.com/news/documentary-says-use-of-homosexual-in-the-bible-is-a-mistake.html.

[20] Giatti, "Documentary filmmaker."

[21] Giatti, "Documentary filmmaker."

[22] Giatti, "Documentary filmmaker."

[23] Giatti, "Documentary filmmaker."

[24] The website for the index is https://www.christianitytoday.com/ct/topics/h/homosexuality/.

[25] B. L. Smith, "Homosexuality in the Bible and the Law," *Christianity Today*, July 18, 1969, 7–10, https://www.christianitytoday.com/ct/1969/july-18/homosexuality-in-bible-and-law.html.

[26] Carl Henry, "Editor's Note," *Christianity Today*, April 26, 1974, https://www.christianitytoday.com/ct/1974/april-26/editors-note.html

[27] "Just Saying 'No' Is Not Enough," *Christianity Today*, October 4, 1999, https://www.christianitytoday.com/ct/1999/october4/9tb050.html.

[28] Andy Crouch, "Sex Without Bodies," *Christianity Today*, June 26, 2013, https://www.christianitytoday.com/ct/2013/july-august/sex-without-bodies.html.

[29] Crouch, "Sex Without Bodies."

[30] Crouch, "Sex Without Bodies."

[31] Ron Sider, "Tragedy, Tradition, and Opportunity in the Homosexual Debate," *Christianity Today*, November 18, 2014, https://www.christianitytoday.com/2014/11/ron-sider-tragedy-tradition-and-opportunity-in-homosexualit/.

[32] Sider, "Tragedy, Tradition, and Opportunity."

[33] Mark Galli, "Six Things To Do after the Supreme Court Decision on Gay Marriage," *Christianity Today*, June 26, 2015, https://www.christianitytoday.com/ct/2015/june-web-only/6-things-to-do-after-supreme-court-gay-marriage-decision.html.

[34] "Here We Stand: An Evangelical Declaration on Marriage," *Christianity Today*, June 26, 2015, https://www.christianitytoday.com/ct/2015/june-web-only/here-we-stand-evangelical-declaration-on-marriage.html.

[35] Greg Johnson "What Comes After the Ex-Gay Movement? The Same Thing That Came Before," *Christianity Today*, September 20, 2021, https://www.christianitytoday.com/ct/2021/october/lgbt-homosexual-identity-what-comes-after-ex-gay-movement.html.

[36] Bekah Mason, "Side B Christians Like Me Are an Asset Not a Threat," *Christianity Today*, December 3, 2021, https://www.christianitytoday.com/ct/2021/november-web-only/same-sex-attraction-gay-marriage-side-b-asset-not-threat.html.

[37] Mason, "Side B Christians Like Me."

[38] Daniel Silliman, "More Evangelical Women Have Had Sex with Women Than You Might Think," *Christianity Today*, October 17, 2022, https://www.christianitytoday.

com/ct/2022/november/same-sex-experience-orientation-affirmation-evangelical.
html.

[39] A sampling of reports on denominational splits include Daniel Silliman, "Brethren Against Brethren: LGBT Fight Divides Peace Church," *Christianity Today*, August 3, 2020, https://www.christianitytoday.com/news/2020/august/church-brethren-southeastern-district-divide-covenant-lgbt.html; Kathryn Post, "Reformed Church in America Splits as Conservatives Form New Denomination," *Christianity Today*, January 7, 2022, https://www.christianitytoday.com/news/2022/january/reformed-church-in-america-rca-alliance-of-reformed-churche.html; Megan Fowler, "Conservative Methodists Launch Global Methodist Church," *Christianity Today*, April 28, 2022, https://www.christianitytoday.com/news/2022/april/global-methodist-church-launch-conservative-umc-lgbt-split.html; Kathryn Pepinster, "Evangelicals Fear LGBT Blessings Proposal Would Split the Church of England," *Christianity Today*, February 6, 2023, https://www.christianitytoday.com/news/2023/february/church-of-england-synod-lgbt-blessings-marriage-evangelical.html; Megan Fowler, "Two Congregations Force LGBT Debate on Evangelical Covenant Church," *Christianity Today*, July 5, 2023, https://www.christianitytoday.com/news/2023/january/awaken-quest-evangelical-covenant-lgbt-division.html; and Kate Shellnutt, "Southern Baptists Expel Two More Churches Over Abuse," *Christianity Today*, February 23, 2021, https://www.christianitytoday.com/news/2021/february/southern-baptists-expel-two-more-churches-over-abuse.html.

[40] Jim Wallis, "A Statement on *Sojourners*' Mission and LGBTQ+ Issues," *Sojourners*, May 9, 2011, https://sojo.net/articles/statement-sojourners-mission-and-LGBTQ+-issues.

[41] See, Jonathan Merritt, "If the Supreme Court Legalizes Gay Marriage in 2015, How Will Evangelicals Respond?" *Sojourners*, January 6, 2015, https://sojo.net/articles/gays-and-lesbians-church/if-supreme-court-legalizes-gay-marriage-2015-how-will-evangelicals; David Gibson, "Why the Supreme Court's Gay Marriage Decision is Not Like Legalizing Abortion," *Sojourners*, July 6, 2015, https://sojo.net/articles/why-supreme-court-s-gay-marriage-decision-not-legalizing-abortion; and Rich Preheim, "Mennonite Church Coming Apart Over Sexuality Issues," *Sojourners*, July 19, 2015, https://sojo.net/articles/mennonite-church-coming-apart-over-sexuality-issues.

[42] Austen Hartke, "7 Things the Transgender People in Your Congregation Wish You Knew," *Sojourners*, January 16, 2016, https://sojo.net/articles/7-things-transgender-people-your-congregation-wish-you-knew.

[43] Mitchell Atencio, "Grace Semler Baldridge is Bringing Queer Stories to Christian Music," *Sojourners*, February 22, 2021, https://sojo.net/articles/culture-news/grace-semler-baldridge-bringing-queer-stories-christian-music.

[44] Atencio, "Grace Semler Baldridge is Bringing Queer Stories to Christian Music."

[45] Lexi McMenamin, "Preach the Gospel. When Necessary, Do It in Drag," *Sojourners*, April 16, 2021, https://sojo.net/articles/preach-gospel-when-necessary-do-it-drag.

[46] McMenamin, "Preach the Gospel."

[47] McMenamin, "Preach the Gospel."

[48] "The Joy of Being Queer and Christian," *Sojourners*, June 2023, https://sojo.net/articles/series/joy-being-queer-and-christian.

[49] Mick Atencio, "The Trinity Delights in My Unique Trans, Nonbinary Identity," *Sojourners*, June 6, 2023, https://sojo.net/articles/joy-being-queer-and-christian/trinity-delights-my-unique-trans-nonbinary-identity.

[50] Mitchell Atencio, "WNBA Star Laysha Clarendon is Keeping the Faith and Breaking Binaries," *Sojourners*, July 23, 2024, https://sojo.net/articles/reconstruct/wnba-star-layshia-clarendon-keeping-faith-and-breaking-binaries.

[51] Wayne Grudem, "The Bible and homosexuality," *World*, April 6, 2013, https://wng.org/sift/the-bible-and-homosexuality-1617738725.

[52] Grudem, "The Bible and homosexuality."

[53] Marvin Olasky, "Blindsided," *World*, June 26, 2015, https://wng.org/articles/blindsided-1618008834.

[54] Olasky, "Blindsided."

[55] Marvin Olasky, "Covering the same-sex debate," *World*, May 7, 2015, https://wng.org/articles/covering-the-same-sex-marriage-debate-1617287430.

[56] Marvin Olasky, "Gays and God," *World*, June 26, 2015, https://wng.org/articles/gays-and-god-1617326722.

[57] See Caleb Kaltenbach, Denny Burk and Heather Lambert, "Homosexuals can change," *World*, January 23, 2016, https://wng.org/sift/homosexuals-can-change-1617252225; Marvin Olasky, "Design and identity," *World*, May 23, 2018, https://wng.org/articles/design-and-identity-1620595521.

[58] Joel Belz, "Gay, but celibate," *World*, September 12, 2018, https://wng.org/articles/gay-but-celibate-1617301664.

[59] Belz, "Gay, but celibate."

[60] Belz, "Gay, but celibate."

[61] Denny Burk, "Is Andy Stanley affirming?" *World*, January 27, 2023, https://wng.org/opinions/is-andy-stanley-affirming-1674823491.

[62] R. Albert Mohler Jr., "The train is leaving the station," *World*, September 18, 2023, https://wng.org/opinions/the-train-is-leaving-the-station-1695036498.

[63] Mohler Jr., "The train is leaving the station."

[64] R. Albert Mohler Jr., "Go and sin no more," *World*, October 3, 2023, https://wng.org/opinions/go-and-sin-no-more-1696305138.

[65] Mohler Jr., "Go and sin no more."

[66] Barton J. Gingerich, "A religious devotion to the left," *World*, August 2, 2023, https://wng.org/opinions/a-religious-devotion-to-the-left-1690973462.

[67] Gingerich, "A religious devotion to the left."

[68] Gingerich, "A religious devotion to the left."

Chapter 12
The 2024 Presidential Election

[1] Chris Hughes, "How Trump and Harris fared with faith voters in 2024," *Baptist News Global*, November 11, 2024, https://baptistnews.com/article/how-trump-and-harris-fared-with-faith-voters-in-2024/.

[2] Michael Gold, "Trump Tells Christians 'You Won't Have to Vote Anymore' If He's Elected," *The New York Times*, July 27, 2024, https://www.nytimes.com/2024/07/27/us/politics/trump-votes-christians.html. The article further explained that a Trump spokesman clarified Trump's remarks by saying the candidate was saying that if Christians, who normally did not vote in large numbers, would vote for him in 2024, he would fix the country so they would not need to vote again to protect their culture and beliefs.

[3] Michael Brown, "Please, please, please, we must all tone things down," *The Christian Post*, July 14, 2024, https://www.christianpost.com/voices/please-please-please-we-must-all-tone-things-down.html; Michael Gryboski, "Trump talks World War III, plans for 'largest deportation' during Fox News town hall," *The Christian Post*, September 4, 2024, https://www.christianpost.com/news/trump-talks-world-war-iii-largest-deportation-during-town-hall.html; Jon Brown, "Trump discusses inevitability of death, says he wants religious revival in US," *The Christian Post*, September 4, 2024, https://www.christianpost.com/news/trump-talks-death-urges-religious-revival-in-us.html?clickType=link-most-popular; CP Staff, "Trump pledges access for faith leaders 'directly into the Oval Office' if elected," *The Christian Post*, November 4, 2024, https://www.christianpost.com/news/trump-pledges-direct-access-for-faith-leaders-in-the-oval-office.html.

[4] Suzanne Bowdey, "How should Christians respond to a watered-down GOP platform?" *The Christian Post*, July 25, 2024, https://www.christianpost.com/voices/how-should-christians-respond-to-a-watered-down-gop-platform.html; Michael Brown, "Donald Trump and the mystery of Project 2025," *The Christian Post*, July 25, 2024, https://www.christianpost.com/voices/donald-trump-and-the-mystery-of-project-2025.html; Ryan Foley, "Pro-lifers slam Trump for calling 6-week abortion ban 'terrible': 'Shouldn't be the GOP nominee,'" *The Christian Post*, September 19, 2024, https://www.christianpost.com/news/pro-lifers-slam-trump-for-calling-6-week-abortion-ban-terrible.html?clickType=link-related-articles; Ryan Foley, "Pro-life leaders react to JD Vance's vow Trump won't sign abortion ban," *The Christian Post*, August 28, 2024, https://www.christianpost.com/news/pro-lifers-react-to-jd-vances-vow-trump-wont-sign-abortion-ban.html; Samantha Kamman, "Does Trump really want a national abortion ban? 3 things he has actually said on the issues," *The Christian Post*, November 3, 2024, https://www.christianpost.com/news/does-trump-really-want-a-national-abortion-ban.html?clickType=link-most-popular.

[5] Ryan Foley, "Trump's selection of JD Vance draws mixed reactions from pro-lifers: From 'exceptional' to 'heartbreaking,'" *The Christian Post*, July 16, 2024, https://www.christianpost.com/news/pro-life-activists-mixed-on-trumps-selection-of-jd-vance.html; Michael Gryboski, "JD Vance shares his journey from atheist law student to practicing Christian," *The Christian Post*, July 19, 2024, https://www.christianpost.com/news/jd-vance-shares-his-journey-from-atheism-to-practicing-christian.html; Melissa Barnhart, "'America felt truth of Scripture': JD Vance talks God, Trump surviving assassination attempt at Butler rally," *The Christian Post*, October 5, 2024, https://www.christianpost.com/news/jd-vance-talks-god-trump-surviving-assassination-at-butler-rally.html.

[6] Anugrah Kumar, "Pastor Jack Hibbs poses question to Evangelicals for Harris after 'wrong rally' rebuke," *The Christian Post*, October 22, 2024, https://www.christianpost.com/news/harris-wrong-rally-rebuke-pastor-jack-hibbs-warns-evangelicals.html; Ryan Foley, "Heritage Foundation pres. Warns Kamala Harris most 'anti-faith' candidate in history," *The Christian Post*, November 2, 2024, https://www.christianpost.com/news/kamala-harris-is-most-anti-faith-candidate-in-history-heritage-pres.html; Ian M. Giatti, "John MacArthur on Kamala Harris rallies after VP response to Christian protestors: 'Jesus isn't there,'" *The Christian Post*, October 23, 2024, https://www.christianpost.com/news/john-macarthur-on-kamala-harris-rallies-jesus-is-not-there.html.

[7] Allie Beth Stickey, "Kamala Harris is a mean girl," *The Christian Post*, August 19, 2024, https://www.christianpost.com/voices/kamala-harris-is-a-mean-girl.html;

Dan Delzell, "Kamala Harris and late-term abortion: A cold-blooded abomination," *The Christian Post*, July 30, 2024, https://www.christianpost.com/voices/kamala-harris-and-late-term-abortion-cold-blooded-abomination.html; Jason Jimenez, "6 Progressive policies of Kamala Harris that should scare you," *The Christian Post*, July 31, 2024, https://www.christianpost.com/voices/six-progressive-policies-of-kamala-harris-that-should-scare-you.html.

[8] Jon Brown, "Billy Graham's granddaughter pens op-ed endorsing Kamala Harris, calls Trump 'megalomaniac,'" *The Christian Post*, October 28, 2024, https://www.christianpost.com/news/billy-grahams-granddaughter-pens-op-ed-endorsing-kamala-harris.html; Jon Brown, "David French endorses Kamala Harris, blasts 'MAGA Christians,'" *The Christian Post*, August 13, 2024, https://www.christianpost.com/news/david-french-endorses-kamala-harris-blasts-maga-christians.html; Michael Gryboski, "Kamala Harris quotes Gospel of Luke, tells AME Church her campaign is 'focused on the future,'" *The Christian Post*, August 28, 2024, https://www.christianpost.com/news/kamala-harris-quotes-gospel-of-luke-in-speech-to-ame-church.html.

[9] Richard D. Land, "To Christian voters, don't be like Pontius Pilate this election with Trump, Harris," *The Christian Post*, October 24, 2024, https://www.christianpost.com/voices/dont-be-like-pontius-pilate-this-election-with-trump-harris.html.

[10] Land, "To Christian voters."

[11] Land, "To Christian voters."

[12] Anugrah Kumar, "Kamala Harris called her pastor on night of presidential run," *The Christian Post*, July 29, 2024, https://www.christianpost.com/news/kamala-harris-called-her-pastor-on-night-of-presidential-run.html.

[13] Kumar, "Kamala Harris called her pastor."

[14] Kumar, "Kamala Harris called her pastor."

[15] Michael Gryboski, "5 Kamala Harris controversies: Extramarital affair, pro-life raid and Knights of Columbus criticism," *The Christian Post*, August 12, 2020, https://www.christianpost.com/news/5-kamala-harris-controversies-extramarital-affair-pro-life-raid-knights-of-columbus-criticism.html?clickType=link-related-articles.

[16] Ian M. Giatti, "'I shouldn't have left': Trump talks 2020, offers prayer to God, calls Harris 'vessel' for 'demonic' Dems," *The Christian Post*, November 5, 2024, https://www.christianpost.com/news/trump-talks-2020-loss-offers-prayer-to-god-for-nation-at-rally.html.

[17] Giatti, "'I shouldn't have left.'"

[18] Giatti, "'I shouldn't have left.'"

[19] Ryan Foley, "Roanoke College women's swim team endorses Trump amid promise to protect women's sports," *The Christian Post*, November 5, 2024, https://www.christianpost.com/news/athletes-endorse-trump-amid-promise-to-protect-womens-sports.html.

[20] Katelyn Webb, "Candace Cameron Bure challenges followers to 'vote like Jesus,'" *The Christian Post*, November 5, 2024, https://www.christianpost.com/news/candace-cameron-bure-challenges-followers-to-vote-like-jesus.html.

[21] Webb, "Candace Cameron Bure challenges followers."

[22] Robert Postic, "Voting Is Important to Me. That's Why, This Year, I Won't Vote," *Christianity Today*, October 25, 2024, https://www.christianitytoday.com/2024/10/voting-is-important-not-voting-2024-election/.

[23] Bonnie Kristian, "The Trump Debate is Dead," *Christianity Today*, January 12, 2024, https://www.christianitytoday.com/2024/01/trump-debate-is-dead-evangelicals/.

[24] Kristian, "The Trump Debate is Dead."

[25] Kristian, "The Trump Debate is Dead."

[26] Daniel Bennett, "Trump's Indictment Demands a Distinctly Christian Response," *Christianity Today*, June 14, 2023, https://www.christianitytoday.com/2023/06/trump-arrest-charges-indictment-ny-fl-evangelical-christian/.

[27] Bennett, "Trump's Indictment."

[28] Bennett, "Trump's Indictment."

[29] Bob Smietana, "Former Southern Baptist leader Russell Moore reflects on the Trump era," *The Washington Post*, July 26, 2023, https://www.washingtonpost.com/religion/2023/07/26/russell-moore-southern-baptist-trump/. See also, Ana Marie Cox, "Russell Moore Can't Support Either Candidate," *The New York Times Magazine*, October 12, 2016, https://www.nytimes.com/2016/10/16/magazine/russell-moore-cant-support-either-candidate.html?searchResultPosition=15.

[30] Sarah Pulliam Bailey, "Could Southern Baptist Russell Moore lose his job? Churches threaten to pull funds after months of Trump controversy," *The Washington Post*, March 13, 2017, https://www.washingtonpost.com/news/acts-of-faith/wp/2017/03/13/could-southern-baptist-leader-russell-moore-lose-his-job-churches-threaten-funding-after-months-of-trump-controversy/.

[31] Ruth Graham, "A prominent Southern Baptist calls on Trump to step down," *The New York Times*, January 8, 2021, https://www.nytimes.com/2021/01/08/us/politics/russell-moore-trump.html?searchResultPosition=7.

[32] Russell Moore, "Mount Zion or Mar-a-Lago?" *Christianity Today*, July/August 2024, 20.

[33] Moore, "Mount Zion or Mar-a-Lago?" 20.

[34] Moore, "Mount Zion or Mar-a-Lago?" 21.

[35] Russell Moore, "Election Day Can Help Break Our Addition to Hope," *Christianity Today*, October 23, 2024, https://www.christianitytoday.com/2024/10/election-day-break-addiction-hope-russell-moore/; See also an earlier piece, by Moore, "Political Homelessness Is a Good Start," *Christianity Today*, March 2024, 30.

[36] Mitchell Atencio, "Faith and Justice Leaders on Facing a Second Trump Term," *Sojourners*, November 6, 2024, https://sojo.net/articles/news/faith-and-justice-leaders-facing-second-trump-term.

[37] Atencio, "Faith and Justice Leaders."

[38] Atencio, "Faith and Justice Leaders."

[39] Atencio, "Faith and Justice Leaders."

[40] Mitchell Atencio, "Trump Falsely Claimed That 'Everyone'—Including Faith Leaders—Opposed Roe," *Sojourners*, June 27, 2024, https://sojo.net/articles/trump-falsely-claimed-everyone-including-faith-leaders-opposed-roe-ecd.

[41] Atencio, "Trump Falsely Claimed."

[42] Atencio, "Trump Falsely Claimed."

[43] Mitchell Atencio, "Meet Vice President Kamala Harris' Pastor, Civil Rights Leader Amos C. Brown," *Sojourners*, July 23, 2024, https://sojo.net/articles/meet-vice-president-kamala-harris-pastor-civil-rights-leader-amos-c-brown.

[44] See, in order, Mitchell Atencio, "Harris-Walz Campaign Hires Veteran Faith and Justice Organizer to Direct Outreach," *Sojourners*, August 30, 2024, https://sojo.net/articles/news/harris-walz-campaign-hires-veteran-faith-and-justice-organizer-direct-outreach; Bekah McNeel, "Harris' Policy Agenda Could reduce Child Poverty, Faith Advocates Say," *Sojourners*, September 3, 2024, https://sojo.net/articles/news/

harris-policy-agenda-could-reduce-child-poverty-faith-advocates-say; and Bekah McNeel, "Harris Says 'One Does Not Have to Abandon Their Faith' to Support Abortion Rights. What Does That Mean?" *Sojourners*, September 12, 2024, https://sojo.net/articles/news/harris-says-one-does-not-have-abandon-their-faith-support-abortion-rights-what-does.

[45] Ken Chitwood, "What Faith and Immigration Leaders Say About VP Harris' Candidacy," *Sojourners*, August 2, 2024, https://sojo.net/articles/what-faith-and-immigration-leaders-say-about-vp-harris-candidacy.

[46] Michael Woolf, "God Isn't a Republican or a Democrat; God is an Immigrant," *Sojourners*, October 17, 2024, https://sojo.net/articles/opinion/god-isnt-republican-or-democrat-god-immigrant.

[47] Woolf, "God Isn't a Republican."

[48] Adam Russell Taylor, "Christian Faith Requires Us to Speak Out Against Fascist Rhetoric," *Sojourners*, October 24, 2024, https://sojo.net/articles/opinion/christian-faith-requires-us-speak-out-against-fascist-rhetoric.

[49] Kaley McEvoy, "A Prayer for Calm Amid an Anxious Election Season," *Sojourners*, November 1, 2024, https://sojo.net/articles/prayer-calm-amid-anxious-election-season; The Editors, "Prayers Lifted: Here's Where You Can Pray for the 2024 Election," *Sojourners*, November 1, 2024, https://sojo.net/articles/prayers-lifted-heres-where-you-can-pray-2024-election; Moya Harris, "This Election is Critical. So Is Taking Time to Rest," *Sojourners*, October 31, 2024, https://sojo.net/articles/opinion/election-critical-so-taking-time-rest.

[50] Bekah McCallum, "Harris gets hip to court Gen Z," *World*, August 13, 2024, https://wng.org/roundups/harris-gets-hip-to-court-gen-z-1723587398.

[51] Denny Burk, "Evangelicals for Harris: Here's what you need to know," *World*, August 14, 2024, https://wng.org/opinions/evangelicals-for-harris-1723629490.

[52] Burk, "Evangelicals for Harris."

[53] Jordan J. Ballor, "Understanding Kamalanomics," *World*, August 21, 2024, https://wng.org/opinions/understanding-kamalanomics-1724236216.

[54] Ballor, "Understanding Kamalanomics."

[55] Hunter Baker, "With abortions and vasectomies for all," *World*, August 23, 2024, https://wng.org/opinions/with-abortions-and-vasectomies-for-all-1724409231.

[56] Carolina Lumetta, "Harris campaign leaving the honeymoon phase," *World*, September 2, 2024, https://wng.org/roundups/harris-campaign-leaving-the-honeymoon-phase-1725307777.

[57] Denny Burk, "Should taxpayers be forced to pay for IVF?" *World*, September 4, 2024, https://wng.org/opinions/should-taxpayers-be-forced-to-pay-for-ivf-1725444281.

[58] Andrew T. Walker, "On abortion, Trump is his own worst enemy," *World*, August 29, 2024, https://wng.org/opinions/on-abortion-trump-is-his-own-worst-enemy-1724927888.

[59] R. Albert Mohler Jr., "Trump and abortion," *World*, September 3, 2024, https://wng.org/opinions/trump-and-abortion-1725360004.

[60] Juliana Chan Erikson, "Transgender ideology drives away longtime Democrats," *World*, September 23, 2024, https://wng.org/roundups/longtime-democrats-crossing-the-aisle-or-refusing-to-vote-1727125797.

[61] Erikson, "Transgender ideology."

[62] Erikson, "Transgender ideology."

⁶³ Jessica Prol Smith, "Where do the candidates stand on LGBTQ+ issues?" *World*, October 11, 2024, https://wng.org/opinions/where-do-the-candidates-stand-on-LGBTQ+-issues-1728590732.

⁶⁴ Smith, "Where do the candidates stand?"

⁶⁵ Robert J. Pacienza, "It's time to sound the alarm," *World*, October 18, 2024, https://wng.org/opinions/its-time-to-sound-the-alarm-1729248224.

⁶⁶ A. S. Ibrahim, "American Muslims and the 2024 election," *World*, October 15, 2024, https://wng.org/opinions/american-muslims-and-the-2024-election-1728934218.

⁶⁷ Denny Burk, "The pro-pornography party," *World*, November 1, 2024, https://wng.org/opinions/the-pro-pornography-party-1730318199.

⁶⁸ R. Albert Mohler Jr., "This is how religious liberty dies," *World*, October 28, 2024, https://wng.org/opinions/this-is-how-religious-liberty-dies-1730113057.

⁶⁹ R. Albert Mohler Jr., "The decision we face," *World*, November 4, 2024, https://wng.org/opinions/the-decision-we-face-1730720497.

⁷⁰ John D. Wilsey, "When it's 'too close to call,'" *World*, October 25, 2024, https://wng.org/opinions/when-it-is-too-close-to-call-1729802159.

⁷¹ George Barna, "2004 Election Research-Report #2," Cultural Research Center at Arizona Christian University, November 13, 2024, https://www.arizonachristian.edu/wp-content/uploads/2024/11/CRC-Release-Post-Election-Nov-13-2024-Christian-Vote-Hands-Trump-Victory.pdf.

Conclusion
Evangelical Publications and the Movement's Future

¹ Martin Marty, "The Protestant Press," in Martin E. Marty, J. G. Deedy, D. W. Silveran and R. Lekachman, *The Religious Press in America* (New York: Holt, Rinehart & Winston, 1963), 8.

² Sean Salai, "Barna Study Suggests 'Christians in Name Only' Skew Political Polls of US Believers," *National Catholic Register*, March 21, 2022, https://www.ncregister.com/news/barna-study-suggests-christians-in-name-only-skew-political-polls-of-us-believers

³ Timothy Dalrymple, "Justice Too Long Delayed," *Christianity Today*, June 10, 2020, https://www.christianitytoday.com/2020/06/justice-too-long-delayed/

⁴ Jeff Brumley, "Politics may drive evangelism to extinction, Galli says in BNG webinar," Baptist News Global, October 9, 2020, https://baptistnews.com/article/politics-may-drive-evangelicalism-to-extinction-galli-says-in-bng-webinar/#.YWOSkmZKg64.

⁵ Russell Moore, "The American Evangelical Church is in Crisis. There's Only One Way Out," *The Atlantic Monthly*, July 25, 2023, https://www.theatlantic.com/ideas/archive/2023/07/christian-evangelical-church-division-politics/674810/.

⁶ Daniel K. Williams, "The Evangelical Diploma Divide," *Christianity Today*, August 7, 2024, https://www.christianitytoday.com/2024/08/evangelical-diploma-divide-election-politics-class-unity/.

⁷ Williams, "The Evangelical Diploma Divide."

⁸ Williams, "The Evangelical Diploma Divide."

⁹ "Modeling the Future of Religion in America: How U.S. religious composition has changed in recent decades," Pew Research Center, September 13, 2022,

https://www.pewresearch.org/religion/2022/09/13/how-u-s-religious-composition-has-changed-in-recent-decades/.

[10] "Modeling the Future of Religion in America."

[11] William Pannell, "Evangelicals and the Social Crisis," *The Post-American*, October 1974, https://sojo.net/magazine/october-1974/evangelicals-and-social-crisis.

[12] This was the subject I explored in my dissertation, Ken Waters, "Toward the Successful Christian Publication: A Descriptive Analysis of Four Independent Evangelical Christian Periodicals," PhD diss. (University of Southern California, 1982).

[13] Moore, "The American Evangelical Church is in Crisis." Note: *The Atlantic Monthly* essay is adapted from his book *Losing Our Religion: An Altar Call for Evangelical America* (New York: Penguin Random House, 2023).

[14] Moore, "The American Evangelical Church is in Crisis."

Index

About the Author

KEN WATERS IS an emeritus professor of journalism at Pepperdine University. His 32-year career included teaching a variety of writing courses, in addition to Intercultural Communication, Communication Ethics and an occasional public relations class. Waters also served a seven-year stint as Divisional Dean for Communication at the university. In that role, he managed 30 faculty and planned classes for nearly 400 majors. His overseas teaching assignments have taken him to London, Lausanne, and Florence. He's also written a dozen journal articles, primarily on the intersection of religious publications and culture.

Waters received a Bachelor of Arts in journalism and history from Pepperdine, and he served as editor of the award-winning student newspaper, *The Graphic*. He also holds a master's degree in religion from Pepperdine, and a PhD from the University of Southern California. He and his wife, Julie, are parents to two adult daughters, Katie and Alison. Waters is a life-long resident of Southern California.

www.ingramcontent.com/pod-product-compliance
Lightning Source LLC
Chambersburg PA
CBHW031457120626
46545CB00005B/1653